Greek Ways

Greek Ways

How the Greeks Created Western Civilization

Bruce Thornton

ENCOUNTER BOOKS
SAN FRANCISCO

First edition published in 2000 by Encounter Books, an activity of Encounter for Culture and Education, Inc., a nonprofit tax exempt corporation.

Encounter Books website address: www.encounterbooks.com

Manufactured in the United States.

The paper used in this publication meets the minimum requirements of ANSI/NISO Z39.48-1992 (R 1997) (Permanence of Paper).

Library of Congress Cataloging-in-Publication Data

Thornton, Bruce S.
Greek ways : how the Greeks created western civilization / Bruce Thornton.
p. cm.
Includes bibliographical references and index.
ISBN 1-893554-03-1 (cloth : alk. paper)
1. Greece—Civilization—Influence. 2. Civilization, Modern—Greek influences. 3. Sexual ethics—Greece. I. Title.
DF78 .T53 2000
949.5—dc21 00-039376

10 9 8 7 6 5 4 3 2 1

Contents

We see with the eyes of the Greeks and use their phrases when we speak.

—*Jacob Burckhardt*[1]

INTRODUCTION

Seeing with Greek Eyes

In 1942, when Edith Hamilton republished *The Greek Way,* her already classic study which had appeared a few years earlier, the survival of the liberal Western tradition was very much in doubt. The atavistic barbarism of fascism appeared poised to wipe out the twenty-five centuries of slow progress the human race had made since a handful of squabbling, parochial Greek city-states had first liberated the human mind from the shadows of superstition and bondage to the irrational. "When the world is storm-driven and the bad that happens and the worse that threatens are so urgent as to shut out everything else from view," wrote Hamilton, "then we need to know all the strong fortresses of the spirit which men have built through the ages."[2] With the world at war, the legacy of the Greeks seemed all the more precious given the real possibility of its extinction.

More than fifty years later, the chief threats to the ideals of freedom and democracy are in abeyance. Not only fascism but communism as well has been shattered against that "fortress of the spirit" whose first bricks were laid by the Greeks. Even those cultures that seem to offer an alternative vision to the West, such as the Islamic states and China, are compelled to admit, if only by their actions, some degree of submission to the Western way. There is no nation in the world, Western or otherwise, that does not desire the advantages of science and technology, such as antibiotics and advanced weaponry, or that does not acknowledge—if only by attempting to suppress them—the powerful ideas of individual autonomy and human rights. What Jacques Ellul said over twenty years ago is even more obvious today: most of the nations of the world are either Western or trying to become so, for they have "inherited the consciousness of and desire for freedom. Everything they do today and everything they seek is an expression of what the western world has taught them."[3] And the first teachers of the West—"the first Westerners," as Hamilton called them—were the Greeks. "The spirit of the West, the modern spirit, is a Greek discovery," she wrote, "and the place of the Greeks is in the modern world."[4]

When Hamilton wrote these words, the place of the Greeks in the pedigree of the West was a truism so obvious that she could confidently assert, "There is no danger now that the world will not give the Greek genius full recognition. Greek achievement is a fact universally acknowledged."[5] If this was true when the Western ideal was threatened with extinction, how much more obvious should it be today, when this century's dominant challenges to that ideal have been defeated, and when academic caretakers of the Greeks enjoy a freedom and prosperity that every day offer proof of the continuing vitality of the "Greek way."

Yet in some elite circles these days, the very phrase "Greek genius" is considered reactionary and "Eurocentric," and those writers like Edith Hamilton who have frankly acknowledged Greek superiority are considered at best naive vulgarizers, or worse, insidious apologists for Western hegemony and oppression. Indeed, "Edith Hamilton" has become a term of opprobrium in the profession of classics, a reflexive smear used to dismiss any affirmation of the heritage left us by the Greeks. (Gary Wills expressed this contempt when he recently scorned the "rather gaga (or Edith Hamilton) idealization of 'the Greek spirit' which he detected in a recent celebration of the Greek achievement.[6]) Such scorn is part of a larger rejection of what one historian of ancient Greece calls, with obligatory sneering quotes, the "now-embarrassing essentialist fantasies about the 'Greek miracle'"—as though the appearance of rational thought or the ideal of freedom in a world that had never known either were not indeed miraculous.[7]

Hamilton can, to be sure, sound at times a bit too earnest for our jaded taste. After all, she was born in 1867, so her prose and her enthusiasm are decidedly late Victorian. A phrase like "a sapphire sea washing enchanted islands purple in a luminous air" seems, to us, overripe. We moderns prefer to affect a cynical, world-weary pose, the better to guard against endorsing naive "illusions." Moreover, Hamilton appears to slight what Nietzsche convinced our century was really most fascinating about the Greeks: the dark, wild, Dionysian forces seething beneath their sunlit, marmoreal repose. Finally, Hamilton says little about the topics our therapeutic culture enjoys brooding over, such as slavery, homosexuality, and the status of women. To her critics, Edith Hamilton's Greeks look suspiciously like staid, late-Victorian bourgeoisie—a self-flattering, presentist fabrication that ignores just how different and irrational and at times unpleasant the real Greeks really were.

Yet Hamilton's critics are confusing two different issues: the historical reality of the Greeks—what they actually did and how they lived; and the influence of the Greeks—the ideas that acquired a life of their own as they were taken up by the Romans, absorbed into Christianity, and "rediscovered" in the Renaissance and the Enlightenment.

The strangeness or irrationality of Greek life and culture, fascinating as it may be, is primarily an issue for the historian. It was taken up early in this century by classicists and social scientists alike. In 1921, Gilbert Murray envisaged a debunker of the Greeks scoffing, "These Greeks whom you call 'noble' have long since been exposed. Anthropology has turned its searchlights upon them."[8] By 1938 the poet Louis MacNeice wrote of the Greeks, "And how one can imagine oneself among them I do not know; / It was all so unimaginably different / And all so long ago."[9] The "strangeness" of the Greeks should be no surprise; every ancient society, inhabiting an uncertain, violent, and harsh world where survival could never be taken for granted, was strangely different from our own.

What was unique about the Greeks, however, was their "spirit," the ideals they introduced into the world, their "sheer originality and brilliance," as Bernard Knox puts it.[10] That those ideals could be contradicted by the Greeks' behavior reflects only the banal truth that humans rarely live up to their own aspirations; it does not mean that the ideals themselves are faulty, or that the Greeks should not be appreciated for articulating them. It is true that while Greeks extolled freedom and individual autonomy, they owned slaves and relegated women to an inferior status—as did every ancient society, and as do many societies still today (though few in the Greek-influenced West). In this, the Greeks were products of their place and time. More important to recognize is that the principles upon which we base our criticism of the Greeks have their origins with the Greeks themselves, in ideals that transcended their particular environment in a way unique among ancient societies, perhaps with the exception of the Hebrews. As interesting as the historical reality of the Greeks is, more relevant for us are the Greek *ideals* that still shape every aspect of our culture. Those ideals—not the particulars of female oppression or the brutal facts of slavery—were the subjects of Hamilton's book.

The more significant reasons for the classics profession's current distaste for someone like Edith Hamilton, however, lie in two intellectual currents that increasingly define scholarly activity in America: postmodernism and multiculturalism, both of which represent a sustained attack on everything that makes the West (and perforce the Greeks) distinct.

Multiculturalism, for all its talk of celebrating cultural diversity, is at heart a species of anti-humanist and anti-liberal identity politics. It locates individual identity in ethnic particularity and scorns the liberal notion of universal human nature as, in the words of one exponent, "an ethnocentric and oppressively universalistic humanism in which the legitimating norms which govern the substance of citizenship are identified most strongly with Anglo-

American cultural-political communities."[11] From this multiculturalist assumption follow two contradictory positions. One is cultural relativism, the belief that all cultures are equal and cannot be compared in terms of superiority or inferiority, since all standards of judgment are locally "constructed" to serve local interests; and there is no consistent "good" or "evil" or "truth." The other is a vision of history as therapeutic melodrama, a saga of Western evils such as sexism, racism, colonialism, imperialism, etc., being inflicted on innocent non-Westerners, who are to be judged only by the privileged standards afforded to victims. Yet opposed as they are, both these positions necessarily deny the existence of something like a "Greek genius" distinct from and superior to the spirit of other ancient cultures.

One multiculturalist tactic for diminishing the Greeks is to deny their originality, asserting that they begged, borrowed, or stole their ideas from other cultures. We need not dwell on Afrocentrism, the idea that the Greeks stole everything good they knew from black Egyptians; the incoherence and historical ignorance of this theory have been amply and repeatedly demonstrated.[12] But even scholars who should know better indulge the current fashion for Greek-bashing by attributing their achievements to a vaguely defined East. Gary Wills, for instance, has asserted that " 'the West' [including the Greeks] is an admittedly brilliant derivative of the East."[13] To which Victor Hanson and John Heath respond, "Can Mr. Wills please demonstrate from what part of the East did the West brilliantly derive democracy, free inquiry, the idea of a middle class, political freedom, literature apart from religion, citizen militias ... and a language of abstraction and rationalism?"[14]

The answer, of course, is "Nowhere"—these were all Greek inventions. There was no polis at Karnak, no Plato in Babylon, no trial by jury in Sardis. That the Greeks borrowed from their Mediterranean neighbors is obvious; no human society lives in a vacuum, untouched by the customs of other peoples with whom they war, trade, and intermarry. The Greeks benefited immensely from a geography that placed them near enough to the great ancient civilizations of Egypt and the Tigris-Euphrates river valleys to be influenced by them, but not so close as to be absorbed into them. More important, however, is what the Greeks *made* of their borrowings. Consider the Greek alphabet, the elements of which were adapted from the Phoenician around the ninth century.[15] The Greek changes—such as using Phoenician consonant letters to signify vowels—made possible in just a few centuries the language of Homer's epics and Sappho's lyrics, a literary speech unrivalled in expressive power, complexity, and sheer beauty by anything found among the few remnants of Phoenician writing.

Another tack taken by the debunkers is to deny that the Greeks were alone in creating their distinctive ideas. For example, Martha Nussbaum has recently argued that *all* societies have had concepts of freedom, human rights, and religious tolerance.[16] But she can make this remarkable case only by defining these in vague and elastic terms, and by ignoring this critical point: it is not enough to find in the historical record behaviors or pronouncements that bear some resemblance to "religious tolerance" or "freedom" or "equality." After all, as Plato reminds us, even thieves divvy up the loot according to egalitarian principles, but such self-interested sharing is hardly the machinery of democracy. Far more crucial is evidence that a particular society recognized these abstractions as *goods* to be rationally defined and consciously pursued apart from the practical and selfish needs of king or priest. Only thus could such goods rise above the accidents of history and geography and the whims of political and religious authorities, to become part of a living, developing intellectual tradition capable of influencing subsequent societies—as did the Greek idea of freedom. The simple fact is that neither Nussbaum nor anybody else can find a society contemporary with fifth-century Athens that left behind a sustained, self-conscious reflection upon freedom or equality as a concept to be rationally analyzed or a principle to be actively cultivated.[17]

If multiculturalist attempts to denigrate the Greeks' achievements or their uniqueness necessarily fail, the attacks deriving from current postmodern intellectual fads are no more successful. One such fashion focuses on the "Other," the despised alien that Westerners allegedly constructed in order to define themselves and justify their oppressive power. Classicist Paul Cartledge devoted a book on the Greeks entirely to demonstrating their wicked indulgence of this nasty habit: "The Greeks . . . in various ways constructed their identities negatively, by means of a series of polarized oppositions of themselves to what they were not."[18]

In itself this would be unexceptional, since every human society defines itself at some level in opposition to those who appear different and strange, perhaps inferior and even subhuman. What is unusual in the Greeks is a real curiosity about people different from themselves and a willingness to consider whether those peoples might have something worthy to offer.

The *Histories* of Herodotus, for example, are filled with just this sort of fascination with the "Other," a fascination unparalleled in the writings of other ancient Mediterranean peoples. The whole second book, concentrating on the Egyptians, examines their customs for the most part with tolerance and even sympathy, going so far as to assert that many Greek practices were borrowed from them. So sympathetic was Herodotus to non-Greek peoples that Plutarch later called him *philobarbaros*, "foreigner-loving."[19]

Plato too recognized the achievements of the Egyptians, and even quoted an Egyptian priest's condescending dismissal of the Greeks as "children," newcomers with no tradition of learning and science.[20]

These are hardly the attitudes of blinkered xenophobes anxious to protect their ethnic identity from contamination by a despised "Other." Indeed, the very notion of cultural relativity—that the differences among cultures cannot be judged or ranked by any transcendent standard—is itself an invention of the fifth-century Greek Sophists, against whom ethical absolutists like Plato and Socrates battled. Twenty-five centuries before today's multiculturalists, the Greek Pindar said that "Custom is the king in all things."[21]

Cartledge's analysis, however, is not so much a historical description as a moral indictment. Speaking of Greek freedom, for example, he says it "was dearly bought . . . at the expense of others, the excluded many: free foreigners and women (Greek as well as barbarian), but above all slaves. . . . Indeed, the exclusion of those various 'outgroups,' the collective Other, was arguably the very condition and basic premise of the Classical Greeks' cultural achievements."[22] In other words, because the Greeks did not immediately extend the idea of freedom to every human alive—because they didn't meet modern expectations (which themselves derive from the Greeks)—we are to consider them undeserving of admiration, and their ideals flawed.

Yet before freedom could be posited as a natural right of all human beings simply because they are human, it had to be identified as a good worth fighting for. The unalterable fact remains that it was among property-owning, Greek citizen males that we find the first recorded identification of freedom as something so essential to human happiness as to be worth suffering and dying for. Once this step was taken, the genie was out of the bottle: the possibility emerged that freedom could one day be seen as a good for *everybody*—which is exactly what happened.

Another postmodern strategy for diminishing the Greeks is to emphasize a radical version of the "strangeness" that became a fashionable theme early in this century. Some scholars turn the Greeks themselves into "Others" whose difference from us is so extreme as to render negligible any influences they may have had on us. (Cartledge, in fact, admits his sympathy with the "intention to defamiliarize the ancient Greeks and so to knock them off the pedestal on which our Roman, Renaissance, Enlightenment, or Romantic forebears once placed them as being essentially like us, only earlier, and thus anticipating and legitimating fundamental characteristics of our own culture."[23]) Scholars who write about Greek social history are especially fond of emphasizing how alien Greek life and culture were.

Some scholars of ancient sexuality, for example, draw upon the radical social constructionism of Michel Foucault, which denies any stable human nature and instead reduces human identity to the expression of local power structures. Thus they see Greek sexuality as a collection of social constructs legitimizing political privilege and exclusion. "Sexual behavior [in ancient Athens]," according to this view, "served to position social actors in the places assigned to them by virtue of their political standing, in the hierarchical structure of the Athenian polity."[24] Hence, sexual practices such as passive sodomy were condemned not because the behaviors themselves were considered unnatural or destructive, but only if they violated the particular protocols and conventions established by the game of Athenian citizenship. Since those protocols were time-bound and culture-specific, nothing the Greeks wrote about sexuality is ultimately relevant to us, whose mores answer the needs of our own, equally oppressive power structures. The Greeks can have only an anthropological interest; they are useful only as career fodder or as occasions for advancing some ideological program or other.

Some postmodern feminist scholars paint the Greeks as arch-misogynists who kept their women locked away in dark, dank quarters while the men cavorted with concubines and boys. For example: "In the case of a society dominated by men who sequester their wives and daughters, denigrate the female role in reproduction, erect monuments to the male genitalia, have sex with the sons of their peers, sponsor public whorehouses, create a mythology of rape, and engage in rampant saber-rattling, it is not inappropriate to refer to a reign of the phallus. Classical Athens was such a society."[25] The bizarre thesis that all women in such a "phallocracy" were sequestered, starved, and nameless can be argued only on the basis of tendentious interpretations of the fragmentary literary and archaeological evidence[26]—and by ignoring the numerous magnificent literary and historical women whom these supposedly women-hating Greeks immortalized. The larger implication of the phallocracy thesis is that on yet another count the Greeks should not be admired, since their ideals of freedom and equality were compromised by their benighted, sexist behavior.

Thus postmodernism attacks or denies the Greek legacy. Postmodernists denigrate rationalism and science—two of the greatest achievements of the Greeks, who first defined man as a "rational animal"; these are regarded not as the means for acquiring truth but rather as arbitrarily constructed "discourses" to justify and legitimize political power. The universal human identity that forms the ground for natural rights is equally suspect, regarded as a fiction masking the West's oppression of all those "Others" who do not fit its tendentious definition of humanity. Yet it was the Greeks who first began to recognize a common humanity more important than local or tribal affiliations. It was the Greek Diogenes who identified himself as a "citizen of the world" rather than just a member of some parochial city-state.[27] Without that recognition of a common humanity, slavery might never have been abolished in the West, women might never have been granted equality (as they still have not in some non-Western countries), and the liberal notion of innate rights possessed by all humans merely by virtue of being human would never have existed.

The pseudo-sophisticated fads of postmodernism and multiculturalism account for the distaste that Edith Hamilton and other celebrators of Greek values arouse in many academic intellectuals. The irony is that fifty years from now these current academic fashions, already beginning to seem somewhat frayed and worn, will appear as quaint and dated as Hamilton's overripe rhetoric. Applied to the Greeks, postmodernist approaches yield little in the way of fresh insights into the continuing vitality of Greek ways, evident everywhere in an increasingly Westernized world. They say much, however, about the crisis of rationalism in higher education, the failure of intellectual nerve that has petrified into an affectation, mastered in graduate school and maintained for the careerist rewards that follow. Intellectuals fervently embrace a congeries of anti-Western clichés, despite the triumph everywhere of the Western way, or at least the discrediting of any viable alternative to liberal democracy and free enterprise.

Ultimately, however, the greatest testimony to the "Greek spirit" so oft derided by the postmodernist or multiculturalist critic is the critic himself, whose life and mind are what they are because of the Greeks. A science whose origins lie among the Greeks has enabled him to survive birth and childhood, grow to maturity well-fed and safe, and live a life of material abundance that people in earlier times would not have dared dream of. He lives free from the arbitrary whims of the priest or aristocratic thug or village big-man, in a polity governed by law and by institutions that follow agreed-upon rules and protocols. He is free to speak his mind and to criticize—not just without fear of reprisal, but even with the expectation of prestige and reward—the very culture that makes him what he is. And *that* is the greatest irony: for the spirit of criticism that among so many academics has fossilized into a pose has its origins nowhere but among the Greeks, who were the first to question critically everything from the gods to political power to their very selves, the first to live what Socrates called "the examined life." No matter what he says, then, the critic of the Greeks has already voted for the Greeks with his feet. As Victor Hanson and John Heath write, "Not one of the multiculturalist classicists really wishes . . . to live under indigenous pre-Columbian ideas of government, Arabic protocols for female behavior, Chinese canons of medical ethics, Islamic traditions of church and state, African approaches to science, Japanese ideas of race, Indian social castes, or Native American notions of private property."[28]

The purpose of this book is not to dwell on postmodernist academics and their discontents, but rather to recover those core ideas invented by the Greeks that have shaped the world we live in and the assumptions we share about human identity and the human good—in short, the ideas that have created Western civilization. For if we look beyond surface forms, we find that the essential ideals of the West—freedom, individualism, consensual government, and the rational pursuit of knowledge—have their origins among the Greeks. Even Hebraism influenced the West only after it passed through the crucible of Hellenism.

But before we identify the unique Greek achievement, we must strip away the modern interpretations that obscure it. I will address the lives of the Greeks and those practices—the treatment of women, sexuality, slavery, and war—most often targeted and distorted by modern critics. The "postmodernist" Greeks are all the rage these days, not just in academe but also in the larger culture, where anti-Hellenism often serves an anti-Western agenda, tracing the alleged sins of the West back to Greek origins. But as we will see, these sins are really the sins of humanity, discoverable in all times and places. Among the Greeks, however, they coexisted with a unique virtue:

the recognition that these practices should not be taken for granted but, like all things, be critically examined.

The modern anti-Hellenists persist in detailing sins of the Greeks that are common to humanity everywhere, while explaining away or ignoring the achievements that set them apart. Seventy-five years ago, Gilbert Murray answered the debunkers of his day:

> We must listen with due attention to the critics who have pointed out all the remnants of savagery and superstition that they find in Greece: the slave-driver, the fetish-worshipper and the medicine-man, the trampler on women, the bloodthirsty hater of all outside his own town and party. But it is not those people that constitute Greece; those people can be found all over the historical world, commoner than blackberries. It is not anything fixed and stationary that constitutes Greece: what constitutes Greece is the movement which leads from all these to the Stoic or fifth-century "sophist" who condemns and denies slavery, who has abolished all cruel superstitions and preaches some religion based on philosophy and humanity, who claims for women the same spiritual rights as for man, who looks on all human creatures as his brethren, and the world as "one great City of gods and men." It is that movement which you will not find elsewhere, any more than the statues of Pheidias or the dialogues of Plato or the poems of Aeschylus and Euripides.[29]

That "movement" is the subject of this study. Yet the reader should not think that this book's celebration of the "Greek spirit" implies that the battle is won and we have reached the "end of history." The tragic view of human life brilliantly imagined by the Greeks forbids us such naiveté. The absolute limits that circumscribe human existence—time, chance, our own passions—could prove greater than the matchless achievements of the Greeks. Perhaps rationalism, science, the free individual, and critical consciousness will prove to be humanity's undoing. If so, then indeed, as Murray posited, Greece will have been the "great wrecker in human history" that "held up false lights which have lured our ship to dangerous places."[30]

I think not: for better or worse, the course the Greeks charted for humanity is the one that has the best likelihood, on this earth and in this life at least, of leading us to our highest fulfillment as human beings. As Goethe said, "Of all peoples, the Greeks have dreamt the dream of life best."[31]

Nor am I asserting that Greek ideals became disembodied Platonic forms in some progressive Grand Narrative of history, floating through time unchanged until Renaissance Italians or Enlightenment Americans could resurrect them. Of course democracy and freedom in Athens were different from their later manifestations, rooted in a particular place and time, attached to any number of pragmatic or selfish expediencies. But as I noted above, an idea like freedom had to start *somewhere* before it could develop further and interact with other traditions, yet retaining a core meaning that transcends any local space and time, and thus influencing and serving the aspirations of peoples radically different from the Greeks.[32] Disbelievers in the continuity of Hellenic tradition are obligated to explain why classical concepts like "democracy," "republic," "tragedy," and "citizen" are vital to our culture today, whereas Hebraic rule by priests, Persian satrapic organization, Germanic tribal structures, and the Egyptian pharaonic cult survive only as objects of antiquarian study.[33]

Defending the Greeks is not a new project, although it has been made more difficult by the decline in our educational system, which ensures that today's critics of the Greeks have an audience ill-equipped to recognize distorted interpretation and false knowledge. That audience is vulnerable to statements like the classicist James J. O'Donnell's claim that the "failure of the dream of western civilization has left us a culture with no ideas"—even while people around the world are risking their lives to possess the freedom and science that lie at the heart of that dream, and that O'Donnell himself takes for granted.[34] The Greeks have always had their critics, from the early Christians who wondered "what has Athens to do with Jerusalem," on through those revolutionary-era Americans who associated classical learning with the dead hand of the aristocratic past and who saw the Greeks as tainted by heathenism, elitism, and slavery. Today the Greek heritage is under assault from both utilitarian and therapeutic critics who see its humane values either as irrelevant to an efficient, high-tech, global economy, or as the root of the West's many sins against the multicultural "Other." At the beginning of the new millennium, then—when it appears that the freedom of the individual has for the moment triumphed, whether as a reality to enjoy or an ideal to aspire to—we need to remind ourselves of the great debt we all owe to those few Greeks who first started the human race down the long, difficult road of its liberation.

Reckless Eros, great curse, greatly loathed by men, from you come deadly strifes and grieving and troubles, and countless other pains on top of these swirl up.

—*Apollonius of Rhodes*[1]

ONE

Eros the Killer

In 1998, President Clinton was impeached for actions he allegedly either took or ordered in an attempt to keep secret certain sexual improprieties he had committed with a White House intern. In the reams of analysis that attended the daily drama unfolding in the House of Representatives and then in the Senate trial, our culture's received wisdom and unspoken assumptions about sexuality were readily apparent. Defenders of the president dismissed the sexual activity as a private matter of no concern to the citizenry, with no implications for his political ability to lead the most powerful nation on earth. They dismissed Clinton's critics as repressed Puritans whose morbid fascination with his private behavior revealed their own unresolved sexual conflicts and fears. No one interpreted the affair the way an ancient Greek would have: as an example of the destructive power of Eros, a turbulent and potentially pernicious force that overthrows the mind and judgment and threatens the social and political orders that make human life possible.

To the popular imagination, such a statement might sound odd. Weren't the Greeks those jolly hedonists, those liberated celebrators of bodily beauty and pleasure, those carefree, "polymorphously perverse" nymphs and satyrs uninhibited by the grim repressions—either exclusive heterosexuality or chastity—that Christianity introduced in its neurotic hatred of the body and its guilty pleasures? This myth of ancient sexual libertinism—"a sentimental paganism which blamed the cold breath of the Galilean for blasting a world of joyous innocence"[2]—cropped up in the nineteenth century, when the mores of the Greeks, with all their cultural authority, were touted as an alternative to the repressive hypocrisies of Victorian society. The myth resurfaced in the sixties when gurus like Herbert Marcuse and the classicist Norman O. Brown preached a Dionysian sexual liberation as the necessary precursor to a politically free, egalitarian utopia. Besides being wrong, this interpretation of ancient Greek sexuality illustrates how the Greeks can be distorted to suit present obsessions—thus obscuring any possible value their ideas might have for us.

No more enlightening are the approaches to Greek sexuality that are fashionable in the academy today. A radical social constructionism, which reduces sexuality and human identity itself to mere epiphenomena of totalizing power networks, has produced an equally distorted view of Greek sexuality. In this interpretation, the Greek "conceptual blueprint of sexual relations . . . corresponded to social patterns of dominance and submission, reproducing power differentials between partners in configuring gender roles and assigning them by criteria not always coterminous with biological sex. Intercourse was construed solely as bodily penetration of an inferior."[3] Only academics could reduce something as intricate, intimate and *interesting* as sex into a boring, depersonalized "system" in which mechanically penetrating or penetrated "subjects" are compelled to act out robotically their politically programmed "roles."

In greek culture, sexuality is considered a force of nature. Like all such forces it is powerful, volatile, amoral, and destructive; it must be controlled by the orders of the mind and the institutions of culture—lest it sweep them away. Like all ancient peoples, the Greeks lived intimately with the powers of nature. The daily imperative to find enough food made them dependent on nature's fickle fertility, while the impact of storms, plagues, predatory beasts, and fires was much more disastrous than it is for us, protected as we are in our cocoon of technology. The passions and appetites of humans were considered natural forces as well, equally destructive, equally in need of restraint and limit.

Plato's image of the soul in the *Republic* illustrates this link of the appetites to nature: the soul comprises a "multifarious and many-headed beast, girt round with heads of animals, tame and wild," along with a lion and a man. The beasts are the passions and appetites; if they gain the upper hand over the "man" (reason), and corrupt the "lion" (the nonrational part of the soul amenable to reason), they will "bite and struggle and devour one another," ultimately destroying the soul.[4] Only by "awing the beast," as Emerson put it, can reason cultivate and tame the nonrational part of the soul so that reason can direct its energy towards ends suitable for human virtue and happiness. The Greeks may have disagreed over whether it is *possible* for reason or culture to control passion, but nowhere in Greek literature is there any evidence of something like our culture's peculiar delusion that liberating sexual passion will lead to the individual's fulfillment and happiness.

In the Greek context, on the contrary, sexuality is an irrational force, full of destructive potential. Greek literature developed a large repertoire of images to communicate the disorder of sex, linking it with storms, fire, disease, insanity, animals, violence, and death. Our Valentine's Day icon, baby Cupid with his bow and arrows, has its origins in a much less benign view of sex that connected it with the violence and suffering of war, and to ancient warfare's most feared weapon, the arrow. The late-seventh-century poet and mercenary Archilochus wrote of passion, "Wretched I lie soulless with desire, pierced through my bones by the bitter pains of the gods."[5] The phrase "pierced through the bones" is from Homer's *Iliad* (5.69), where it describes the effect of an arrow; thus it links the experience of desire to the danger and misery of battle. The soldier

Archilochus, unlike most of us, knew first-hand what edged steel can do to human flesh, and his metaphor, although dead for us, forcefully described the lethal consequences of desire to the soul.

Other Homeric phrases that describe the fallen warrior's experience are similarly applied to sexual passion. In another fragment Archilochus writes, "For such was the passion for lovemaking that twisted itself beneath my heart and poured a thick mist over my eyes, stealing the tender wits from my body."[6] Readers of Homer will recognize the "dark mist" over the eyes as one of his striking images for the dying warrior's experience. Another phrase that describes death, "limb-loosening," is often used to convey the loss of rational control that accompanies desire. Hesiod (late eighth century) calls the god of sexual passion, Eros, the "limb-loosener" who "conquers the mind and shrewd thoughts of all the gods and men."[7] The seventh-century poet Sappho uses the same epithet in a fragment that records for the first time that old standby expression, "bittersweet": "Once again Eros the limb-loosener shakes me, that bittersweet, irresistible creature."[8] The linking of desire to death emphasizes how high the stakes of passion are: one's self-control, mind, humanity itself are all at risk.

Other sexual imagery in Greek literature links passion to the forces of nature. Fire is particularly significant since, like sexuality, it is necessary for civilization even to exist—remember that Prometheus saves the human race by stealing fire from heaven. Yet fire obviously is destructive as well. Sappho's catalogue of erotic symptoms includes a "delicate fire running beneath the skin."[9] Apollonius of Rhodes (third century) says of Medea's fierce passion for Jason—incited by Aphrodite so that Medea will betray her father and help Jason steal the golden fleece—"Coiling round her heart secretly burned Eros the destroyer."[10] For us, fire might be a harmless prop in a romantic tableau; for the Greeks, who used fire every day and knew intimately its destructive potential, the fire of sex could wipe out whole cities, just as the illicit passion of Helen and Paris led to the burning of Troy.

Disease and insanity are also used as metaphors to describe the baneful effects of sexual passion. In his play *Hippolytus* (429),

Euripides tells the story of an austere, ascetic intellectual who hates the disorder of sex and the body and so considers himself naturally chaste, in effect denying his own sexuality. This angers Aphrodite, the goddess of sex, "mighty among men," whose power extends over every creature that lives and must reproduce, and who "trips up" those who "think big" against her. So she sets out to destroy Hippolytus by making his stepmother Phaedra conceive an overwhelming sexual passion for him. Euripides brilliantly manipulates his culture's repertoire of sexual imagery to dramatize the destruction of Phaedra's soul. When she first is brought on stage, she is literally out of her mind, "wracked with fever," as her nurse describes her, wasting away, a victim of "sheer madness, / that prompts such whirling, frenzied, senseless words."[11] Phaedra drifts in and out of sanity, struggling to fight against her disease and tormented by her powerless sense of shame. She finally kills herself after her nurse's attempt to arrange a liaison with Hippolytus ends in a humiliating rejection; but first she destroys Hippolytus, accusing him of rape and thus leading his father Theseus to curse him.

For us, being "lovesick" or "crazy" about someone is harmless, even agreeable. To the Greeks, however, such metaphors conveyed the awesome power of sexuality, a force that, unregulated, could overthrow the mind and civilization itself. Excessive sexual desire wasn't *like* a disease, it *was* a disease. No wonder the aged Sophocles, when asked if he missed the pleasures of sex, responded, "I feel as if I had escaped from an insane and furious despot."[12]

GREEK HOMOSEXUALITY HAS ALWAYS BEEN one of the major battlefields in the war over the Greek legacy. To early Christian Europe the sexual proclivities of the Greeks were part and parcel of their general pagan corruption, graphic evidence of their fallen status. Once the Hellenic heritage was assimilated into Christian culture, Greek practices like pederasty became guilty secrets available only to the learned. In the Victorian heyday of idealizing the Greeks, their homosexuality was explained away or rationalized, as when the German scholar Ulrich von Wilamowitz interpreted Sappho's fragment 31 as a heterosexual wedding song, rather than a brilliant description of the poet's powerful sexual attraction to a girl. When middle-class sexual liberation began in the late nineteenth and early twentieth centuries, a cult of sentimental homosexuality idealized the Greeks as inventors of the worship of male beauty and youth, something scorned by a Philistine, heterosexual Victorian establishment.

Today we have our own received wisdom about "Greek love." According to the social constructionists in the academy, the Greeks regarded various sexual acts such as homosexual sodomy with indifference, as neutral practices obtaining meaning only in the context of the game of political power and citizenship. Sexual objects, one theorist tells us, were determined not so much "by a physical typology of sexes as by the social articulation of power."[13] The implication is that our most important cultural arbiters, the Greeks, are now spokesmen for some modern version of gay sexual "liberation." Their practice allegedly legitimizes any and all sexual practices, none of which is inherently good or bad, natural or unnatural, constructive or destructive, since all bear merely a contingent meaning as required by a particular culture's power structure, by the way it distributes the prizes of citizenship. The evidence from Greek literature, however, tells a different story.

Consider the story Plato has Aristophanes tell in the *Symposium* about the origins of heterosexuality and homosexuality: Humans once were double creatures with four arms and four legs; some were male, some female, and others both. In their arrogance these wheel-like creatures conspired against the gods, who punished them by splitting them in two. Consequently we have a powerful drive to seek our lost "other half"—descendants of the all-males seek men; of the females, women; and of the mixed sex, their opposite. Aristophanes' obvious implication is that people are born either heterosexual or homosexual; the latter marry and have children, says Aristophanes, not because of "nature" (*phusei*) but because of "custom" (*nomou*).[14] Ancient Greek natural philosophers also explain homosexuality as a phenomenon resulting either from nature or from individual habit, rather than from arbitrary social "constructs." The *Problems,* doubtfully attributed to Aristotle, explains what the author considers the oddity of men enjoying passive sodomy by postulating a physical deformity, arising either naturally or from abuse, that causes semen to collect in the anus. The fluid collects and creates desire that cannot be gratified because the semen cannot be discharged. Hence the passive homosexual seeks out anal intercourse to relieve the pressure.[15] Aristotle also accounts for what he calls "diseased practices"—compulsive behavior such as pulling out one's hair, nail-biting, eating coals or earth, or "sex between males"—by attributing them to either "nature" or "habit."[16] These passages show that some Greeks, at least, saw homosexuality both as a type of deviant behavior and as a phenomenon of nature, albeit a deformed nature.

The Greek view of Eros as an indiscriminate force implied that most people would gratify their imperious desire by means of just about any object available. Euripides' Laius, in a fragment from the lost play *Chrysippus,* explains his rape of the boy Chrysippus—the act that starts the chain of disaster culminating in Oedipus' crimes—by saying, "Nature drove me on."[17] But contrary to the Christian-influenced view that any sexual act between males is a sin, the Greeks mainly condemned the passive homosexual; they saw the male who would submit to penetration by another male as having abandoned the soul to destructive passion. The active male was faulted if he was excessive or outrageous or chose the wrong partner, as did Laius.

Occasionally one finds condemnation of active same-sex acts. In the philosopher Prodicus' allegory concerning Heracles' choice between a personified Virtue and Vice, the former accuses the latter of "using men like women."[18] But the Greeks' harshest censure was reserved for the male who played the woman's role in sex. Such a man was called a *kinaidos,* a word whose range of meaning goes from the specific—the effeminate, penetrated male; to the general—someone whose excessive sexual appetite compelled him to behave in shameful and degrading ways. Since the Greeks defined humanity as the rational control of appetite, anyone who willingly gave in to shameful pleasures—to a compulsive "itch," as Socrates described it—had sacrificed not just his manhood, but his humanity itself.[19]

Similar opprobrium met the adulterer, the man who so lacked self-control that he would seduce a citizen-wife—at the risk of his life, since a wronged husband could legally kill an adulterer. As the Cynic philosopher Antisthenes asked, who but a senseless man would risk his life in such a way when gratification was available on every corner for a pittance?[20] Another traditional punishment for adultery, sticking a radish up the offender's anus, suggests that the Greeks viewed the adulterer and the passive homosexual in the same light: as creatures of appetites that drove them to destructive behavior. Aristophanes specifically connects the two in the *Clouds* (423), where the Athenian audience is scorned as utterly dissolute, their "wide assholes" evidence of either buggery or the radish punishment.[21] Such men were considered unfit to wield political power, for all their decisions would reflect the tyrannous demands of appetite rather than a rational assessment of the state's best interest.

The contempt that the Greeks felt for the *kinaidos* is reflected in the insulting epithets that focus on the anus stretched out by buggery. Words such as *katapugôn,* "passive homosexual/lecher," and *euruprôktos,* "wide-anused," formed from the words for "rump" and "anus," were obviously derived from the experience of being buggered, and were used to describe the worst examples of sexual incontinence even when homosexuality was not at issue. Other, similar insults included "gapers," "gaping-assed," and "cistern-assed."[22] When applied to men, they often were accompanied by derogatory references to effeminacy and "softness" (*malakos,* still an insult in modern Greek), since the man who would play the woman's role during sex was thought to cultivate on purpose a woman's appearance and to share her characteristic weaknesses. Thus in the *Laws* Plato can assume that the passive homosexual will be a coward, since the man who is sexually penetrated like a woman will display a woman's timidity.[23] The implication of these insults is that the man who plays the woman's role in sex has sacrificed not only his masculinity but even his humanity to bestial pleasure.

Aristophanes' comedies are full of characters, many based on historical models, who are ridiculed for passive homosexuality and effeminacy. The tragic poet Agathon, a late-fifth-century contemporary of Euripides and Socrates, is pilloried for his effeminate dress, his habit of depilating himself, and the unsavory sexual practices that his appearance suggests. In the *Women at the Thesmophoria* (411), a play about Euripides' trial by the Athenian women who are angry over the playwright's alleged misogyny, Agathon is described as wearing a woman's robe and hair net, as well as being "fair of face, white, clean-shaven, woman-voiced, soft, pretty." Since men in Athens didn't shave their beards, anyone clean-shaven was assumed to be effeminate not just in appearance but in sexual practice as well. When the character of Euripides wants to disguise an old relative of his as a woman to infiltrate his accusers' counsels, he borrows Agathon's razor and singes off the unfortunate elder's pubic hair, not just because Athenian women singed their pubic hair, but because passive homosexuals were assumed to depilate their anuses. (Another mocked effeminate, Cleisthenes, is accused of "plucking the hairs from his anus among the tombs"—cemeteries being notorious trysting spots.[24])

The old relative of Euripides, Mnesilochus, has no doubt that Agathon's sexual practices reflect his appearance: when the tragedian sententiously announces that misfortune must be met with "endurance," literally "things suffered," Mnesilochus snorts, "Yeah, and you, oh sodomite, are wide-anused not with words, but with the things you've suffered."[25] Plato also, in the midst of one of the most famous encomia to same-sex Eros, the *Phaedrus,* assumes that a boy who cultivates a girlish appearance and lives an "unmanly and delicate way of life" would be capable of sexual practices too shameful to mention.[26]

Jokes of this kind take for granted that most of the Athenians in the audience would find men who are effeminate in appearance and sexual behavior to be natural objects of scorn and ridicule. Aristophanes, however, is not just trying to get a laugh. He has a more serious political point: that the corruption of Athenian politics, evident in the growth of the Athenian Empire and in the destructive, costly war with Sparta, resulted from unrestrained greed for power, wealth and self-gratification—from an inability to exercise self-control, whose most potent metaphor is the male who submits to buggery. The passive homosexual functions as the concrete image for *all* the destructive appetites. He is linked as well to the late-fifth-century "new man," whom Aristophanes regarded as evidence of Athenian decline from the hardy generation that stopped the Persians at Marathon. The "new man" included "the smooth-talking orator and Sophist, the lupine careerist and ambitious demagogue, the 'laconizing'—pro-Spartan—snooty aristocrat, all of whom promote war and weaken the fabric of society for private gain and the gratification of appetite."[27]

Several of Aristophanes' comedies link a corrupting greed to sexual excess, especially passive homosexuality, in order to explain the decline of Athenian society. In the *Knights* (424), the vulgar Sausage-Seller's rise to political preeminence is partly attributable to his indiscriminate sexual appetite. He tells the story of how, as a boy, he stole some meat and hid it between his buttocks. An orator who witnessed this obvious reference to buggery commented, "That boy is certain to go far; he's bound for public office."[28] In other words, thieving, lying, and enduring buggery are prime qualifications for political success.

Later, the Sausage-Seller confirms that in his youth he was "fucked" in the marketplace for money. His rival for the affections of Demos, the personified Athenian citizenry, is the Paphlagonian: his anus lies "among the Gapers," those whose anuses have been stretched out by constant buggery. When the Paphlagonian claims that he cut down on the number of "fucked ones," passive homosexuals, the Sausage-Seller retorts that his opponent was simply reducing the number of both his sexual and political rivals. Finally, the contest between the Sausage-Seller and the Paphlagonian is compared to the rivalry between two men for the affections of a "boy-love"—the implication being that the winner will get to "fuck" the city both literally and metaphorically.[29] In other plays as well, Aristophanes links the corruption of politics, of language, of mores, even of theater itself to the unnatural "itch" to be sodomized. The moral is clear: the man who so lacks self-control that he will submit to such shameful practices merely because of a sterile pleasure will submit to any and all desires, and will put the city and its institutions at risk in order to gratify his appetites.

This view of passive homosexuality is not unique to the humorous requirements of comedy. Among the orators and philosophers, too, a soul-destroying lack of self-control finds its worst manifestation in the *kinaidos*. The orator Aeschines' politically motivated attack on Timarchos (345) accused him of selling his body to men for sex; this was damaging because in Athens, being a prostitute barred one from holding political office. Throughout the speech, a link is made between "excessive incontinence," whose worst manifestation is committing a "woman's sins" (passive sodomy), and unfitness to participate in the machinery of government. As a "slave to the most shameful pleasures," including heterosexual excess, gambling, and gluttony, a man such as Timarchos is not fit to be trusted with the business of the city, for his lack of self-control will make him vulnerable to every form of corruption. The man who will abandon his body to shameful pleasures will sell out his country as well.[30]

But surely a philosopher like Plato, who wrote two of the most famous paeans to homosexual Eros, must think differently from the comic poet or the orator, both of whom must play to the prejudices of their audiences? In fact Plato, like other writers who praise pederasty, does not thereby condone *physical* gratification between males, but condemns it as "shameful" and "unnatural." In the *Phaedrus* Plato describes the soul attracted to a beautiful boy's body instead of his soul as "not ashamed to pursue pleasure contrary to nature."[31] Likewise, in the *Erotic Essay* attributed to the fourth-century orator and statesman Demosthenes, the "just lover" neither does to nor requests from a boy anything "shameful"; rather, he "associates chastely" with him and gives him the benefits of love "without shame." So too Socrates, in Xenophon's *Symposium* (set in 421), calls acts of physical gratification between males in a pederastic relationship "the most thoroughly shameful things."[32]

Aristotle defined shame as a "pain or disturbance in regard to bad things ... which seem likely to involve us in discredit"—the "bad things" including "carnal intercourse with forbidden persons."[33] This concept of "shame" was critical for the ancient Greeks, who lived their lives much more publicly and valued public esteem far more than we do. Their persistent references to shame in connection with passive homosexuality belie the modern notion that they were indifferent to sodomy as long as certain social and political protocols were observed. On the contrary, the anxiety about shame arising from passive homosexuality permeates even the writings of the pederastic apologists, who must continually ward off the charge, apparently widespread, that the pedagogical and character-building rationale for the relationship between an older male and a teenager is nothing more than a pretext for illicit sex. Hence Pausanias, depicted in Plato's *Symposium* as Agathon's lover far beyond the age considered respectable for the younger partner in a pederastic couple, admits that the sexual gratification practiced by the "vulgar" lovers, those unconcerned with building a noble character, is responsible for the view of "some" that it is "shameful to gratify a lover."[34]

The characterization of passive sodomy as "contrary to nature" (*para phusin*) used by Plato in the *Phaedrus* marks out the passive homosexual as someone whose appetites deform his natural humanity. Thus Aeschines in his speech against Timarchos accuses him of "outraging his body contrary to nature." And in the *Laws,* the Athenian Stranger outlines for his utopia sexual laws similar to those that existed "before Laius," the father of Oedipus, whose rape of Chrysippus was often considered the origins of pederasty—that is, laws forbidding sex with men "like women" *(kathaper thêleiôn)*. Such laws Plato describes as "following nature" *(tê phusei),* while sexual practices like adultery and homosexuality are called "contrary to nature" *(para phusin)*.[35] Some modern commentators go into interpretive contortions in their attempts to explain away the obvious implication of the phrase "contrary to nature": that at least Plato and Aeschines viewed sex as having a natural function, procreation, which by its absence rendered homosexuality "unnatural." And Aristotle would seem to agree, for his abovementioned efforts to account for the desire to be sodomized assume that such strange behavior results from a deformity, and represent it as a compulsive anomaly, like eating earth or tearing out one's hair. This is hardly the view that one modern scholar has attributed to the Greeks: that they "did not see a gulf between a desire to penetrate and a desire to be penetrated."[36]

Sexual passion to the Greeks, then, was a potentially destructive force of nature, a power that, if indulged to excess, could destroy not just the individual soul but the political and social institutions of civilization itself. This is not to say that the Greeks did not recognize and appreciate the beauty and pleasure of sexual desire, for they certainly did. "What life, what joy," the seventh-century poet Mimnermus asked, "without golden Aphrodite?"[37] The breast-band of Aphrodite, which Hera borrows in the *Iliad* to seduce her husband Zeus, is embroidered with "allurements" and "dalliances" and "the whisperings of maidens" and "smiles."[38] Hesiod tells us that "Sweet delight" is Aphrodite's "portion."[39]

But that delightful pleasure is exactly what makes sexuality so dangerous: the sweetness of sexual pleasure too often masks the bitter, destructive power of Aphrodite. To keep that power in check, sex has to be contained and regulated—and its creative energy exploited—by the mind and by the institutions, customs, and laws that the mind projects to order the world. To be sure, the Greeks disagreed about whether or not these controls could contain Eros. To Socrates' contention that knowledge can create virtue, Euripides famously responds with the despairing cry of Phaedra, wracked by the disease of lust: "We know the good and recognize it, but we cannot do it."[40] Still, both the philosopher and the poet recognize that the seductive power of Eros, once unleashed, leads not to fulfillment but to destruction.

How is this awesome force to be contained? The philosophers look to reason, the truly humanizing part of human identity, to control the volatile, chaotic forces of the body and its appetites. The latter are indiscriminate, with no innate ability to recognize their own proper limits or ends. As Plato says, they are "infinite . . . and never have in [themselves] a beginning, middle, or end of [their] own."[41] Elsewhere he uses the Pythagorean image of the incontinent soul as a "jar perforated because of its insatiable desires." After death, such a soul is condemned to the never-ending task of filling its leaky jar with a sieve, since in life he devoted his power and energy to gratifying desires that can never be permanently sated and so always demand more and more.[42] Such desires and their pleasures, Plato tells us, are the soul's "disease," one "endless and insatiate of evils."[43]

These appetites and passions are also bestial and slavish, as Aristotle describes them, ruling like a tyrant or despot the soul that gives in to their pleasures.[44] The well-ordered soul, however, makes reason its "steersman," the guiding intelligence that sees the proper ends of the appetites and exploits their energy just as a steersman uses the power of wind and wave to guide the ship to its goal.[45] An important tool for effecting this control is "self-control/temperance" (*sôphrosunê*), a rational virtue that brings thought and calculation to bear on the body's appetites and passions. Its main purpose is to be the ruler "over the desires and pleasures of food and drink and sex" so that they do not become excessive and thus destroy the soul.[46] Likewise Aristotle sees "self-control/temperance" as concerned with the "slavish and brutish" pleasures of touch and taste, those like eating and drinking and sex that belong to our animal natures.[47] The latter is a particularly volatile and potentially destructive appetite, the indulgence of which earns one the epithet "licentious," the vice directly opposed to "self-control/temperance." Thus Aristophanes, in a lost play, brought on stage the character Katapugôn, "sodomite/lecher," as a personification of vice, in opposition to Sôphrôn, a personification of "self-control/temperance."

Certainly, sexual self-control was the preeminent virtue that made Socrates the ancient paragon of *sôphrosunê*. In Plato's *Symposium,* Alcibiades' famous praise of the philosopher gives many examples of his mastery over his body: going about barefoot in the dead of winter during the campaign at Potidaea during the Peloponnesian War, standing all day in one spot while he pondered a philosophical conundrum, and surviving the Athenian rout at Delium by keeping his head while the panic-stricken were slaughtered all around him. But the prime example of Socrates' temperance was his resistance to the handsome Alcibiades' youthful attempt to seduce him. After spending the night with Socrates wrapped in a cloak, says Alcibiades, he awoke the next morning as chaste as if he had spent the night with his father or brother. Alcibiades marveled at the "self-control/temperance [*sôphrosunên*] and manliness of his [Socrates'] nature."[48] The ability to control one's sexual appetite is the touchstone of the truly self-controlled, virtuous man.

SOCIETY'S INSTITUTIONS ALSO WORK TO CHANNEL and control the power of sex. The premier social structure for ordering human sexuality, of course, is marriage. In marriage the natural exuberance of sex, as fraught with danger as it is alluring, is channeled into the household, the fundamental building block of the state—which is why Aristotle begins his treatise on the state, the *Politics,* by first considering the household. He defines this as "the union of those who cannot exist without each other; namely, of male and female, that the race may continue.... The family is the association established by nature for the supply of men's everyday wants.... Seeing then that the state is made up of households, before speaking of the state we must speak of the management of the household."[49] The emphasis on procreation points to marriage's important function in ancient Greece: to exploit sexual energy to keep a society going beyond one generation, and to provide the legitimate citizens who will run the state and inherit its property.

This channeling and regulating function of marriage is obvious in the agricultural metaphors the Greeks used to describe it. Agriculture was central to the lives of the ancients in ways lost to us modern Westerners, who take it for granted that safe, abundant food will always be available in the market. Most Greeks were small farmers, intimate with the struggle to wrest nutrition from a recalcitrant nature that has defined most of humanity's experience, until this century's advances in chemical fertilizers and pesticides liberated people in the industrialized West from the backbreaking work of providing themselves food. Hence for the Greeks, agricultural metaphors powerfully communicated the central drama of human existence: surviving in a natural world utterly indifferent, if not actively hostile, to human beings. Moreover, survival depended on humanity's ability to exploit the energy of nature, to impose a rational order on it so that its fertility was more predictable and reliable, and its destructiveness minimized. Against that most volatile of natural forces, Eros, the social and political institution of marriage regulated human sexuality to control its potential destructiveness and exploited it in order to create the next generation of citizens.

The metaphor of plowing, used to describe conjugal sex, exemplifies this likening of marriage to agriculture. The image was part of the traditional marriage ceremony: "I give you my daughter for the plowing of legitimate children," the father of the bride would tell the groom, an expression as evocative of marriage in Greek literature as our "for better or worse" is for us.[50] Marriage could be described as "sowing arable land," and the wife could be designated a "furrow," an image Sophocles exploits in the *Oedipus Turannos* when the chorus wonders how a "father's furrows" could stand Oedipus' incestuous marriage to his mother, Jocasta.[51] Oedipus' father, Laius, despite the oracle that predicted his son would kill him and marry his own mother, nevertheless "sows a child while drunk and full of lust."[52] These farming metaphors, typically used to describe licit marital intercourse, here intensify by contrast the horror of Laius' and Oedipus' sexual crimes, whose results are civic chaos: the curse that not only destroys Oedipus' family but nearly wipes out the whole city of Thebes with a blight of infertility.

An analogy to farming also expressed the Greeks' view of procreation, wherein the male is the active depositor of the seed in the female, who, as Plato puts it, "imitates the earth."[53] A notorious example of this mistaken attribution of sole creative power to the male occurs in Aeschylus' *Oresteia.* To the Furies' argument that Orestes should die for killing his mother—crimes against blood relatives being theirs to punish—Apollo counters by asserting that the mother is not the parent but merely the "rearer of the new-sown embryo." The true parent is the "mounter," the father, while the mother "preserves the sprout."[54] In this view, both marriage and farming work by ordering and controlling nature so that its fertility can be exploited. In Apollo's logic, the relationship created by the social institution of marriage, paternity, takes precedence over the relationship created by nature, maternity.

In addition to marriage, many religious festivals in ancient Greece linked nature's fertility to female sexuality, subjecting both to social and civic controls. One of the more significant in this regard was the Athenian Thesmophoria, which took place in late October at the olive harvest, when the seed for the next year's grain was prepared for planting. The myth central to the festival tells the story of Demeter, goddess of the earth and its products, and her daughter Persephone, who is kidnapped by Hades and taken into the underworld. There she must live for four months of the year, and during that time nothing grows, for Demeter is mourning her lost daughter. This myth allows for many interpretations, but the central and obvious one concerns the life cycle of vegetation, especially grain, which grows, is cut down in early summer, and then is "buried" in late fall, coming to maturity in the spring. Yet the story of Persephone also links the life of plants to that of the young girl, whose spring-like life as a virgin—"the sweetest life known to mortals," as Sophocles' Procne puts it[55]—must end in marriage so that her sexuality can bear fruit; she undergoes a symbolic "death" to her old life, followed by rebirth into her role as wife and mother in the social structure of the household.

A fragment of Sappho, probably from one of her epithalamia or "wedding songs," also uses an agricultural metaphor to capture the necessary loss of the girl's sexual innocence: "As the sweet apple blushes on the top branch, the top of the highest branch, the apple pickers have forgotten it; they haven't forgotten it, but they couldn't reach it."[56] The image's poignancy comes from our knowledge that whether the pickers can reach it or not, the apple is ripe and so must fall, just as the girl must marry and become a mother.

What we know about the Thesmophoria confirms this link of female sexuality to natural fecundity.[57] Only Athenian citizen-wives participated in the three-day festival; men, children, concubines, prostitutes, and virgins were excluded. The wives were supposed to remain chaste, eating garlic to make this easier. On the first day the women assembled, organized their "government," and transported the sacrificial animals and material they would need to build the "city" they would inhabit, separated from their husbands. On the second day the political business of Athens was suspended and the women participating in the festival fasted, sitting on mats woven from a plant that was supposed to inhibit sexual desire and promote menstrual flow. Probably toward the end of the second day, pigs, fecund animals par excellence, were sacrificed, and the "things laid down" were brought forth by "Balers," women who had abstained from sex for three days before the festival. These mysterious "things" consisted of an unpleasant melange of rotting sacrificed pigs mixed with dough models of human genitalia and snakes, which had been deposited in caverns during a festival celebrated earlier, before midsummer. This compost would later be mixed with the seeds for next year's grain crop. Little is known about the activities of the third day, Kalligeneia, the day of "beautiful offspring," but the name implies a day of feasting and celebration after the two days of fasting, a joyful anticipation of the fertility to come, both of the women and of the crops.

Any religious festival has complex and intricate meanings, but clearly the Thesmophoria, through abstinence and sympathetic magic, was a civic ritual that ordered and focused the citizen-women's sexual energy and the fertile powers of nature to ensure that there would be food to eat and citizens born to continue the city's life. Like agriculture, the political ritual organized natural sexual power so that it served society rather being an end in itself.

MORE THAN ANYTHING ELSE, PEDERASTY has earned the ancient Greeks their reputation for either enlightened tolerance or depraved license. This ritualized, transitory, quasi-pedagogical relationship between a boy in his late teens and an older male was by the late fifth century a minority pursuit of an embattled aristocracy and those who aped their fashions. The small farmers and "good ol' boys" of Aristophanes' comedies certainly view it that way: as a Spartanesque affectation, like long hair, of a nobility disillusioned with democracy and its radical egalitarianism. In the *Wasps* (422), it is the old veterans of Marathon who mock the younger generation's "curls and wide-arse-ishness."[58] But even among those writers who frankly approve of the pederastic relationship, the fear of Eros' destructive power and anxiety about turning the boy into the dreaded *kinaidos* ring the relationship with numerous prohibitions, particularly that against a "shameful" physical gratification.

What we see is not a celebration of a mutually gratifying physical and emotional bond, but rather a mechanism for channeling homosexual desire into a social institution that limited its expression while exploiting its energy to train the citizen-elite who would fight in the city's armies and hold its offices.[59] In short, like marriage or religious festivals, pederasty was a "technology" that controlled and sublimated sexual energy for the benefit of the city by instructing its future leaders. Thus Euripides called Eros the most important teacher of wisdom and inspirer of virtue.[60]

Pederasty, then, attempted a delicate balancing act between using the sexual attraction for teenaged boys as the energy driving their education, and avoiding even the hint of sexual activity that would lump the boy with the despised *kinaidos*. Numerous formal and informal prohibitions existed to protect the boy's sexual integrity—for example, laws that prohibited the teacher or head of a gymnasium, one of the prime locales for pederastic courtship, from opening before sunrise or staying open after sunset.[61] Boys were expected to behave modestly and play hard-to-get. Plato makes reference to fathers having slaves watch over their boys, and older youths often reproached boys who were too attentive to wooers.[62]

More important, perhaps, were the ethical boundaries of pederasty created by the fear of "shame" and "outrageous excess" *(hubris)* that would arise from sexual indulgence, and by the insistence on "temperance/self-control/chastity" as the virtue that would protect the relationship's integrity. In pederastic literature, the bogey of "shame" and "outrage" is used repeatedly to define by contrast a relationship as a "just Eros." Xenophon's *Symposium* presents a vignette of such a relationship, between the young athlete Autolycus and his admirer Callias, who are attending the banquet on the occasion of the youth's victory in a sport called the pancratium, a brutal combination of wrestling, boxing, and kicking. The narrator describes Autolycus' beauty as "kingly" because it is joined to "a sense of shame/sobriety and chastity/self-control" *(sôphrosunês),* and Callias' demeanor as admirable because it reflects a "chaste Eros" *(sôphronos Erôtos)*. The relationship is so aboveboard that Autolycus' father is present. Socrates later explains that the manly Autolycus, in contrast to the *kinaidos,* is not corrupted by "softness/effeminacy" *(malakia)*. Rather, he displays "bodily strength, endurance, manliness, and self-control/chastity [*sôphrosunên*]." This somewhat anxious insistence on self-control clearly functions to distance the relationship from the chaos of Eros and its mind-destroying pleasure—not even a kiss is allowed the "self-controlled/chaste" lover.[63]

The most famous examples of the attempt to exploit the physical force of Eros for a nonsexual purpose can be found in Plato's *Phaedrus* and *Symposium*. In these dialogues the aristocratic institution of pederasty, whose function is ultimately to benefit the city politically by training its elite, is now put to a much different service: the lifting of the rational soul above the shifting mire of change and decay that is the material world, until it can soar in the empyrean of pure, timeless Truth and Goodness and Beauty. In the *Phaedrus,* the famous image of the soul as comprising a charioteer (reason) in a chariot driven by two horses—one "good" because it is a "lover of honor along with self-control/chastity and shame/modesty," the other bad because it is the "companion of outrage [*hubreôs*]"—reprises the idealized ethics of pederasty. When the soul is incited by the divine Beauty shining forth from the boy, the good horse restrains itself while the bad leaps forward to seek "favors of sexual pleasure." The charioteer and the good horse recoil from such "awesome and unlawful things," and restrain the bad horse until it is trained to see the beloved with "reverence/shame and fear."

Only thus can the soul avoid the shameful disorder of sex while exploiting its energy in order to acquire knowledge of true Beauty—the immaterial, pure, abstract Beauty "all breathing human passion far above," to borrow Keats' phrase.[64] Once more, erotic energy is not an end in itself, but merely a force to drive the soul to enlightenment.

So too in the *Symposium,* the soul's ascent of the "ladder of beauty," fueled by erotic desire, leads ultimately beyond the body and its passions. The man attracted to a beautiful boy will be inspired to speak of virtue and goodness and to inculcate these in himself and in the beloved. Yet this typical pederastic pedagogical aim is only the beginning, for experiencing the beauty of one body should lead to the recognition of a more general, abstract beauty, in which beautiful material things partake imperfectly, thus pointing beyond themselves. Then, the lover will disdain the mere physical, erotic beauty of the beloved, for his still-sexual desire is for the *idea* of beauty, which all beautiful bodies share.[65]

The ladder of beauty does not stop there. The soul so inspired will proceed from the beauty of bodies to the beauty of souls, thence to the beauty of laws and customs, and from there to the beauty of all knowledge, each step departing further and further from the "petty" and "cheap" embodiment of beauty in one mere boy. If lucky, the lover will proceed to a vision of absolute, essential Beauty, immortal and unchanging, and finally the "pure and unmixed" Beauty that is not "infected with the flesh and mortal colors and much other mortal nonsense"—Beauty seen not with the mortal eyes but with the immortal, rational soul.[66] We are no longer concerned with harnessing Eros in order to exploit its procreative energy and minimize its destructiveness. Eros' energy has somehow been distilled from the body and put in the service of the individual soul's journey towards knowledge. In Plato's homoerotic metaphysics we find the most extreme example of the mind's attempt to control the disorder of the body and its most volatile appetite, by appropriating its energy to transcend this world of change and decay.

WE HAVE COME A LONG WAY FROM THE GREEK VIEW of sex as a force of nature, volatile and destructive if left uncontrolled. Plato's idealization of sexuality is the distant starting point for the West's long fascination with sexual idealism, a debased version of which permeates our culture today in film, advertisement, supermarket romance, pop lyric, and television show. The Greeks knew better. They realized that the powerful beauty and pleasure of sex were dangerous, in need of controls and prohibitions. To them, sex could never be a "private" affair, of no concern to the larger political community; nor was it a mere "social construct" reflecting the structures of power and privilege, a contingent phenomenon to be restructured at will by social engineers. Rather, it was one of those absolute limits on human identity and aspiration, a powerful force of nature—and like all such forces, necessary for human survival yet requiring rational and social limitations. They would never have imagined undertaking the experiment we have embarked on: trivializing the power of Aphrodite—who, as she warns in the *Hippolytus,* destroys those who "think big" against her—by loosening and weakening those controls, such as marriage and shame. The results are all too obvious today, from the talk-show sexual freaks to the sordid spectacle of casual sex and unleashed narcissism in the White House. Whether we can survive this novel experiment remains to be seen; but whatever its outcome, we cannot say the Greeks didn't warn us.

For a man acquires nothing better than a good wife, and nothing worse than a bad one, a meal-stealer who roasts her man without a fire, for all his strength.

—*Hesiod*[1]

TWO

The Best and Worst Thing

At the beginning of the new millennium, millions of women in the world are still subjected to the brutal power of nature and of men. In China, female babies are aborted en masse to control population and increase the number of more highly desired sons. In India, women are regularly beaten and murdered over inadequate dowries. Across the Middle East and Africa, as many as two million women a year are subjected to genital mutilation ranging from clitoridectomies to infibulation—the complete excision of all external genitalia, after which the wound is sewn up, sometimes with acacia thorns. And everywhere outside the industrialized nations, women with no access to modern medical care suffer death as well as painful complications from prolonged or difficult labor.[2]

In those countries that have inherited the legacy of the Greeks, however, the lot of women is quite different. Medical science has liberated them from the tyranny of nature with its ruthless reproductive imperative, which in ages past subjected them repeatedly to painful and often lethal childbirth. Technology has freed most women from the back-breaking drudgery of daily life that was traditionally their responsibility for most of history. Women have gone to colleges, universities, and professional schools in growing numbers, and now comprise the majority of enrollees in some fields. Women currently enjoy the same political, economic, and legal rights as do men. True, the perennial human evil of the stronger brutalizing the weaker means that women are still victims of abuse and rape, as are children; yet our whole society has been sensitized to these crimes and is making changes that lessen their incidence. Women live longer, healthier lives than do men, and are less likely to be victims of violent crimes. All in all, in the last fifty years women lucky enough to live in the advanced nations have seen their daily lives bettered to a degree unimaginable to earlier generations.

This improvement can be attributed to the long, slow triumph of the Enlightenment ideals of individual human rights and scientific rationalism, which in turn were shaped by the recovery and development of trends initiated by the Greeks. Yet the fashionable anti-Westernism rampant among intellectuals has made the oppression of women a staple charge in the litany of Western crimes against humanity. Even the obvious role of science and technology in bettering women's lives is reduced to a mere instrument of patriarchal hegemony. A book recently published under the imprimatur of a prestigious university press asserts that modern obstetrics—which has saved the lives of millions of women and their infants—is nothing more than "technobirth," a "medical hegemony [that] both reflects and displays the power still vested in the patriarchal capitalist system . . . and American society's profound fear of nature and wistful, uneasy confidence in the technological products of culture."[3] And the origin of this Western blight of technophilia and sexism is found with the Greeks, who despised and oppressed their women, subjecting them to what one feminist scholar has called the "reign of the Phallus."

The details of this sexist "reign" are well known. Greek men, so the story goes, devised a political system based on a paradigm of dominance and submission that gave power only to male citizens. They rationalized their arbitrary and unjust exclusion of women by defining them as volcanoes of sexual appetite ready to erupt at the slightest provocation. Women were deficient in the humanizing faculty of reason, and hence defined as bestial in opposition to the truly human—the rational male, suited to exercising political power.

Yet women were necessary for breeding new citizens and heirs; and so, to insure against bastardy, they had to be strictly controlled, locked away in the dank recesses of the household, protected from the penetrating "gaze" of other men waiting to take advantage of their lecherous proclivities. True friendship and sexual affection being impossible with such lubricious creatures, men turned instead to their peers' comely sons, with whom they conversed and flirted and copulated at the *palaistra,* the wrestling school, a public space where males congregated and enjoyed their superior status; and at the *symposion,* the private drinking party celebrated in the men's quarters, to which their wives and daughters were strictly forbidden entrance. As one recent popular survey puts it, Greek women were "closed off in the internal part of the house to which the men did not have access," and their lives were "empty" and "deprived of interests and gratifications"; they were "excluded from love . . . which . . . found its highest expression in relationships between men."[4]

As we shall see, there is a kernel of truth in this tale. In the literary remains, Greek men do portray women as more closely linked to nature than themselves, and with a more volatile sexuality. But the complexity of Greek attitudes is reduced these days to a simplistic melodrama in order to suit the ideological concerns of postmodern academics. In fact, this tale of Greek sexism has roots among Victorian scholars, against whose exalted (and sexist) standards the Greek treatment of women fell short. The motif, for example, of the "dark and dank" women's quarters in which Greek wives were presumably locked away recurs like a Homeric epithet in Victorian indictments of Greek sexism. In 1923, F. A. Wright, who attributed the Greek world's decline to "one main cause, a low ideal of womanhood and a degradation of women," called the Greek wife a "harem prisoner" secluded in a "small, dark, and uncomfortable" house where she was subjected to a "long round of monotonous work."[5]

In our own time, Sarah Pomeroy likewise has disapproved of the "dark, squalid, unsanitary" homes of Athenian citizen-wives.

The description found its *reductio ad absurdum* in Eva Keuls, who discovered a Greek "phallic ethos" under which Greek women were compelled to spend "their lives wrapped in veils, nameless, concealing their identity, and locked away in the dark recesses of closed-in homes."[6] Of late, scholars have begun to question the basis for this common belief, citing evidence that adultery was commonplace, which implies a measure of mobility and freedom for women, and a lack of archaeological evidence for separate "men's quarters."[7] Yet the "seclusion thesis" still dominates.

WOMEN IN ANCIENT GREECE DID NOT, IT IS TRUE, enjoy the same political, legal and economic rights as did men—nor did they anywhere else in the world. The melancholy truth of human nature is that the stronger enjoy privileges denied to the weaker; and for most of human history, given the harsh environments in which people have lived, physical strength and martial aggressiveness have been advantages for survival. Typical of ancient male attitudes is the following law from twelfth-century Assyria: "A man may flog his wife, he may pull out her hair, he may damage and split her ears. There is nothing wrong in this."[8] Or consider the law of the ancient Israelites that condemned to death by stoning the bride who could not prove her virginity.[9] If we judge the Greeks by the standards of their own age, rather than by ours (which, by the way, are ultimately derived from the Greeks), we find that they are worthy of notice *not* for their unexceptional denial of certain political and economic rights to women, but for their unique recognition of women's complex humanity.[10]

It is true that negative stereotypes of women abound in Greek literature. The reason for this must be found in the larger Greek view of nature and sex, discussed in the previous chapter; for women were considered more subject to those chaotic natural forces upon which humans depend, more passionate and less rational, and thus more volatile and potentially destructive unless subordinated to the controls of reason and culture. At the same time, women are lovely and alluring, shining with the pleasures of Eros and the charms of Aphrodite; they possess a power upon which men are dependent, and to which they are intensely attracted. In short, the power of woman is the power of Eros, the creative and destructive force of nature both inside our souls and out in the world, a force terrible and beautiful—"death and undecaying life," as Sophocles describes Aphrodite.[11]

A look at two famous women from Greek literature reveals just this ambiguity. Pandora is the first woman, created by Zeus in revenge for Prometheus' salvation of humanity by stealing fire from heaven. She is fashioned by Hephaistus, the craftsman god, as an "evil thing" hidden in the semblance of a "bashful maiden." Athena teaches her the woman's arts of needlework and weaving, while Aphrodite gives her sexual allure, the power to arouse "cruel longing and limb-devouring cares." And the trickster god Hermes provides her with a "bitch's mind and a deceptive character" and "lies and wily words." This "sheer trap" is the ancestress of women, a "plague to men who eat bread."[12]

The details of Pandora's creation reveal what is so troubling about her to men: her sexual power, both attractive and duplicitous, but also necessary for humanity in order to reproduce and have the children who will protect them from what Hesiod calls "deadly old age."[13] Man's dependence on nature and its procreative power animates this fear of women, for women seem to be more intimate with that ambiguous power, creative and destructive all at once. Continually in Greek literature women, like Pandora, are linked to the procreative yet volatile forces of nature. A notorious poem of Semonides from the seventh century B.C. comprises a misogynistic bestiary in which various kinds of bad women are linked to animals or nature: the "sow-woman" is fat and dirty, the "vixen" moody and inconsistent, the "bitch" a gossip, and the "she-ass" lazy and indiscriminately promiscuous. All these women are characterized by appetitive excess and emotional instability. And a man is bound to this "unbreakable fetter," Semonides tells us, because of a sexual desire that compels him to "gape" after his wife, to the amusement of his neighbors. The good woman, on the other hand, is likened to the honeybee, which in antiquity was considered asexual and thought to have an innate disgust towards sexual matters. Semonides writes that "on her alone blame does not settle. She causes his property to grow and increase, and she grows old with a husband whom she loves and who loves her."[14]

Pandora, then, is the ancestress not simply of woman, but of sexually attractive woman, with a power men fear and depend on, and often have trouble clearly seeing beneath an alluring surface. Women's power is the power of nature, to which they are closer than are men. The prevalence of the vital fluid, blood, in their lives and life-changes—from menarche to defloration, menstruation to childbirth—links them with the mysterious world of nature. Their minds also are considered to be more vulnerable than men's to the procreative imperative. Ancient medical writers attribute numerous female ailments to the inadequate discharge of menstrual blood, especially in virgins or in women with abnormally narrow cervixes: When the menses can't flow out of the vagina, it backs up into the chest, where the ancients believed the mind was located, and causes psychological disorders ranging from insanity to anxiety or even suicidal and homicidal tendencies.[15] In more extreme cases, the womb becomes detached and wanders about the body—the origin of our word "hysteria," literally "wombiness"—usually because it is angered by the woman's failure to procreate. (The Hippocratic corpus says, "Women who have intercourse with men are healthier than women who abstain.")[16] This peripatetic womb can cause suffocation if it blocks the lungs, as well as torpor and even foaming at the mouth.[17] Thus, their minds being more vulnerable than men's to nature and the procreative imperative, women are considered less able to control their appetites and more prone to irrational disorders of all sorts unless restrained by the order of culture.

The most famous woman from Greek myth, Helen, perhaps best exemplifies woman's double character—her seductive allure and destructive capacity. Helen is not just the most beautiful woman, but the most *sexually* beautiful woman in the world. Her sexual power is almost supernatural, akin to that of her patroness, Aphrodite. When Helen appears on the walls of Troy to identify the Greek champions for Priam, the old men remark of her beauty, "Terrible is the likeness of her face to immortal goddesses."[18]

A fragment from an archaic poem about women who married gods says that Helen's beauty is that of "golden Aphrodite," her eyes the eyes of the Graces, Aphrodite's attendants.[19] This beauty attracts all the heroes of Greece as suitors, and so vehement are they in their lust for her that her mortal stepfather, Tyndareus (Zeus was her actual father), makes the heroes swear an oath to recover Helen if anyone ever runs off with her. That's one reason why they all end up at Troy. Indeed, so powerful is Helen's sexual allure that her cuckolded husband, Menelaus, understandably on the point of killing her after the sack of Troy, drops his sword when he catches sight of her naked breast.[20] In another version of this scene, the whole Greek army is ready to stone Helen until her loveliness changes their minds.[21]

In the legends surrounding Helen her sexual power is the dominant motif, and always it is characterized as voracious and destructive. In one myth, the promiscuity of Helen and her sisters Clytaemestra and Timandra is explained as a punishment of Tyndareus for some offense or other: his daughters are cursed into being "twice-wed and thrice-wed and husband deserters."[22] Helen's three husbands are Menelaus, Paris, and his brother Deiphobus, whom she marries after Paris dies. But other traditions give Helen even more partners. The Hellenistic poet Lycophron, in a bizarre poem describing Cassandra's prophecies when Paris is born, calls Helen the "five-times-married possessed woman."[23] One partner linked to Helen is Theseus, the legendary king of Athens who kidnaps Helen at the tender age of seven, inciting her brothers Castor and Polydeuces to invade Attica and sack Athens.[24] And her last "husband" is Achilles, the greatest warrior at Troy, who enjoys a secret liaison with Helen during the war, and who, after his death, spends eternity with her on the White Island at the mouth of the Danube—the premier exemplar of martial violence wed to the premier exemplar of sexual power.[25]

The most famous destructive consequence of Helen's sexual appetite, of course, is the sack of Troy. Everywhere in Greek literature the destruction of Troy is attributed to the sexual crime of Helen and Paris. Odysseus' swineherd Eumaeus tells his disguised master that Helen "loosed the knees of many men," a powerful metaphor for describing not just death but, as we saw earlier, sexual desire as well.[26] Odysseus in the underworld says the same thing to Agamemnon's shade, which still bears the gashes inflicted by his treacherous wife Clytaemestra: "Many of us were destroyed because of Helen."[27] The sixth-century poet Alcaeus attributes Priam's "bitter grief" to Helen's "evil deeds," and the playwright Aeschylus created a memorable pun on Helen's name, which sounds like a Greek word that means "destroy": she was "hell on ships, hell on men, hell on the city *(helenaus, helandros, heleptolis)*."[28]

Euripides' Trojan plays, which focus on the sufferings of the innocent survivors of the city's sacking, are filled with epithets that locate Helen's sexuality in the savage realm of chaotic natural forces. In her are concentrated all that is seductive and destructive about women and nature, a nature that resides in men as well, else they would not be so terribly attracted and vulnerable to woman's beauty. And this, I think, is what is interesting about women in Greek literature. They are not alien "Others" to be locked away and despised; rather, they display most intensely the problem of *human* identity: how to control the volatile forces that, unleashed, bring destruction and suffering, but are necessary and often beautiful as well.

That this problem is not just a female but a human one is evident in the myths that link female and male sexual destructiveness. Paris, Helen's paramour, is also characterized in terms of unbridled sexual appetite. His brother Hector scorns him as "Evil Paris, most noble in appearance, woman-mad, beguiler," adding, "would that you were unborn and had died unwed."[29] In Euripides too, Paris is the "great ruin of Priam's city," and Lycophron calls him a "wolf" and a "pirate of Kypris [Aphrodite]."[30] Likewise the myth of the Lemnian women who murder their husbands in a fit of jealousy exemplifies not just the destructive power of thwarted female Eros, but of male desire as well, for the women are provoked by their husbands' taking of concubines. Another notorious example of a depraved female, Clytaemestra is driven to kill her husband not just by her own sexual crime—her illicit affair with Aegisthus, which, she chillingly tells us, will be spiced by the murder of Agamemnon—but also by her husband's sexual appetite. After all, he returned from Troy arrogantly parading his spear-won concubine, Cassandra.[31]

The vulnerability of men to the powers of female sexuality that speak to their own passions is best evident in the mythic culture-hero Heracles. On the one hand, his twelve labors represent the power of masculine culture to organize a chaotic natural world. Yet at the same time, Heracles is famous for his enormous appetites, particularly sex. Like his father Zeus, he enjoys many consorts and fathers numerous children—in one tradition, he deflowers the fifty daughters of a certain Thestius in five days.[32] Indeed, Heracles dies because of his sexual appetite, which drives him to sack the city of Oechalia to possess Iole, the daughter of the city's king Eurytos. When Heracles' wife, Deianira, finds out, she attempts to win her husband back with a love potion, which turns out to be a horrible poison that melts his flesh. Heracles dies in agony, immolating himself on a funeral pyre, the metaphoric fire and disease of lust having become literal.[33] Heracles is burned by the fire of his own lust, just as Troy is burned by the lust of Helen and Paris.

In Greek tragedy we see most sharply defined this problem of human identity: how the failure to control the passions leads to personal and social destruction. We have already met Phaedra, who is driven to suicide and the indirect murder of her stepson Hippolytus because of sexual madness. Yet Hippolytus is partly responsible for his own destruction; his arrogant dismissal of Aphrodite and his delusional belief that he is "chaste by nature" reflect an irrational blindness to the defining limits of his own humanity.[34] While he may celebrate self-control in the play, Hippolytus explodes in irrational anger when the nurse approaches him regarding a liaison with Phaedra. It is that humiliating tirade, overheard by Phaedra, which precipitates her actions.

So too Euripides' Pentheus, in the playwright's brilliant last play the *Bacchae* (405), is vehemently disgusted with the sexual irregularities he suspects the women of Thebes are indulging while they worship Dionysus in the mountains, serving not the god but "the beds of men."[35] He is ultimately lured to a horrible death by Dionysus, who exploits the mortal's sexual ambivalence, irrational obsession, and voyeuristic impulses. The god dresses Pentheus up like a woman and entices him to the mountains by promising him a sight of the women's sexual orgies. Instead, Pentheus is pulled down from the tree in which he has hidden and torn to pieces by the frenzied women, including his mother, who returns to Thebes cradling her son's head in her arms. As with Hippolytus, Pentheus' own irrational impulses collude with those of women to bring about a destruction that threatens the city itself; the play ends with the people of Thebes marching off into exile.

Heracles, Hippolytus, and Pentheus all magnify the contradiction inherent in human identity: natural passions and appetites battling and subverting the order of mind and culture. In the case of women, their subjection to the procreative imperative sharpens that conflict. But *all* humans are defined by this struggle between the creative chaos of the irrational and the controlling order of the mind—a truth obscured by our postmodern melodrama of patriarchal oppression.

THE MOST NOTORIOUS FEMME FATALE in Greek literature is Medea, who murders her own children in a fit of rage against her husband, Jason, because he plans to bring to their household a younger, politically connected wife. Medea's speech at the beginning of Euripides' play has often been interpreted, however, not as a representation of Eros' destructive power, but as a powerful indictment of patriarchal marriage and its evils: the dowry with which a bride must "buy" a husband, the girl's painful adjustment to a new household, her confinement at home where she risks death in childbirth. "Three times," Medea asserts, "I would rather stand in the front line of battle, than bear one child."[36]

Yet Medea's complaint does not reflect her own experience. Her father did not arrange her marriage to Jason. In fact, stricken by a powerful sexual attraction, she ran off with him, betraying her father and country and murdering her brother—in some versions of the story cutting up his body and throwing it into the sea so that her pursuing father must stop to gather up the pieces, thus allowing her getaway. The driving force in her life is passion, not her father's wishes: "In opposition to her father," the poet Pindar wrote, "Medea decided on her own marriage."[37] Her famous speech describes not so much her own experience as that of the Greek women whose sympathy she is enlisting. She admits as much when she says to them, "Yet what applies to me does not apply to you. / You have a country. Your family home is here. / You enjoy life and the company of your friends."[38] Medea's life exemplifies the consequences of destructive sexual passion and wounded aristocratic honor, rather than the effects of "patriarchal" marriage. As she acknowledges, for most Greek women their marriage and household and city give them benefits denied to a "spear-won" barbarian bride like herself.

Marriage to the Greeks was, as noted in the last chapter, the obvious social and cultural institution for containing and exploiting the energy of Eros. But any discussion of this subject must begin with two caveats. First, I am speaking here of ideals deduced from literary remains. How these relate to actual, everyday life is nearly impossible to say, given the fragmentary nature of the literary evidence, and the absence of evidence from private life such as diaries and letters. Moreover, "Greek marriage" covers a broad range of households from a long span of time: Dark Age feudal manors, small farms, city homes, and even suburban households in the Hellenistic period. And most of the evidence reflects narrow social classes, the aristocratic or citizen households from the fifth and fourth centuries. The experience of wives in these situations would have been radically different from that of peasants or the urban proletariat. But my concern here is with identifying the idealized images that the Greeks left behind, not with what marriage was really like.

Second, we must beware of projecting modern assumptions back onto a people who never entertained them. Most of us think of marriage in romantic terms: people fall in love and marry because they are passionately attracted to one another and want to spend their lives together. The validity of the marriage is expressed by the intensity of the sexual passion. Marriage is personal, a relationship whose worth is often measured by the opposition it encounters in the larger society, as in our great foundation myth of romantic marriage, Shakespeare's *Romeo and Juliet.* In the Greek context, however, such a marriage was fraught with dangers, for anything predicated on the volatile force of passion was uncertain and vulnerable to changing circumstances. This is exactly what we see in the *Medea:* a marriage built on intense sexual attraction, which, when Jason's ardor is cooled by his ambition, is transformed in an instant into an equally intense and destructive hate. The result is the complete annihilation of two households, Jason's and King Creon's.

Greek literature typically depicts marriage as much more of a social institution, a basic building block of the larger political order. This is particularly true of fifth- and fourth-century Athens, from which much of our evidence comes. Athenian citizenship had a high value: only citizens could hold political office, participate in most religious ceremonies, or even inherit property, and being a citizen required that both parents be citizens. This made legitimacy an important concern, which explains some of the anxiety about female sexuality that crops up in our sources. Courtroom speeches from ancient orators provide us with evidence linking anxiety about woman's sexuality to the social importance of legitimacy. An oration of Lysias from the early fourth century presents the defense of a certain Euphiletus, indicted by the relatives of his wife's lover, whom he had murdered. Euphiletus evokes the seldom-acted-upon law that allows a husband to kill an adulterer, arguing that the purpose of the law is to uphold the conjugal affection that is strengthened by sex and that in turn strengthens the household. Moreover, the adulterer weakens the body politic by creating uncertainty about who is and isn't a legitimate citizen.[39]

That sexual disorder in the household could have wider implications for society is clear too from another oration, *Against Neaira,* attributed to the fourth-century statesman and orator Demosthenes. This complicated case involves a suit brought against Neaira accusing her of being a prostitute who masquerades as a legitimate citizen-wife. Part of her alleged scam involved her so-called husband shaking down her customers—who apparently were titillated by thinking they were having sex with a citizen-wife—by demanding payment to preclude the sanctions against adulterers, which as we have seen could include death. The litigants, by graphically detailing Neaira's sexual career, hammer home the point that such sexual license is incompatible with citizen status, and that such a creature should not have been allowed to participate in the city's religious festivals that are reserved for legitimate, chaste wives. They ask the jury to consider what their wives would say if they acquitted Neaira: those of "most self-control/chastity" would be angered that a woman without sexual self-control could enjoy the civic privileges that belonged to legitimate wives, who presumably controlled their sexuality; and the promiscuous wives would think they had been given a license for wantonness, since those privileges could now be enjoyed by both the chaste wife and the unchaste.[40]

This case makes clear that the household and the sexuality of the wives within it were intimate concerns of the city-state. The speaker in the oration makes this explicit when he says, "This is what it means to set up a household with a woman, with whom one has children, and one introduces the sons to the clan and *deme* [parish], and betroths the daughters to men as one's own. Courtesans we have for pleasure, concubines for the daily care of our bodies, and wives to bear legitimate children and to be the trusty guardians of the household."[41] This passage has frequently been distorted into saying that wives function *only* for procreation, which is absurd; the same logic would mean concubines function *only* for domestic maintenance and not sexual pleasure. The function of wives is inclusive of the other two—they provide sexual pleasure, domestic management, *and* legitimate children. Rather than a private pleasure of concern only to the couple, conjugal sex is the energy that binds together the household so it can play its role in the larger political and economic order of the city, by providing legitimate citizens who will marry other citizens and someday participate in the city's religious, civic and political institutions.

The household, then, is the defining context of Greek marriage. And the household is considered an institution that exists because of the complementary natures of male and female. We have heard Aristotle's statement that the household is "the union of those who cannot exist without each other; namely, of male and female, that the race may continue.... The family is the association established by nature for the supply of men's everyday wants."[42] Not only are humans "pairing creatures" by nature, but male and female possess different though complementary qualities and abilities that work together productively, a primitive division of labor that prefigures the more complex one making up the state. Thus man and woman together create a "communal thing," a common enterprise larger than the sum of its individual members. The *Economics,* attributed to Aristotle, likewise states that "a common life is above all things natural to the female and to the male.... But it is impossible for the female to accomplish this without the male or the male without the female."[43] In the *Politics,* Aristotle identifies the talent each sex possesses: the man's is for acquisition, the woman's for nurturing and preserving what is acquired.[44] Thus marriage is a natural state in which male and female find their fulfillment, that is, a "good life."

An important work of Xenophon, the *Oeconomicus* or *Household Management,* illustrates this same point. This work takes the form of a conversation between Socrates and a young man named Ischomachus, who has recently married and is explaining to Socrates how he is training his young wife. (In ancient Greece a bride could be half the age of her husband, so a certain amount of patronizing is to be expected.) Before speaking with Ischomachus, however, Socrates establishes the importance of husband and wife working well together in comments he makes to Critobolus, whom he criticizes for ignoring his wife, even though Critobolus has admitted that there is no one to whom he entrusts more of his important business. Socrates regards Critobolus' inattention as dangerous, for "the wife who is a good partner in the household is equivalent to the man in respect to its good." Like Aristotle, Socrates attributes this partnership to the complementary natures of male and female: "The property/wealth come to the house through the man's exertions, but the dispensing depends mostly on the economy of the woman." As Ischomachus says a bit later, man and woman share a "communal thing," a unit of that larger "communal thing" that is the state. Husband and wife, uniting their complementary qualities and abilities, must work together as a team to maintain and increase the household's wealth, and this in turn depends on both exercising "self-control," a capacity for which both male and female possess. "Self-control [*sôphronôn*] in a man and a woman is acting in such a way that their property will be the best possible, and that as much property as possible shall be justly and fairly added."[45]

Thus the woman's sphere of influence, authority, and honor is the household, which she oversees. Unlike our private homes, the household in ancient Greece was a large enterprise, including extended family and slaves, and much of what the family consumed was produced in the household. The wife had to manage and dispense the household's goods; oversee their production, particularly the spinning of wool and weaving of cloth items; and supervise and train the slaves—not to mention, of course, raising and educating her own children. There were, too, important religious rituals that went on in the household and were the purview of the wife, especially those concerning marriage, birth, and death. To keep this enterprise running smoothly, the wife could not be the timid, beaten-down recluse of modern imagination, but rather had to be a skillful manager and organizer. To assign women the "space" of the household, then, was to give them a much larger and more important social and religious function than might be the case for a modern suburban housewife in a nuclear family.

But what about affection? Even if women were afforded respect and esteem for their managerial roles in the household, weren't such marriages "rarely . . . a focus of love for either party," as one critic recently put it?[46] If this were so, one would be hard-pressed to explain the many inscriptions on grave stones that testify to a husband's love for his wife, as in this one from fourth-century Athens: "Farewell, tomb of Melite; a good woman lies here. You loved your husband Onesimus; he loved you in return. You were the best, and so he laments your death, for you were a good woman."[47] Greek literature as well abounds in evidence that shows men finding affection and fulfillment in their relationships with their wives. Odysseus' father Laertes grows old before his time, grieving not just for his lost son but also for his dead wife Antikleia, whom he held in such esteem that he refused to sleep with the household nurse Eurykleia, and whose death "gave him to a green untimely / old age."[48]

Hesiod, Semonides and Theognis all record what must have been a proverb, that "nothing is better [or sweeter] than a good wife."[49] Sophocles in a fragment likewise says, "But what house among mortals was ever thought happy / without a good wife, though it was loaded with luxury?"[50] Euripides' play the *Alcestis* (438 B.C.), about a woman who dies in her husband's place, details Admetus' hysterical grief over the loss of his beloved wife: "When you die, nothing is left. In you we [he and the children] exist, both to live and not to live, for we reverence your love." He swears never to remarry and banishes all festivity from his household.[51] Or consider the end of Xenophon's *Symposium*. The entertainment for the evening is two actors portraying the marriage of Ariadne and the god Dionysus. They do such a good job of acting out the passion between the two that the men in the audience are aroused: "The unmarried men swore that they would marry, while the married men mounted their horses and rode home to their wives, so that they could find pleasure with them."[52] If the men just wanted sex, why didn't they grab a serving boy or flute girl?

That men need *affectionate* sex—the sort of sex that people enjoy who share a life—is the whole point of the plot of Aristophanes' *Lysistrata* (411). The title character, disgusted with the long, destructive Peloponnesian War that has drained the Greek states of men and treasure, calls a Panhellenic conference of wives to implement her plan to force the men to negotiate peace: the older women will seize the treasury on the Acropolis, and the younger will go on a sex strike. If Greek men found sexual affection in boys and concubines, why would they care if their wives withheld sex? Why not find release in their boy-loves or prostitutes? But the point of the play is that men want and need affectionate sex; as Aristotle says, intercourse is a means to achieving the end of affection.[53] Lysistrata understands this as well, which is why she advises the women that if their husbands force them to have sex, they should not enjoy it, for "a husband never really enjoys himself if he isn't getting along with his wife."[54] It is not the power to withhold sex that the Athenian wives are wielding, but the power to withhold affectionate sex. And this power must have really existed for Aristophanes' plot to have any psychological believability at all.

THE ARCHETYPAL WIFE IN ANCIENT GREEK LITERATURE is Penelope from the *Odyssey*. In her character we see all the ideal qualities of a wife, and in her marriage with Odysseus all the characteristics of a good marriage, which we have already encountered in later authors writing under much different social and economic conditions from those of early Archaic Greece (late eighth century), when Homer's epics were most likely written. Significantly, the hallmark of Penelope's character is the virtue that was most capable of reining in the power of Eros, the virtue most important for a wife to possess: rational self-control, the ability to restrain her appetites out of loyalty to her husband and her household. Throughout the *Odyssey,* Penelope is given epithets that emphasize her powers of self-control: she is "very wise/of sound understanding," she "knows well counsels/arts in her mind," and she is *periphrôn,* "prudent/of good sense," a common epithet formed—like the word for "self-controlled," *sôphrôn*—from the word for "mind."[55] So linked to self-control is Penelope's character that when one of the women in Aristophanes' *Women at the Thesmophoria* is castigating Euripides for all the promiscuous women he puts on stage, she asks him why he never writes about a "self-controlled" woman like Penelope, who obviously is the proverbial exemplar of this virtue.[56]

Yet the wife's self-control is not the only ingredient for a good marriage. In Book Six, Odysseus himself defines for us the essence of the ideal marriage. After washing up battered and naked on the island of the Phaiacians, Odysseus approaches the princess Nausicaa and begs her for help, wishing for her in return "a husband and a household, and noble like-mindedness. For nothing is more powerful or greater than this, when a husband and wife, being like-minded in their thoughts, hold the household."[57] The word translated "like-minded" *(homophrosunê)* derives from the same word for "mind" as does "self-control" *(sôphrosunê)*. Elsewhere in Greek literature it has a range of meanings that includes the ideas of cooperation, honesty, communication, affection, and shared values.[58] Notice that Odysseus makes the foundation of a good marriage not, as we sometimes do, sexual passion, but rather a *mental* quality—a similarity of character and values, an agreement about what is important, and a willingness to communicate that, together, bind the couple into a harmonious whole. Sexual passion is subordinate to qualities of character and shared values.

The marriage of Penelope and Odysseus illustrates just the sort of marriage that Odysseus wishes for Nausicaa. Attentive readers of the *Odyssey* will notice that Penelope is very much like Odysseus, sharing as she does his two most representative qualities: endurance and cunning. As for the first, she has endured not just her husband's twenty-year absence, but also 108 armed suitors occupying her house for three years, corrupting her maids and plotting to kill her son. And Penelope is Odysseus' equal in cunning and trickery—she puts off the suitors for a year by postponing a decision until she has woven her father-in-law Laertes' burial shroud, unweaving at night what she has woven by day. Most important, however, are the values she and Odysseus share, especially the commitment of each to their household and to each other. Penelope, after all, has remained faithful for twenty years despite the importunities of the suitors, the impatience of her son Telemachus, and her uncertainty over whether Odysseus is even alive.

Odysseus likewise is committed to Penelope and his household, which is why he undergoes such hardship and suffering to return home. And Calypso, the goddess who has detained him for seven years, understands the object of his longing: If you knew what he had to suffer, she says to Odysseus, "you would stay here with me and rule this house, and you would be immortal, even though you desire to see your wife, for whom always you long all your days."[59] Yet not even the promise of immortality or the spectre of further suffering can keep Odysseus from struggling to return to Penelope, for their relationship is an essential part of his identity. Humans are what they are because their passions are contained by a specific cultural milieu, by institutions and rational virtues that both limit those passions and provide a context for their expression. To be human is to live within a cultural order that defines human relationships; and any life outside it—even a life of eternal sexual dalliance with a goddess—is no human life at all.[60]

The best illustration of Penelope and Odysseus' "like-mindedness," however, is in the way they together bring about the destruction of the suitors, even before Penelope knows Odysseus has returned. Penelope is no passive, immobile, helpless female awaiting rescue by her knight. Without her planning, Odysseus could never destroy the suitors, for the odds are against him: they number 108 aristocrats trained in the use of arms, and Odysseus has only Telemachus, Eumaeus, and Philoitios, another herdsman, as allies. Moreover, the suitors physically occupy his hall. Odysseus needs surprise, and he needs a weapon that can overcome large numbers.

Penelope provides Odysseus with the opportunity he needs. As she speaks with Odysseus, who is disguised as a lowly beggar, she intuits that the man before her might be her husband, so she thinks up a stratagem that only he could exploit. She suddenly announces to Odysseus that she will hold a contest the next day to decide who will be her new husband. Penelope will marry whoever can string Odysseus' bow and send the arrow through twelve lined-up axes with some sort of hole in their heads. As soon as Odysseus hears his wife's plan to marry another man, he excitedly replies, "No longer put off this contest in the halls. For crafty Odysseus will be back here before these men, handling the polished bow, shall stretch the string and shoot an arrow through the iron."[61] Odysseus knows—and he knows Penelope knows—that no one but he can string that bow. Penelope has cleverly rigged the contest to make sure the suitors fail. Moreover, if the stranger *is* Odysseus, she knows he will find a way to get his hands on the bow and use it to offset the much greater numbers of the suitors. In the event, this is what happens. The suitors can't string the bow. Odysseus, helped by Penelope, gets his hands on the bow, strings it, and sends the first arrow through the neck of the most powerful suitor, Antinoös.

Because of Penelope's Odyssean cunning, and Odysseus' Penelopean fidelity to their marriage and household—because of their "like-mindedness"—they can destroy the suitors, renew their household and, since Odysseus is the king, renew as well the whole society of Ithaka. The symbol of this ideal marriage is the bed whose corner-post is an olive trunk still rooted in the earth, the unmoving center of Odysseus' identity and also of Ithakan society. There he and Penelope enjoy a night of love lengthened by Athene. Sexual passion, contrary to our romantic expectations, *results* from "like-mindedness," the shared character and values that fortify the marriage, rather than preceding the strength and integrity of the bond. For passion to be productive for human flourishing, it must be subjected to the larger cultural and rational order that allows us to be human at all. And marriage is a key element of that order.

Was marriage the only venue in which women could transcend the stereotypes that limited them to their procreative functions? On the contrary, throughout Greek literature and history we find women whose complexity, achievements, and sheer human magnificence belie the commonplaces of Greek misogyny. Remember that Medea's powerful indictment of patriarchal marriage, with its sympathetic insights into a woman's lot, was written by a man and presented in a public theater filled with men. So too was Sophocles' lost *Tereus,* in which this patriarchal male presents us a sensitive recognition of the fate of young girls "who are pushed out and sold, away from [their] paternal gods and from [their] parents, some to foreign husbands, some to barbarians, some to joyless homes, and some to homes that are opprobrious."[62] Indeed, in tragedy after tragedy, the women—from Aeschylus' Clytaemestra to Euripides' Hecuba—are usually more congenial, more insightful, more powerful, and more *interesting* than the men. Outside of literature as well, we encounter women recognized and praised for their achievements. The poet Corinna was memorialized for defeating the famous Pindar in competition five times.[63] Plutarch and Pausanias both tell of how, when Sparta was attacking Argos after killing most of the city's fighting men, the poet Telesilla organized and armed the women and put them on the walls, where they turned back the Spartan attack.[64]

Two literary women in particular stand out as examples of the Greeks' sympathetic interest in the predicament of women: Sophocles' Antigone and Aristophanes' Lysistrata.

Antigone is the daughter of Oedipus who defies at the cost of her life her uncle Creon's edict that her brother Polyneices, who died attacking the city of Thebes, should lie unburied. At one level, through Antigone's passionate commitment to the claims of family and the gods at the expense of male political power and civic law, Sophocles asserts the importance of women's world and the familial relationships with which they are intimately concerned, a world that men like Creon slight at their peril. Moreover, in the confrontation between Antigone and Creon, it is the latter who comes off as petty and paranoid, insecure not just about his new power but about his masculinity itself: "So I must guard the men who yield to order, / not let myself be beaten by a woman. / Better, if it must happen, that a man / should overset me. / I won't be called weaker than womankind."[65] And it is Creon whom the city, including his son Haemon, declares wrong.

Yet Antigone is no mere spokesman for a narrow female view; she is a unique, magnificent *individual,* a strong-willed, passionate defender of her own honor. As much as any Homeric hero, she is willing to punish and humiliate those who dishonor her, in order to achieve the glory owed to one of her exalted birth ("And yet what greater glory could I find / than giving my own brother funeral?").[66] Her public defiance of Creon, her exposure of his weakness as a ruler, are her revenge—as powerful a motive as her desire to honor family and gods. Through Antigone, Sophocles explores a perennial *human* problem: the power of our will and passions, even when we are right, to destroy us just at the moment of our triumph. That a young woman, utterly without social, political, and economic power, is given this moment of tragic grandeur, acknowledges the humanity of women, their capacity for experiencing the same spectacular triumph and failure as do men.

On the comic stage, Aristophanes' Lysistrata makes the same point by organizing a seizing of the treasury and a sex strike by Athenian wives in order to compel the men to bring an end to the Peloponnesian War. The plot turns on the reversal of a fundamental Greek sex stereotype: rather than the women being less able to control themselves sexually, it is the men, barely able to walk because of their mammoth erections, who ultimately are driven to give in to their wives' demands. Moreover, the standard Greek ideal of woman's obligation to keep quiet about matters outside the house is mocked and rejected for perpetuating the bad decisions the men have been making, most specifically the disastrous Sicilian expedition of 415. Lysistrata says to the men, "If you'd wanted to listen to us for a change / while we told you what was proper, and if you'd shut up, instead of us, / we could have set you straight."[67] Such a profound, if comic, challenge to prevailing sex norms is remarkable, and could not have happened anywhere in the ancient world other than in Greece.

Moreover, all the women, Lysistrata in particular, display remarkable skills of management and organization—skills of governing usually considered masculine—that help them pull the whole thing off. These skills historically would in fact have been applied by Athenian women in running their own households and putting on the many religious festivals for which they were responsible, such as the Thesmophoria discussed in the previous chapter. The talents developed in running the household are invoked by Lysistrata in an analogy that compares managing Athens and its allies to preparing wool for spinning: cleaning out (the same way a fleece is untangled and cleaned) the disaffected citizens who plot in their subversive political organizations, and then blending fairly and harmoniously the interests and contributions of citizens, foreigners, allies, and subjects, "and from that / you weave a cloak for the people."[68]

The experience gained by managing and participating in religious festivals is invoked by the chorus of women when the chorus of men criticizes them for bothering with the business of the city: "All citizens! We shall now undertake / some words of true benefit to the state — / rightly, since in comfort and in splendor she has nourish'd me." The women then enumerate all the festivals in which they have participated since girlhood and the civic duties that women perform for the city's good, duties as important as holding office and voting. And they ask, "Does the city not deserve the benefit of my advice?"[69]

The moral is clear: these Athenian women are citizens, lovers of the city, beneficiaries of its power, contributors in their own ways to its life and its flourishing—and not only because they provide the sons who hold its offices and fight in its wars, and suffer the absence and loss of those sons and husbands. Their voices deserve to be heard. Every stereotype about women—and men, for that matter—is turned on its head in this play. And the result is a richer, more complex vision of woman's identity, one that was publicly celebrated in the very center of the presumably misogynistic city.

MANY OTHER WOMEN IN GREEK LITERATURE—virtually all of it written by men—challenge misogynistic stereotypes by asserting the complex humanity of women, and exposing the limitations of the authors' own preconceptions. Even Plato, notorious for his dismissive comments about women, proposed in the *Republic* that women be made "guardians" of the state and undergo the same "nurture and education" as men. And later, in the *Laws,* he goes even further. "In education and everything else," he proposes for his utopia, "the female sex should be on the same footing as the male." For a state to do otherwise is to develop "only half its potentialities, whereas with the same cost and effort, it could double its achievement."[70] The Stoics too rejected the old notion that women were less rational than men, as evidenced by the title of a book (now lost) by the philosopher Cleanthes: *On the Thesis That the Same Virtue Belongs to Both a Man and a Woman.*[71] Although suggestions of this kind were clearly speculative and were considered impossible to effect, the fact that philosophers even *made* them was revolutionary.

That willingness to recognize and question their own assumptions about sex roles is ultimately what was unique about the ancient Greeks, not their subordination of women, a practice typical of every society before the modern period. Such peoples, living more intimately with nature and more vulnerable to its power, always one harvest or one generation away from extinction, had reasons for confining women's destiny within the ruthless biology that impacted their lives every day, holding them to an unyielding procreative imperative.[72] But only the Greeks saw far enough beyond the necessity of nature to recognize the human depths behind the stereotypes, and the possibilities for tragedy and achievement every bit as grand for women as for men. And if women in the West today enjoy legal equality with men and freedom to choose their destiny apart from biology, it is largely because of those self-critical questions the Greeks first raised.

The deity gave liberty to all men, and nature created no one a slave.

—*Alcidamas*[1]

THREE

The Roots of Emancipation

EVERY PRE-MODERN SOCIETY known to history practiced slavery in some form or other. From China to India, Africa to the New World, the ownership of humans by other humans was a ubiquitous evil.[2] Indeed, slavery still exists today: in March of 2000, the human rights group Christian Solidarity International purchased 4,968 children out of bondage in the Sudan.[3] Yet in the West, slavery was eradicated by the beginning of the modern age, with the exception of the Spanish colonies and the American South; and Americans fought a long, bloody civil war partly because the continued existence of chattel slavery was considered an atavistic barbarism incompatible with both Christianity and the progress humanity had made. One of the remarkable stories of human history is how an institution once so commonly accepted as an inevitable fact of life is now practiced in only a few parts of the world—and even there is kept hidden, in recognition of its universal condemnation.

The story of emancipation begins among the Greeks, yet as we noted earlier, many scholars today see slavery in ancient Greece as proof of hypocrisy. Such attitudes are not new. In 1935, R. W. Livingstone noted that "some people put the Greeks out of court at the outset because they owned slaves," a fact that presumably "deprives their life of significance for us."[4] Livingstone went on to point out the flaws in such thinking, not the least being that judging a society so removed in time requires a superhuman wisdom and impartiality. And when the terms and assumptions underlying our criticism derive mostly from the Greeks—when it was Greek humanistic ideals of rational inquiry and freedom of dissent that started humanity down the long road of emancipation—it shows a peculiarly arrogant ingratitude and lack of historical perception to condemn the Greeks for owning slaves. As Moses Finley, the great historian of ancient slavery, put it, "Slavery is a great evil: there is no reason why a historian should not say that, but to say only that, no matter with how much factual backing, is a cheap way to score a point on a dead society to the advantage of our own."[5]

Another impediment to understanding ancient slavery is the tendency of most people to think of bondage in terms of American slavery, an emotional topic in our public discourse, bound up as it is with contemporary issues of racial equality. Any attempt to address the complexities and ambiguities of slavery often invites the charge that one is apologizing for it or failing adequately to acknowledge its full horror. Yet slavery in Greece was very different from slavery in the American South, which was based on race and limited to an easily identified minority considered to be incapable of rational thought and hence less than human. Slavery was thought to be a condition justly suited to such a minority, and therefore a fate that would never be experienced by whites. The barrier of skin color separated the free and unfree, making it difficult for the former to sympathize with the latter's experience, or to acknowledge their common humanity.

In the ancient world, on the other hand, slavery was an evil that anyone potentially could suffer. Although theories of natural slavery such as those of Isocrates and Aristotle postulated that some peoples, especially non-Greeks, were by nature suited to slavery, and although many slaves in fifth-century Athens were not Greeks, throughout the historical period Greeks were enslaved not just by foreigners but by fellow Greeks as well (the latter practice one that

Plato condemns in his utopia).[6] Such a fate could befall anyone, no matter how exalted his status. In the *Odyssey,* Odysseus' swineherd Eumaeus was the son of a king who had been kidnapped by Phoenicians, who sold him to Odysseus' father.[7] In addition to being kidnapped by slave-traders and pirates, children sometimes were sold by their parents, and people were frequently enslaved for debt—both practices abolished in Athens by Solon as part of his reforms of 594.[8] And if we can believe the Stoic Posidonius, some people even sold themselves into slavery, ensuring that at least their material wants would be taken care of.[9]

War, of course, was the common catastrophe that enslaved many people, especially women and children after a city was sacked; as the philosopher Heracleitus said, "War has made some slaves, others free."[10] Frequently in Greek literature the pitiful fate of enslaved women and children is sympathetically described. One of the most touching instances occurs in Book Six of the *Iliad,* when Hector, taking a brief respite from the fighting to speak with his wife, Andromache, foresees the doom of Troy and says, "But it is not so much the pain to come of the Trojans / that troubles me . . . / as troubles me the thought of you, when some bronze-armoured / Achaian leads you off, taking away your day of liberty."[11] In the *Odyssey* too, a grieving Odysseus is compared to a woman weeping for her dead husband, "while the men behind her, / hitting her with their spear butts on the back and shoulders, / force her up and lead her away into slavery, to have / hard work and sorrow."[12]

Nor was this disaster merely a literary one: the reality was experienced by many Greeks, at the hands not only of "barbarians" but of other Greeks. Thucydides describes several occasions during the Peloponnesian War when the Athenians punished their rebellious subjects by enslaving their women and children, including the Samians, the Skionians, the Mytileneans, and most notoriously the Melians. Contrary to American slavery, then, in the ancient world the possibility of ending up the property of somebody else was part of a larger tragic necessity that defined the human condition, not just the destiny of an alien race. In Greece, the gulf between master and slave was not so great as to close off any possibility of empathy.

Another important difference between American and ancient slavery is the higher level of education and training of some ancient slaves, who served as government clerks, skilled craftsmen and tutors, as well as domestics and laborers. For example, surviving records concerning the workmen on the Erechtheum, a building on the Acropolis, reveal that about a quarter were slaves who worked alongside citizens and free resident aliens for the same pay.[13] A slave tutor, or *paidagôgos*, was more than just an attendant; he also had responsibility for shaping his charge's character. Konnidas, the tutor of Theseus, legendary king of Athens, was honored along with his master at the Athenian festival dedicated to Theseus.[14] Another famous slave tutor was Sicinnus, the teacher of Themistocles' sons. At the battle of Salamis, Themistocles entrusted Sicinnus with the false message to the Persians that tricked them into fighting the sea battle in the narrows, where the Greeks had an advantage. After the war Themistocles freed Sicinnus, enrolled him as a citizen of Thespiae, and made him a rich man.[15] Such an event involving an American slave is unthinkable. The belief in the natural inferiority of African slaves necessarily meant that they could not be educated, let alone entrusted with shaping the character of their masters' sons. To do so would disprove the assumptions of intellectual inferiority by which slavery was justified. In ancient Greece, on the other hand, at least some slaves had a chance for education; a few even became philosophers, the most famous being the Stoic Epictetus.[16]

In addition to being better educated, slaves in the ancient world had much greater opportunities for manumission than did slaves in the South.[17] Sometimes military service would earn freedom—slaves who fought at Marathon in 490 were freed before the battle.[18] Before the critical naval battle at Arginusae in 406, the Athenians enlisted slaves as rowers and then freed them after the victory.[19] Indeed, in the *Frogs* of Aristophanes, this act of emancipation and enfranchisement is praised and recommended as a sound policy to follow in the future. To be sure, these were exceptional events made necessary by pressing circumstances, yet the contrast with the South is instructive: nothing frightened Southern slave-owners more than the thought of arming their slaves, something they never did, even during the darkest days of the Civil War.

More typically, ancient slaves had to buy themselves from their masters. They could save their own money, be "sold" to a god who became a sort of supervisory authority over the transaction until the price was repaid, or borrow money from associations *(eranoi)* that advanced to slaves the price of manumission.[20] Sometimes several people would form a consortium and advance the money, as did the former lovers of Neaira, as we saw in the previous chapter. Unwilling to see their former mistress under the control of a pimp, they advanced her part of the purchase price; the balance she provided herself from the gifts of other lovers.[21]

Though freedmen in Greece did not suffer the permanent stigma of race that black freedmen in America did, they were still hemmed in by contractual obligations to their former masters, who remained their legal patrons. A contract surviving from Delphi from the first century A.D. states that the slave Onasiphoron will upon emancipation have to remain with her former master Sophrona until the latter dies. She will have to do whatever Sophrona says, and provide her with a child.[22] For their part, former masters were obliged to intervene, on the pain of a fine, if anyone tried to re-enslave the freedman. All in all, though, a freedman's existence was more precarious than a citizen's, and his freedom was far from absolute. In Athens, freedman status was similar to that of a "metic" or resident alien: freedmen could not become citizens or own land, but they had to pay taxes and serve in the military. And always their status could be challenged, or they could be called to account for failure to fulfill their obligations to their former masters.

Yet despite these liabilities, the absence of physical differences between freedman and free meant that emancipated Greek slaves had greater opportunities for improving their status than did American ex-slaves. A certain Nicomachus, whose father was a slave, became an Athenian commissioner for recording the laws.[23] Two slaves in Athens manumitted by their masters, Pasion and Phormion, even became citizens. And eventually the freedman's descendants at least could become indistinguishable from the free.[24] The fourth-century-B.C. comic poet Anaxandrides illustrated the role of providence in each man's life by saying, "There are many who are not free right now, but tomorrow they will be registered as citizens."[25] The possibility, however remote, of free men becoming slaves and slaves, free men made it easier to acknowledge the slave's humanity and understand his lot than was the case with the race-based slavery of the South.

Perhaps nothing, however, distinguishes Greek slavery from American more than the ancients' greater willingness to practice and acknowledge sexual relations between slave and free. In the South, although sex between master and slave was common, it was a guilty secret—for as Faulkner understood, mixed-race children more than anything gave the lie to the theory that Africans were subhuman. In the ancient world, sex with female slaves, whether prostitutes or domestics, was widespread and openly acknowledged: injunctions to free men to avoid sex with their slaves, such as Plato's in the *Laws,* are clearly presented as idealistic. In the *Women at Assembly* (392), Aristophanes' fantasy about women seizing political power, the women's utopian legislation includes forbidding slave-girls from sleeping with free men, which must have been a frequent complaint on the part of legitimate wives.[26] The Sophist Gorgias, whose wife was jealous of his passion for his maid, was tweaked for preaching concord among the Greeks when he could not even persuade his wife and maid to get along.[27]

Sex between free women and slaves, something horrifying for antebellum Southerners even to contemplate, is also mentioned in the ancient evidence. In *Women at the Thesmophoria,* Euripides' spy Mnesilochus, disguised as a woman, reminds the women of their possible recourse to slaves for sexual pleasure when nothing better is around—a sexist slur, no doubt, but one that must have had some basis in fact.[28] The Hellenistic writer Herodas, fragments of whose realist "slice-of-life" short pieces have survived, describes a free woman's angry outburst against her slave-lover Gastron for sleeping with a neighbor's slave. With painful realism Herodas details the humiliating abuse of the poor slave, including threats of torture and branding: "You must realise that you are a slave and I paid three minas for you.... Bind his elbows tightly; saw them off with the ties.... See that he doesn't slip free. Take him to the executioner's, to Hermon, and order him to hammer a thousand blows into his back and a thousand into his belly."[29]

As well as reflecting the sexual needs of individual women, such relationships sometimes were pragmatic responses to catastrophes that reduced the population of free men. In his dialogue *Slavery and Freedom,* Dio Chrysostom, a first-century-A.D. philosopher, has the slave state that "many Athenian women have become pregnant by foreigners or slaves, because of the absence or unavailability of citizens, some without knowing the man's status and others quite aware of it."[30] Several stories in the ancient world concerned communities that after some catastrophe or other were revitalized by intermarriage between slave men and free women, as happened at Argos around 500 after the city's defeat at the hands of the Spartans, who had burned alive most of the male citizens.[31]

Slaves are by definition property, and thus to some degree necessarily considered less than human. But in the ancient world slaves were not completely without legal protections. Killing a slave was illegal, even if the killer was the slave's master. Plato's dialogue the *Euthyphro* takes as its starting point Euthyphro's prosecution of his own father for the death of a slave whom he had left bound in a ditch as punishment for killing another slave. Slaves could not be subjected to unjustified blows or injuries; doing so could lead one to being prosecuted for *hubris,* the charge that covered acts of wanton violence against persons.[32] These legal safeguards, as well as the fact that slaves were outwardly indistinguishable from free men, led the late-fifth-century conservative "Old Oligarch" to grouse that among the slaves in Athens "there is the greatest uncontrolled wantonness; you can't hit them there, and a slave will not stand aside for you."[33]

Of course, some of those legal protections may have arisen from the utilitarian need to protect a citizen's property and status. Aeschines explained that the law against hitting a slave was a prophylactic against violence towards citizens, not a reflection of a concern with slaves per se. Writing about the slave revolts in Sicily in the first century, Diodorus Siculus blamed them on the maltreatment of slaves, and he drew the practical moral that slaves should be treated gently to avoid disorder in the household and the state.[34] But comparison with the very different conditions of slaves in the South indicates a further assumption behind ancient thinking: that slaves were still human beings, considered a part of the family in a way most African slaves were not. As Yvon Garlan points out, the ancient slave was "ritually associated with his master's house. Here he received a new name, was welcomed, like a bride, with a showering of nuts and fruits, symbols of prosperity, and took part in the cult of the household gods."[35]

Pointing out these differences, however, should not lead one to think that slavery in the ancient world was anything other than a degrading evil. Slaves were frequently the sexual playthings of their masters, and were subject to their fits of rage—the medical writer Galen reports he once saw a man stick a reed pen in a slave's eye.[36] Runaways could be branded, and often entire populations were marked, as the Athenians did to the Samians they enslaved. Of course, slaves were routinely bullied and humiliated, as the abovementioned scene from Herodas illustrates, and they could be whipped and beaten as punishment; a common joke was to derive the word "boy" *(pais),* typically used of a slave, from the word for "beat" *(paiô).*[37] Comedy too found humor in jokes about beating slaves.[38] The stage no doubt reflected everyday practice. In Xenophon's *Memorabilia,* after Socrates mentions that some masters fetter slaves to keep them from running away and beat them with whips, he asks his interlocutor Aristippus how *he* controls a recalcitrant slave. Aristippus replies casually, "I inflict every kind of punishment upon him . . . until I can force him to serve properly."[39] Worse, slaves could be tortured for evidence, since it was believed that they would tell the truth only under severe compulsion.

Many slaves, moreover, rather than being domestics or skilled craftsmen or clerks, were put to brutally hard labor as agricultural workers or, crueler still, as miners. The silver mine at Laurium, which financed much of the spectacular cultural grandeur of Athens, was worked by slaves whose iron fetters have been found by archaeologists. The shafts lacked air circulation and light, and were scarcely bigger than the miner himself. Slave-boys also worked in the mines, hauling out the baskets or sacks filled with ore. These slaves' experience was no doubt similar to that of the Egyptian mine workers described by Diodorus Siculus. These unfortunates—boys, men, women—laboring in near darkness with crude tools, had to

> work at their task unceasingly both by day and throughout the entire night, enjoying no respite . . . and at this task they labour without ceasing beneath the sternness and blows of an overseer. . . . [N]o man can look upon the unfortunate wretches without feeling pity for them because of the exceeding hardships they suffer. For no leniency or respite of any kind is given to any man who is sick, or maimed, or aged, or in the case of a woman for her weakness, but all without exception are compelled by blows to persevere in their labours, until through ill-treatment they die in the midst of their tortures.[40]

Yet although the Greeks could accept the cruel and hard conditions imposed on slaves, they also recognized that the slave's humanity was diminished in his degradation and suffering: "Zeus of the wide brows takes away one half of the virtue / from a man, once the day of slavery closes upon him," Homer says (a proverb Plato misquoted as "half his mind").[41] This recognition gave emotional power to the Trojan princess Polyxena's lament, in Euripides' *Hecuba* (425 B.C.), where she welcomes the fate of being sacrificed to the shade of Achilles:

> And now I am a slave.
> It is that name of slave, so ugly, so strange,
> that makes me want to die. Or should I live
> to be knocked down to a bidder, sold to a master
> for cash . . . doing the work of a drudge, kneading the bread
> and scrubbing the floors, compelled to drag out
> endless weary days?[42]

Such sentiments, voiced in the public theater during the Peloponnesian War when many Greeks indeed were being enslaved and suffering the very fate Polyxena describes, are unparalleled anywhere in the ancient world. They reflect a unique consciousness of the common humanity shared by slave and free, a consciousness that made possible the first halting steps toward the abolition of slavery.

Scattered throughout Greek literature is evidence that some Greeks viewed slavery in a critical light, as something troubling and even tragic. There are indications of a belief that once upon a time slavery didn't exist, that it was not a universal, naturally occurring phenomenon. The historians Timaeus and Herodotus wrote that in ancient Athens the Greeks were not served by slaves.[43] And according to Athenaeus, the second-century-A.D. compiler of quotations from Greek literature and history, the fourth-century historian Theopompus claimed that the Chians were the first Greeks to buy and sell slaves, implying there was a time when chattel slavery, at least, did not exist. Athenaeus goes on to say that the god "punished the people of Chios for this—for in later times they were engaged in a long war because of their slaves." Later, Athenaeus refers to the enslavement of the Chians by Mithridates, and concludes "in this way God [*sic*] truly showed how angry he was with them because they were the first people to use human chattels that had been bought." The Chians would deserve retribution only if chattel slavery was considered evil.

Athenaeus was no doubt influenced by Stoicism, which we will discuss later. But his quotations of earlier Greek comedies in which prehistoric utopias are described as slave-free also reveal the view that slavery is a necessary evil in a wicked world that has degenerated from a better one: "The poets of the Old Comedy [from the fifth century B.C.], when they tell us about life in primitive times, set forth such lines ... to show that in those days no use was made of slaves."[44] In the comic imagination those "primitive times" were a "golden age" when all the ills of contemporary society—injustice, war, greed, treachery, hard work, and slavery—were absent because objects and animals had the power to prepare themselves for man's use. Crates, imagining a utopia that will reprise the Golden

Age, attributes the absence of slaves to animated furniture and food. The speaker in Athenaeus concludes, "If things were like that, what need had we of domestic slaves?"[45]

Clearly, the comic writers saw slavery as an evil made necessary by the harsh world they lived in, a world where all the scarce, good things must be acquired and prepared by dint of hard work. Pherecrates in the *Savages* says that in the old days there were no slaves, and so the women had to do all the housework themselves.[46] And obviously, no one even considers the possibility of giving up his slaves and working for himself. But whatever their selfish or utilitarian motives, these writers still see slavery as an evil, however inevitable or necessary, that characterizes a fallen world. Thus in several ancient utopias, slaves do not appear—the best of all possible worlds is a world without slaves.[47]

An ancient festival revealing the idea of a distant past without slavery was the Cronia, so named from Cronus (the Roman Saturn), the deity who presided over the Golden Age until Zeus (Jupiter) usurped it, ushering in the Iron Age in which we live. This festival was very likely similar to the Roman Saturnalia celebrated in December. The first-century-A.D. satirist Lucian connects the Cronia to the Golden Age: Cronus himself explains that once a year he returns for a week to remind people of what life was like during his reign, when wine flowed in rivers, milk could be had from springs, everybody was good, and there was no slavery. Thus during the festival the slave is considered as good as the free man; "equal honor" is given to all, slave and free, rich and poor.[48] Moreover, slave and free exchange places, as "nearly everyone joyfully prepares banquets and each one serves his slaves."[49]

Athenaeus lists several Greek communities in which the reversal of slave and free roles was a part of the festival.[50] Rooted in a time beyond history and recovery, these festivals no doubt served to reinforce the idea that slavery was inevitable in the present world, and made handling slaves easier for masters by relaxing the burdens of servitude at least for one week. Yet the acknowledgment that slavery once did not exist, along with the reversal of roles during the Cronia, suggested that slavery was a tragedy of chance rather than a destiny of race, an institution not really in the natural order of things, and so perhaps not necessarily permanent—a view unlikely in the antebellum South, where slaves were forever branded by race.

COMEDY AND TRAGEDY FREQUENTLY PRESENTED SLAVES as characters. In these depictions, viewed by citizens at a public festival, the scope of slaves' humanity was widened, and there arose as well the possibility of sympathetic understanding on the part of the spectators. This is not to say that the slaves in ancient theater mirrored the typical lives, behavior, and characters of actual slaves or masters. Rather, putting slaves on stage and having them speak and interact with others enlarged their identities beyond their servile status, making them more human and less alien—a necessary first step to questioning the institution.

Many of the slaves in comedy reflect what no doubt were stereotypes in which free people traded. Of Aristophanes' slaves, Joseph Vogt says that "the great majority of his slave-girls are described as stupid, the men are boorish; good and trustworthy slaves are overwhelmingly outnumbered by the vast crowd of their lazy, insolent, randy, cowardly, thieving and dishonest companions."[51] An example is in *Frogs* (405), about the god Dionysus' journey into the underworld to bring back the shade of the recently deceased Euripides, where Dionysus' slave Xanthias has a conversation with a slave of Plouton, master of Hades, in which the two swap the pleasures of slaves: cursing their masters behind their backs, gossiping about them, prying and eavesdropping.[52] Yet in Aristophanes' later comedies, including the *Frogs*, the greater complexity in slave characters and the larger importance of their roles give evidence of a growing recognition that slaves' humanity and potential were not limited by their servile status.

Many readers have noted a new dimension to the theatrical role of slaves in the character of Dionysus' slave Xanthias. Right from the start Aristophanes calls attention to the conventional use of slaves in comedy—to complain and to receive beatings—only to reject such reductive humor:

XANTHIAS	Shall I give them the usual jokes, master? You know, the ones that are always good for a laugh?
DIONYSUS	Go ahead. *Any* of them. Except, "what a day!" Don't give them that one. It's gone awfully sour.
XANTHIAS	But something witty, like . . .
DIONYSUS	*Any*thing. Except "my poor back."[53]

From then on, the relationship between the god and his slave subverts the usual expectations about slave character, as well as the theatrical jokes of which slaves were supposed to be the butt. Xanthias, as K. J. Dover says, "does more than laugh at his master; he dominates him, as the braver and more resilient of the two, makes a fool of him, and splendidly gets the better of him in the scene where both are beaten by the Doorkeeper."[54] The scene to which Dover refers occurs when Xanthias, who has taken over the disguise of Heracles that Dionysus discarded out of fear, persuades the doorman of Hades to torture the god, who is now playing the part of Xanthias' slave, for evidence.[55] Both characters end up getting whipped, with the slave taking it much better than the god.

This scene, and others such as the one in which a whining Dionysus begs his slave to put on the disguise of Heracles, challenge the commonplace assumptions about slave and free that the nearly twenty thousand Athenians in the audience no doubt depended on to legitimize slavery. By the fourth and third centuries B.C., in the so-called "New Comedy," the clever slave who is wilier, smarter, funnier, and simply more interesting than his naive or oafish owner becomes a stock character upon whose wits and ingenuity the happy resolution of the plot depends.[56]

Fantasy reversals such as these, of course, are a safe way to laugh at one's secret fears. Many in the audience probably laughed at Dionysus or the thick-headed "juveniles" of New Comedy, and then went home and abused a slave. Yet the by-play between god and slave, the common humanity revealed by their relationship, the reversal of their identities, all called into question the distinctions between slave and free, suggesting that beneath those differences we all are humans, all driven by the same appetites, fears, contingencies, and instincts for survival. The enlistment of slaves in the Athenian fleet before the battle of Arginusae may have contributed to this shift in attitude, for the similar experiences of training and rowing and facing together danger and death would have invited the reflection that slaves could be as good as free men—exactly what happened to some Northerners' attitudes during the Civil War when ex-slaves and freedmen were taken into the Union Army.[57]

However, depictions of slaves in tragedy even before the unusual circumstances that led to the enlistment of slaves in the fleet suggest that a more sympathetic attitude was developing, especially in the tragedies of Euripides produced during the Peloponnesian War when the Athenians were enslaving other Greeks. As in comedy, slaves in tragedy also have stereotypical roles to play: they perform menial tasks and highlight by contrast the noble characters. They are frequently assumed to be inferior. When Orestes mentions to Pylades that his mother is defended by slaves, Pylades snorts, "What are slaves worth in a fight with men / who were born free?" When the battle starts, a terrified Phrygian (i.e. Trojan) slave runs out, hysterically speaking pidgin Greek, and later cravenly begs for his life, offering to grovel in Persian fashion.[58] Euripides here indulges Greek stereotypes about the debased character of both slaves and effeminate Easterners.

Yet some slave characters manage to break through these boundaries. The misery of a slave's lot is frequently expressed, allowing for the possibility that a theater-goer would empathize with the slave. Thus when Hecuba's daughter Polyxena is sacrificed to Achilles' ghost, Euripides' chorus tells the suffering queen of Troy, "This is what it means / to be a slave: to be abused and bear it, / compelled by violence to suffer wrong." One wonders how many Athenians, remembering their own unjust violence against their slaves, squirmed at such lines. Later the chorus of Trojan captive women pitifully wonder where their new home will be, where they will "live a slave, / forced to a foreign land, / torn westward out of Asia / to a marriage that is death!"[59] In the *Andromache,* about the Trojan Hector's widow and her suffering as the concubine of the Greek Neoptolemus, the chorus of Greek women openly sympathizes with Andromache: "A sight for compassionate eyes—my heart said—woman of Troy, you / Entered my masters' home. Fear keeps me dumb, / And yet I'm all sorrow."[60] To be sure, these are proud and once-powerful nobles now suffering an ignoble servitude, and much of the pathos comes from that reversal of fortune; but many ordinary Greeks during this time were suffering the same fate. In democratic Athens, moreover, the nobles were more often objects of scorn than of pity. In any case, sympathy must start somewhere. Once the enslaved noble's lot is made the object of empathy and compassion, the possibility is created that other slaves too can appear more human, and their suffering worthy of attention.

Slaves of good or virtuous character also appear in Euripides, and they challenge the easy assumption that slavery is a reflection of innate ignobility. Andromache's slave-girl willingly risks her life to help her mistress, now a slave like her: "What's my life, that I should care / What happens now? A slave's life, and a woman's."[61] Here a slave is given the courage to choose goodness and death over a mean life, to show a virtue characteristic of the free. In the *Helen,* about Menelaus' rescue of Helen from Egypt where Theoclymenus has tried to marry her forcibly, his own slave prevents Theoclymenus from killing his sister for helping Helen escape. "You are not to judge what I do," Theoclymenus thunders, to which the slave responds, "If I am in the right, I must." Even when threatened with death, the slave refuses to allow Theoclymenus to commit such a crime.[62] These examples could be multiplied; as Philip Vellacott writes, "The slaves in Euripides, more than twenty individuals and a chorus, are loyal, honest, brave, sympathetic, and shrewd, and in only two cases unscrupulous . . . [and] their behaviour and moral judgement are clearly on a higher level than that of most of the free men and women."[63]

In Euripides the assumption that the free are inherently more courageous, rational, and virtuous is frequently overturned, an inversion that challenges the conventional, legitimizing distinctions between slave and free. Even if these scenes in the theater had no immediate effect on the everyday life of Athenian slaves or caused anybody to question the legitimacy of the institution, the mere fact that they were presented sowed the seeds of critical questioning that some day would bear fruit.

THE NEW ATTITUDES EVIDENT IN THE COMEDY and tragedy of the late fifth century reflect developments in Greek philosophy that would some day lay the groundwork for a wholesale challenge to the institution of slavery. Plato and Aristotle, however, accepted without question the need for slavery, and assumed that slaves were more or less deficient in reasoning power. A speaker in Plato's *Laws* says that "there is no element in the soul of a slave that is healthy. A sensible man should not entrust anything to their care."[64] Slaves "will never be friends with their masters."[65] In the philosopher's utopias, laws concerning slaves are proposed that are much harsher than the actual laws or practices of his times. In the *Laws* he suggests that

> slaves ought to be punished as they deserve, and not admonished as if they were freemen, which will only make them conceited. The language used to a servant ought always to be that of a command, and we ought not to jest with them.... [T]his is a foolish way which many people have of setting up their slaves, and making the life of servitude more disagreeable both for them and for their masters.[66]

Plato's pupil Aristotle agreed that a deficiency in reasoning power made some people naturally fit to be slaves and submit to the greater rationality and authority of a superior:

> One who is a human being belonging by nature not to himself but to another is by nature a slave.... For he is by

> nature a slave who is capable of belonging to another . . . and who participates in reason so far as to apprehend it but not to possess it. . . . Hence there are by nature various classes of rulers and ruled. For the free rules the slave . . . for the slave has not got the deliberative part [of the soul] at all.[67]

Slaves are also necessary for doing menial tasks, thus freeing citizens to pursue the good life for both themselves and the state. Hence as a thing apart from the master used for his benefit, the slave is a "kind of instrument," or as Aristotle puts it in the *Eudemian Ethics*, "a slave is as it were a member or tool of his master; a tool is a sort of inanimate slave."[68] He concludes, "It is clear, then, that some men are by nature free, and others slaves, and that for these latter slavery is both expedient and right."[69] As Peter Garnsey summarizes Aristotle's position, "The net result of his analysis is that there is very little humanity in his natural slave."[70]

Yet in the *Politics* we find evidence of a different point of view, and some ambivalence in Aristotle's position. His remarks in the *Politics* are in part a response to a very different position apparently significant enough for him to answer: "There are others, however, who regard the control of slaves by a master as contrary to nature. In their view the distinction of master and slave is due to law or convention; there is no natural difference between them: the relation of master and slave is based on force, and being so based has no warrant in justice."[71] Later, just following his endorsement of "natural" slavery, Aristotle agrees that war captives who become slaves are not necessarily natural slaves, and so should not be enslaved, for "no one would ever say that he is a slave who is unworthy to be a slave."[72] The problem then becomes determining the criteria by which natural slaves could be distinguished from those unjustly enslaved. Aristotle's solution is to designate barbarians as natural slaves, an idea that flattered Greek xenophobia. As Euripides' Iphigenia says, accepting her sacrifice to further the Greek expedition against the barbarian Trojans, "It is / a right thing that Greeks rule barbarians. . . . They are bondsmen and slaves, and we, / Mother, are Greeks and free."[73] Yet the existence of numerous Greek slaves made Aristotle's theoretical discussion an implicit indictment of slavery, at least as it was actually practiced by Greeks, for many slaves were Greeks who had perforce been enslaved unjustly. At any rate, we see in Aristotle the consequences of making slavery an object of rational analysis. Once that happened, it could become an object of criticism as well.

The "others" Aristotle mentions give further evidence that slavery was not completely taken for granted as natural and just among Greek thinkers. They very likely were the Sophists, those philosophers of the late fifth century who inquired critically into traditional beliefs and received wisdom, often advancing a relativism that saw human institutions and customs as reflecting force or chance or other arbitrary causes rather than innate right or justice. Perhaps the influence of the Sophists can best be seen in the tragedies of Euripides. The idea that slaves are inferior by nature and thus deserving of their status is contradicted by a passage from the *Ion,* a play about a noble temple slave; the line is spoken by an old, faithful slave: "A slave bears only this / Disgrace: the name. In every other way / An honest slave is equal to the free."[74] So too in the *Helen,* Menelaus' slave says, "I, though I wear the name of lackey [bondsman], yet aspire / to be counted in the number of the generous [noble] slaves, for I do not have the name of liberty / but have the heart [mind]."[75] Merely modifying the noun "slave" with the adjective "noble" in itself was a striking challenge to conventional views.

Fragments from lost plays suggest sentiments like those found in extant tragedies. One fragment goes so far as to discount entirely the equation of innate value with free status: "The name of slave does not exclude quality. Many slaves are worth more than free men."[76] Judging from the surviving fragments, it appears that Euripides' lost play the *Alexander* (ca. 415), about the Trojan prince's upbringing at the hands of slave shepherds after being exposed by his mother, Hecuba, centered on debates about the justice of slavery. After Paris bests his noble brothers at the games, a debate ensues on the issues of nobility and natural slavery. His brother Deiphobus indulges the common stereotypes about slaves as appetite-driven and reason-impaired (slaves "only think about their bellies, and have no thought for the consequences of their actions"). Paris retorts by invoking the Sophists' argument that contingencies are responsible for slave or free status, whereas true nobility and freedom derive from an individual's character: "vile people like you have become slaves in all but name, for Fortune [chance] has made you so." The chorus of shepherds endorses Paris's view: "Nature's creation is equally base and noble; / it is Custom, and Time, which make people proud of their rank. / True nobility lies in good sense and judgment, / and God alone, not wealth, bestows it."[77]

A fragment from a play by Sophocles, the *Tereus,* makes the same argument, suggesting that these ideas were widely discussed in Athens:

> Mankind is one tribe; one day in the life of father and mother brought to birth all of us; none was born superior to any other. But some are nurtured by a fate of misfortune, others of us by prosperity, and others are held down by the yoke of compulsion that enslaves us.[78]

Servile status, rather than reflecting innate inferiority, is an accident of chance, just as nobility is, and all humans are united by their common subjection to fortune. For Sophocles, a slave with a noble character is a possibility, one that undermines the kind of rationalization for slavery that would be articulated by Aristotle.

These scattered references tell us that in Athens of the late fifth century, ideas were circulating that challenged the prevailing justifications for slavery. As we see in the passages from Euripides, the idea that the quality of one's character and mind, rather than the status of one's body, makes one genuinely free was widespread enough by this time to appear in the public forum of Athenian tragedy. This focus on character changes the meaning of "natural slave": the free man can be a slave if he submits his reason to appetites and passions, and the slave a free man if he displays the right sorts of rational virtues. He will be, as a fragment of Sophocles puts it, "Servile in body, but the mind is free."[79] Two hundred years later, Bion would write, "Good slaves are free, but bad free men are slaves of many passions."[80]

This view of slavery as a condition of the soul rather than the body, implicit in the imagery used by Plato and Aristotle to describe the soul of the man dominated by appetite, became widespread in Stoicism. According to this Greco-Roman philosophy, the world is an orderly structure reflecting a divine, providential intention, a rational structure in which all humans—who by virtue of being human hold a spark of divine reason within them—have a duty to play whatever role providence has given them in order to further the good of the whole. True freedom is the choice of the wise man to do his moral duty. As Diogenes Laertius paraphrases Stoic doctrine, "Only he [the wise man] is free, but the bad are slaves. For freedom is the power of autonomous action, but slavery is the lack of autonomous action."[81] Moreover, everybody is rational and capable of virtue. "All men have natural tendencies to virtue," said Cleanthes (c. 260), and so potentially can learn to make the right choices and hence be free.

Even if such ideas tended indirectly to legitimize slavery as something beyond our control, and irrelevant anyway to our souls in their submission to whatever sphere providence has assigned us, they repudiated the notion of natural slavery. As the late-fourth-century comic poet Philemon put it, "No one by nature ever becomes a slave, but chance enslaves his body."[82] Stoic doctrine broke down the absolute distinctions between slave and free assumed in the theory of natural slavery, stressing instead their similarities in the common human condition—something more difficult to do in the race-based slavery of the American South.

The most important development in the nascent critique of slavery was the Stoic idea of the "brotherhood of man." The Stoics recognized a shared human nature transcending the accidental differences of environment, language, ethnicity or civic status, based on the common possession of reason and leading to affinity for other humans. "The mere fact of their common humanity requires that one human should feel another man to be akin to him," the Roman Stoic Cicero put it.[83]

This idea of human kinship has antecedents in earlier Greek thought. The late-fifth-century Sophist Antiphon said,

> For by nature we are all in every way made in the same fashion to be either barbarians or Greeks. That is what is shown by the things which are by nature necessary to all men. All men, in similar fashion, have the possibility of enjoying them and in all this no man is marked out as a barbarian or a Greek. We all breathe the air through our mouths and nostrils, and we all eat with our hands.[84]

A few decades later the orator Isocrates, in his *Panegyricus* (380), defined Greekness not as a matter of common blood but as one of common culture: "the name 'Hellenes' suggests no longer a race but an intelligence, and ... the title 'Hellenes' is applied rather to those who share our culture than to those who share a common blood."[85] Human identity rests on universal natural needs and abilities, together with a peculiar kind of culture that anyone can learn and embrace. Just as Greekness is not inborn, neither is slavery a reflection of innate racial or ethnic inferiority, but rather an accident of chance. And freedom, as the Sophist Alcidamas says in this chapter's epigraph, is a natural possession of every human being.

In the Stoic brotherhood of man, the common possession of divine reason binds all men together. Of course, some people have more reason than others, and humans can be hierarchically divided between the superior few who develop their reason to its maximum potential, and the foolish many who let their divine potentiality slumber unused. Still, if Plutarch can be believed, Zeno, the fourth-century founder of Stoicism, wrote that "our life should not be based on cities or peoples each with its own view of right and wrong, but we should regard all men as our fellow-countrymen and fellow-citizens, and that there should be one life and one order, like that of a single flock on a common pasture feeding together under a common law."[86] If Zeno did not actually intend the "world state" idea that Plutarch perhaps reads back into his work, certainly later Stoics, living in the more unified, cosmopolitan world created by Alexander and later the Romans, envisioned a human community not defined by artificial distinctions of ethnicity or status. The slave Epictetus, in the late first century A.D., best articulated this idea when he advised that we identify ourselves not as citizens of Athens or Corinth or some other state but as "citizens of the world," since our true human identity as rational beings comes not from our families or local communities but from God, and so the one true community is that of rational humans and God.[87]

These philosophical ideas carried with them obvious implications for how slaves should be treated, even if they did not frontally challenge the institution itself. Epictetus asked slave-owners, "Don't you remember what you are, and over whom you rule, that they are kinsmen, that they are brothers by nature, that they are the offspring of Zeus?"[88] A generation before Epictetus, the Roman Stoic Seneca, in one of his literary letters, criticized the dehumanizing abuse of slaves ("We abuse them as one does pack animals, not even as one abuses men") and invoked their common humanity: "Remember, if you please, that the man you call slave sprang from the same seed, enjoys the same daylight, breathes like you, lives like you, dies like you. You can easily conceive him a free man as he can conceive you a slave." Since a larger order beyond the individual's deserts determines whether one is slave or free, Seneca advised his correspondent to "treat your slave with compassion, even with courtesy; admit him to your conversation, your planning, your society."[89] Though neither Seneca, himself a slave-owner, nor anybody else in the Greco-Roman world called for the abolition of slavery, nonetheless these sentiments would in time help build the critical mass necessary to end human bondage.

NOWHERE ELSE IN THE ANCIENT WORLD—in the Near East, Asia, or northern Europe—can one find slaves and slavery discussed in this critical way. Works like the dialogue *Slavery and Freedom,* by the first-century philosopher Dio Chrysostom, in which a slave vigorously, intelligently, and passionately challenges the received wisdom of his free interlocutor, are unheard of outside Greece. There the debate began, and once the Greeks made slavery an object of free thought, analysis and discussion, the possibility of challenging the institution itself opened up. We should no more chastise the Greeks for not taking the next step, the abolition of slavery, than fault them for knowing the earth is round but not sailing to America.

M. I. Finley economically summarizes the significance of Greek thinking about slavery: "Shot through with ambiguity, and not rarely with tension," the Greeks' attitudes were articulated in an "academic conflict," to be sure, "but no society can carry such a conflict within it, around so important a set of beliefs and institutions, without the stresses erupting in some fashion, no matter how remote and extended the lines and connections may be from the original stimulus."[90] Much had to happen historically—the rise of Christianity is important here—before the seeds sown by the Greeks bore fruit. Yet rather than criticize the Greeks for a practice universally accepted in the ancient world, we should instead acknowledge them as the first to question it, thus pointing humanity down the road of emancipation.

War is both king of all and father of all, and it has revealed some as gods, others as men.

—*Heracleitus*[1]

FOUR

The Father of All

In September of 490, the Persian king Darius, long vexed by the stubborn recalcitrance of the self-governing Greek cities on the edge of his empire, landed an army of thirty thousand men at the Bay of Marathon, about twenty-six miles northeast of Athens. The Athenians, ten thousand strong, along with one thousand soldiers from the nearby city-state of Plataea, took up their position on the hills overlooking the plain where the Persians had encamped. After a close debate, the Athenian Miltiades persuaded the other generals to attack despite being outnumbered three to one. To achieve surprise and minimize the effect of the Persian archers, the Greeks either jogged for a mile or ran the last couple of hundred yards, to the amazement—and gratification—of the awaiting Persians. "For it seemed to them suicidal madness," wrote Herodotus, "for the Athenians to risk an assault with so small a force—at the double, too, and with no support from either cavalry or archers."[2] The Persians broke through the attenuated center of the Greek line, but the Greek wings turned the Persian flanks, then joined together behind them and routed the whole army, driving it into the sea. The Greeks lost 192 men, the Persians 6,400.

Ten years later, Darius' son Xerxes marshaled an enormous avenging army over a quarter-million strong, crossed the Hellespont on a pontoon bridge built of boats, and marched into Greece from the north, drinking rivers dry on the way, according to Herodotus. The confederated Greeks sent an army under the leadership of the Spartan king Leonidas to Thermopylae, the "Hot Gates," a narrow pass between the mountains and the sea in northeast Greece. After the Persians tried unsuccessfully for two days to force the pass, a treacherous Greek showed the Persians a route through the mountains that outflanked the Greek position. Discovering the betrayal, Leonidas sent the bulk of the Greeks away, remaining behind with 299 Spartans and several hundred other Greeks from Thespiae and Thebes. On the third day, after beating back wave after wave of the enemy and watching the Thebans defect, the remaining surrounded Greeks died fighting, literally buried by the swarms of Persian soldiers and missiles. Herodotus rises to Homeric heights in his description of the Spartans' glorious end: "Here they resisted to the last, with their swords, if they had them, and, if not, with their hands and teeth, until the Persians, coming on from the front over the ruins of the wall and closing in from behind, finally overwhelmed them."[3]

These two key battles demonstrate the peculiar Greek spirit and genius which, when turned to warfare, developed an ethic and technology of fighting unparalleled in the ancient world, a way of waging war that gave the Greeks an influence in the Mediterranean well out of proportion to their numbers and natural resources. These victories reveal as well the unique values that helped the Greeks withstand two major invasions by the huge, wealthy Persian Empire, securing the independence and freedom of the Greek city-states and hence creating the space in which the distinctive Hellenic intellect flowered.[4] If the Greeks had lost the battle of Salamis (September 480) that followed a few weeks after the defeat at Thermopylae, and had they then been absorbed into the autocratic Persian Empire as a satrapy, not only the subsequent history of Greece but that of the whole world would have been radically different.[5] Moreover, the Greek way of war shaped the manner in which later Western societies fought, initiating a tradition that made the West the most militarily powerful and successful—and the most destructive—civilization in the history of the planet. Today there is no society, no matter how anti-Western or technophobic, that does not desire Western advanced weaponry or military science. It is a paradox of history that some of humanity's highest ideals developed in tandem with some of its most brutally efficient means of destroying other human beings—and the origins of that paradox lie among the Greeks.

FROM THE NEOLITHIC AGE ONWARD, the willingness of men to kill and maim their fellows for any number of reasons, both rational and not, has been a sad constant of human history. Just about every pre-Greek society that scholars have studied, whether primitive or complex, shows evidence of organized violence, from the prehistoric raids memorialized on the walls of caves in Spain, to the martial boasting of Egyptian pharaohs carved on marble stelae. With the rise of large, complex, hierarchically organized civilizations around the Nile and the Tigris and Euphrates rivers, huge armies comprising cavalry, infantry, and chariots were fielded in order to further the ambition, greed, and thirst for glory of the various autocrats and elites who dominated the ancient Near East. At the battle of Kadesh in 1285 B.C., one of the earliest for which we have reliable information, Pharaoh Ramesses II and the Hittites mustered between them almost forty thousand men—a huge number compared with most armies before the military behemoths of the nineteenth and twentieth centuries.[6]

Yet the revolutionary advances in war-making that changed the course of history began not with the mighty pharaohs but in the tiny, seemingly insignificant Greek city-states some time in the late eighth or early seventh century. Prior to that time, during the Mycenean period that came to a violent end around 1200, Greek warfare was similar to the practice of Near Eastern civilizations. Aristocrats fought from chariots with the support of a motley collection of ground troops and skirmishers armed with javelins, slings, and bows. Massed chariots were used as platforms from which to fire arrows or launch spears. Armor was often made of linen and wicker, and weapons were made of bronze. Some time around the twelfth century, the Mycenean palace-centers were destroyed by the "Sea Peoples," invaders who fought on foot in mass formation. By the end of the "Dark Age" (1100–800), the lessons learned from these destructive warriors, along with an increased availability of iron, had led to the abandoning of the massed chariot attack with hit-and-run tactics, in favor of heavily armed infantrymen who fought at close quarters.

Readers familiar with Homer's *Iliad* no doubt remember the battle scenes, which probably reflect an amalgam of idealized Mycenean practice, Dark Age tribalism, and the new, evolving form of infantry battle of the early polis (ca. 700). In Homer, aristocrats do drive into battle on chariots and carry the towering, rectangular Mycenean shields, but the chariots function as little more than taxis. The poet emphasizes the one-on-one duel between warriors, who dismount from their chariots and hunt down other aristocrats deemed worthy of being killed. After some banter and genealogical boasting, they hurl their spears. If the spears miss their targets, the warriors fight with swords at close quarters, sometimes throwing a rock. The duel ends when one of the combatants suffers death or a wound.

Yet along with these romantic memorials of single combat, we also find in Homer oblique references to masses of infantrymen arrayed in rows, closely packed together—"Shield leaned on shield, helmet on helmet, man against man, / and the horse-hair crests along the horns of the shining helmets / touched as they bent their heads, so dense were they formed on each other."[7] The *Iliad* presents as well what appears to be a reference to the collision of phalanxes: "Now as these [Greeks and Trojans] advancing came to one place and encountered, / they dashed their shields together and their spears, and the strength / of armoured men in bronze, and the shields massive in the middle / dashed against each other, and the sound grew huge of the fighting."[8]

The type of fighting to which Homer alludes involved the hoplite, or heavily armed infantryman, who fought in a phalanx, the tightly packed rows of warriors that centuries later would terrorize the Persians at Marathon.[9] A combination of new technology and new tactics created this devastatingly effective style of making war. The hoplite got his name from the *hopla* or "panoply," the components of which included a round, concave, yard-wide, sixteen-pound, bronze-covered wooden shield that the front-line soldier held by an arm strap and handgrip, and the soldier behind hunkered into, resting the lip on his shoulder. His head was protected by a bronze helmet that covered the back of the neck and the cheeks and was fitted with a horsehair crest; the seventh-century poet from Lesbos, Alcaeus, wrote lovingly of the "bright helmets, down from which nod white horse-hair plumes, adornments for men's heads."[10] The thighs were protected by the shield, and the shins were covered with bronze greaves. Finally, there was a thirty- to forty-pound breastplate comprising two pieces of bronze, an inch and a half thick, connected at the shoulders and curving out at the hips to protect the chest and belly. Sheathed in these fifty to seventy pounds of stifling bronze, the hoplite warrior wielded what Anacreon called the "tearful spear": a pole of ash or cornel wood from six to eight feet long, fitted with an iron tip and a bronze butt-spike.[11] In addition he carried a short sword to use when the spear shattered.

Along with the bronze panoply came the phalanx, a new tactic of massing the fighters and sending them into shock assault. The hoplites were put into rows, usually eight shields deep, but sometimes as many as fifty, the shield of one man overlapping that of the man to his right like the scales on a reptile. With the spears of the first three rows projecting beyond the front line, the whole looked, as Plutarch put it, like a "ferocious beast, as it wheels at bay, [and] stiffens its bristles."[12] The seventh-century Spartan poet Tyrtaeus has left us a vivid description of arrayed hoplites awaiting the enemy:

> [L]et him take a wide stance and stand up strongly against
>   them,
> Digging both heels in the ground, biting his lip with his
>   teeth,

> covering thighs and legs beneath, his chest and his shoulders
> under the hollowed-out protection of his broad shield,
> while in his right hand he brandishes the powerful war-spear,
> and shakes terribly the crest high above his helm.[13]

When battle between two phalanxes was joined on a hot summer day on flat ground, each line marched toward the other to the accompaniment of a flute, then ran the last few hundred yards to give more impetus to their spear thrusts, colliding in a horrendous dusty din of clashing bronze and wood, splintering shields and spears, war cries, prayers, shouts of help and encouragement, and screams of agony.

Then came the scrum-like "push." As Tyrtaeus described the action, the engaged lines shoved against each other "toe to toe and shield against shield hard driven, / crest against crest and helmet on helmet, chest against chest; / let him close hard and fight it out with his opposite foeman."[14] Inches away from their enemies' faces, the front lines grappled and jabbed and stabbed while their comrades in the lines behind leaned into their shields and shoved forward, trampling and stabbing the fallen wounded with the butt-spike. The men in the front fought with their spears, if they still had them, or used their swords to stab the enemy wherever he was vulnerable—in his face and neck, or under his shield in the belly or groin (Tyrtaeus describes a white-haired front-line warrior "holding in his hands his testicles all bloody").[15] The struggling hoplites wrestled, pushed, scratched, yanked hair and beards, gouged, tripped, did anything possible to carve a gap into the opposing line and break its cohesion until that critical moment came, sometimes after a mere half-hour, when one side perceived it was losing, panicked, and broke and ran, the men tossing aside their heavy shields, each soldier offering "his back, a tempting mark to spear from behind."[16] After it was all over and the dust cleared, a horrific spectacle greeted the survivors. In the aftermath of Coronea (394), Xenophon saw "the earth stained with blood, friend and foe lying dead side by side, shields smashed to pieces, spears snapped in two, daggers bared of their sheaths, some on the ground, some embedded in the bodies, some yet gripped by the hand."[17]

Such fighting required remarkable courage and fortitude in order, says Tyrtaeus, to "endure to face the blood and the slaughter, / go close against the enemy and fight with his hands," or as the late-seventh-century poet Callinus described it, to "go straight on / forward, spear held high, and under his shield the fighting / strength coiled ready to strike in the first shock of the charge."[18] The armor trapped the heat like an oven; the helmet closed off sight and hearing and, without padding, offered little protection against concussions from the clanging blows; the soldiers' churning feet raised the choking dust into Simonides' "harsh cloud of war."[19] Surely the willingness to brave this "storm of spears,"[20] to stand in broiling armor inches from the foe and hack away at him, came from the hoplite-citizen's knowledge that he was fighting not for the glory or aggrandizement of some big-man or lord, but for his own "land and children and wedded wife," as Callinus put it.[21]

For two hundred years, from about 700 down to the Persian conflicts which radically altered the Greek practice of warfare, disputes between city-states, usually over contested borderlands, were often settled by this brief, horrific slaughter on flat ground. The premier infantrymen were the Spartans, whose elite citizens began their military training at the age of seven, living in barracks and organized in regiments under the critical and watchful eyes of older boys and veteran hoplites. All their time was spent developing few skills or talents other than the physical and psychological ones needed to stand unflinching in the line across from the gleaming bronze and bristling spears of the enemy, and then to endure the collision of bronze and iron until victory or death—but never flight—settled things. Sending her son to war, the Spartan mother pointed to his shield and advised, "Come home with that, or on it."

Nothing was more frightening to an enemy than the spectacle of the advancing Spartan phalanx: the shining shields emblazoned with the lambda (L for Lacedaemon, the ancient name for the region around Sparta), the scarlet cloaks, the long, carefully groomed hair of the soldiers, the whole phalanx "one solid mass of bronze and scarlet," as Xenophon described it,[22] while the men advanced calmly and precisely to the weird music of the flutes. It was the grim composure of the Spartans that perhaps more than anything else unsettled their enemies. Herodotus records the astonishment of the Persian spy at Thermopylae who witnessed the vastly outnumbered Spartans calmly exercising and combing their hair, and of Xerxes, who asked Demaratus, the exiled Spartan who accompanied him, what it meant. Demaratus explained that his countrymen intended to defend the pass to the death and would not surrender or retreat, for they always groomed their hair when they were about to risk their lives.[23]

The innovative phalanx style of fighting, at first limited to border disputes between city-states, was remarkably successful against the motley, polyglot, badly armored Persian army. For centuries it made the Greek hoplite an indispensable mercenary throughout the Mediterranean—Alexander killed as many hired Greek soldiers as Persian during his rampage through the Persian Empire. Success in turning back the Persians in the fifth century, and the necessity of resisting the ever-present threat of another invasion from Persia, created the conditions that would change Greek warfare from a brutal but economical way of settling disputes between neighbors into an instrument of expansion and conquest far beyond the city-state, culminating in the carnage of the Macedonian Alexander, whose conquests, despite the rhetorical patina of proselytizing Hellenism, were nothing more than one immense raid for plunder.[24]

As important as the Greek innovations in warfare were on the battlefield, the social and political circumstances surrounding the rise of the hoplite warrior are more significant for us, touching on themes to be developed in subsequent chapters, such as freedom and constitutional government. For the hoplite came into being at the same time as a new kind of man, never seen before in the autocratic kingdoms of the ancient Near East: the citizen freeholder of the polis who worked and lived on his own small plot, who held an equal place in the Assembly where decisions were debated and made, and who donned his armor to go out and occupy his position in the phalanx when his city quarreled with a neighbor. Neither an aristocratic horseman, nor a peasant conscript who, like the innumerable, anonymous Persian soldiers, had to be whipped into battle to fight and die for reasons not his own, the hoplite-farmer was of the "middle," and the manner of fighting he engaged in was designed to protect as efficiently and with as little waste of lives and property as possible his own economic and political interests rather than the self-aggrandizing schemes of big-men, elites, and priests. Our ideals of constitutional government, civilian control of the military, private ownership of property, individual freedom, egalitarianism, and self-sufficiency have their roots in the simultaneous rise of the middling farmer and the hoplite fighter.[25]

These landowning hoplite-farmers, however, began to be transformed during the fifth century under the stresses of the Peloponnesian War, fought between the atypical city-states of Sparta and Athens. The growth of the maritime Athenian Empire and its radical democracy created conditions in which the landless acquired political power and influence through service in the fleet. The heavily armed infantry was by itself insufficient to the demands of protecting a far-flung empire, which required, as well, rowers in the fleet, marines, archers and horsemen, not to mention military options other than the brief, decisive clash of foot-soldiers on flat ground. These changes paved the road for the conquering armies of Alexander, his Hellenistic successors, and later the Romans, creating a military might directed towards gaining territory and plunder, at a much higher cost in lives and treasure than that exacted by the intensely brutal yet parochial clashes of the Greek city-states.

In addition to this efficient military lethality, as Hanson and Heath show, the Greeks handed down several key traits that contributed to the triumphant dynamism of Western warfare: improved technology, superior discipline and training, the drive to learn and improve fostered by a tradition of free thought, a preference for citizen-soldiers and civilian control of decisions, the settlement of disputes by the decisive head-on encounter, an emphasis on infantry, and efficient accumulation of capital to finance war.[26] Some of these will be the focus of later chapters. Here I want to discuss the way the Greeks made war an object of analysis, and at times criticism—an intellectual engagement unique in the ancient world.

We should not expect to find anti-war sentiment in Greek thought. Pacifism is the transitory luxury of a people whose security has been earned by the bravery and militarism of earlier generations. Like slavery, warfare was absent only in the Golden Age, or among fabulous peoples like the Hyperboreans or the Scythian Argippaei. In the actual Iron Age world, war was considered a non-negotiable constant of human life, a necessity deriving from the innate violence and greed of humans or from the scarcity of resources in a harsh natural world. Thus Plato said, "Every city is in a natural state of war with every other."[27]

So it is no surprise that war permeates the poetry, philosophy, and art of the Greeks, and that many of their philosophers, writers, and artists experienced first-hand the brutal work of killing human beings. During the Peloponnesian War, Socrates fought at Potidaea, where he saved Alcibiades' life, at Amphipolis, and at Delium, where during the disastrous, panicked Athenian retreat he kept his head and never turned his back on the enemy. According to the general Laches, who was with Socrates at Delium, "If others had only been like him, the honour of our country would have been upheld, and the great defeat would never have occurred."[28] Although Aeschylus wrote nearly a hundred plays, in his epitaph he ignored his artistic achievement and memorialized instead his presence at Marathon: "The grove of Marathon, with its glories, can speak of his valor in battle. / The long-haired Persian remembers and can speak of it too."[29]

The ubiquity of war in the lives and imaginations of the polis Greeks did not, however, lead to a wholesale idealization or glorification of killing, much less any sort of glossing over of the brutality of war, whose god, Ares, is "most-hateful of all gods who hold Olympus."[30] No matter how necessary, war was still a horror to be avoided if possible. "To those without experience," wrote

Pindar, "war is sweet, but he who has experienced it fears in his heart its approach."[31] Similarly, Herodotus has the Lydian king Croesus say, "No one is fool enough to choose war instead of peace—in peace sons bury fathers, but in war fathers bury sons."[32] And in Sophocles' *Ajax,* produced a decade before the Peloponnesian War, the chorus of soldiers sings a bitter lament over the miseries of war: "Whoever it was that first revealed to Hellas / Their common scourge, detested arms and war, I curse him."[33]

Even Homer, who sings the glorious deeds of warrior heroes and their thirst for martial glory, does not ignore war's brutality or sugar-coat it with chivalry. In the *Iliad* the horrific effects of edged steel on human flesh are graphically portrayed in 147 wound descriptions, like these:

> Now the son of Phyleus, the spear-famed, closing upon [Pedaios]
> struck him with the sharp spear behind the head at the tendon,
> and straight on through the teeth and under the tongue cut the bronze blade,
> and he dropped in the dust gripping in his teeth the cold bronze.

> Next he [Diomedes] killed Asynoös and Hypeiron, shepherd
> of the people, striking one with the bronze-heeled spear above the nipple,
> and cutting the other beside the shoulder through the collar-bone
> with the great sword, so that neck and back were hewn free of the shoulder.

> He [Diomedes] spoke, and threw; Pallas Athene guided the weapon
> to the nose next to the eye, and it cut on through the white teeth
> and the bronze weariless shore all the way through the tongue's base
> so that the spearhead came out underneath the jawbone.

These deaths are a few of the many just in Book Five, and the effect of so many graphic wound descriptions by the time Hector dies in Book Twenty-two is to replicate the gruesome monotony of war, as well as document its harsh violence.

Warfare among the Greeks is seldom mentioned without some implicit or explicit recognition of its terrible human cost, the brutality it brings, the suffering it leaves in its wake. One can see the uniqueness of the Greeks in this regard by comparing their treatment of war to references in the literature of other ancient societies, for whom martial violence was accepted as a necessary and even desirable and glorious means of augmenting territory, serving a god, acquiring possessions, and furthering the power and prestige of kings.

An Egyptian hymn to Ramesses II praises "he who treadeth down the land of the Khatti, and maketh it a heap of corpses like Sekhmet [goddess of war]. . . . [E]veryone that encountereth it [Ramesses' might] becometh ashes—he, King Ramesses."[35] In Deuteronomy, dating from about the time of Homer (around 700), the "rules of war" are set out for the Israelites, such as this instruction regarding an attack on a city:

> But if [the city] refuses peace and offers resistance, you must lay siege to it. Yahweh your God shall deliver it into your power and you are to put all its menfolk to the sword. But the women, the children, the livestock and all that the town contains, all its spoil, you may take for yourselves as booty.[36]

This is the fate of distant towns. The cities closer to the Israelites are to be destroyed utterly: "You must not spare the life of any living thing." This matter-of-fact attitude towards total war as a necessity can be found too among the imperial Assyrians. Inscriptions from the mid-ninth century celebrate the cruelty and destruction inflicted on Assyria's enemies by Assurnasirpal, "mighty king, king of the universe, the king without a rival," who "overcame all his enemies and fixed the bodies of his foes upon stakes." The king boasts that he "slew great numbers of [enemies]; their spoil, their possessions and their cattle I carried off . . . with their blood I dyed the mountain red like wool; with the rest of them I darkened[?] the gullies and precipices of the mountain; their cities I destroyed, I devastated, I burned with fire."[37]

Anyone familiar with Homer's *Iliad* knows that there, war is more problematic than it is in Hebrew texts with their God-sanctioned slaughter, or in the arrogant boasts of the pharaoh or the Assyrian king. Homer's numerous wound descriptions are accompanied not just with the victim's name and lineage, but often with some brief biographical detail that personalizes him and reminds us that a human being, a unique individual with a family and a history, has passed from the earth. That Pedaios who bit the bronze spear-tip was Antenor's illegitimate son "who, bastard though he was, was nursed by lovely Theano / with close care, as for her own children, to pleasure her husband." Diomedes pursued and killed Polyidos and Abas, "sons of the aged dream interpreter, Eurydamas; / yet for these two as they went forth the old man did not answer / their dreams."[38] These poignant details—a woman who cared for her beloved husband's bastard, a dream-interpreter who could not foresee his own sons' deaths—humanize the enemy, reminding us of all that is lost when someone dies.

The human cost and dehumanizing brutality of war constitute one of Homer's major themes in the *Iliad*. We see this most clearly in the character of Hector, the defender of Troy who knows that the city's survival depends on his own, for Troy cannot fall as long as Hector lives. Unlike the Greek heroes, who live the camp life with their comrades and concubines, Hector is shown interacting with his whole family and fellow citizens, which emphasizes what is at risk every time he goes into the fighting. The famous scene from Book Six in which Hector, having returned briefly from the fighting, speaks with his wife Andromache captures beautifully the psychological burden not just on the warrior who knows how much he must protect, but on the wife gnawed with anxiety every time her husband leaves to fight. After reminding Hector that Achilles has killed her father and seven brothers, she pleads,

> Hektor, thus you are father to me, and my honoured mother,
> you are my brother, and you it is who are my young
> husband.
> Please take pity upon me then, stay here on the rampart,
> that you may not leave your child an orphan, your wife a
> widow.[39]

No one who has read the scene can forget Hector's infant son, Astyanax—doomed after the sack of Troy to be hurled from the city's wall—shrinking in terror from his father's helmet "and the crest with its horse-hair / nodding dreadfully," only suffering to come to his father's arms when the warrior has removed the helmet.[40] Here Homer powerfully shows us that the warrior must discard his humanity when he puts on his armor to go and kill, even in defense of his fatherland, and that he regains it when he takes his armor off. And remember, this sympathetic insight is extended to an enemy of the Greeks whose descendants Homer's aristocratic audience fancied themselves to be.

The development of Hector's humanity climaxes in the few moments before his duel with Achilles, who has now been turned into an inhuman killing machine by his rage and grief over the death of his beloved Patroclus. Hector's father and mother plead with their son from the wall, Priam evoking his own brutal end when the dogs he has nurtured "will lap my blood in the savagery of their anger," and Hecuba baring her breast, which symbolizes every human's dependence on others and the ties of obligation by which we are all bound. Hector, all too human in the few moments before Achilles arrives, talks to himself, expressing his fear, his doubt, his shame over his arrogant miscalculation that cost so many of his warriors' lives. When Achilles approaches he panics and runs, stopping only when Athena disguises herself as his brother Deiphobus and promises to stand by him. And when his first spear-cast misses and he turns to his brother for another spear and his brother is not there, when he realizes that his doom has been sealed by the gods, he rises to magnificence and says, "But now my death is upon me. / Let me at least not die without a struggle, inglorious, / but do some big thing first, that men to come shall know of it." Yet the glory of this last charge is tempered by our knowledge of the price Hector is willing to pay for his own honor and glory: the deaths of his father and brothers and son, the enslavement of his wife, and the complete destruction of a whole glorious civilization.[41]

The price of martial glory and the inhumanity that war fosters are perhaps Homer's major themes. Certainly the character of Achilles, the "best of the Achaians," illustrates this. For all his dazzling excellence, Achilles is a terrible force of destruction, not just to the Trojans but to his own comrades and ultimately to the one human he loves the most, Patroclus. His obsession with honor and glory, driven by his wrath at the dishonor inflicted first by Agamemnon and then by Hector's killing of Patroclus, is starkly exposed to us for what it is: a threat to the conditions of our humanity itself. For violence is not all there is to being human; there are, as Achilles' tutor Phoinix reminds him in Book Nine, the ties that bind, the obligations we have to those who have benefited us, the affectionate connections between other humans that create society and the possibility of our human identity. In Homer, the emotion that reflects these ties is pity, our response to the suffering not only of those we love, but even of our enemies.

In the character of Achilles, a destructive wrath struggles with a human capacity to care for others, a struggle that ends when the last person he cares for, Patroclus, is killed. Achilles is left an inhuman killing machine, choking the rivers of Troy with her myriad dead. Yet after Hector's death, he returns the body to Priam and recovers his humanity—if only briefly, for his own death is nigh—when he pities the old king whose sons he has slaughtered. For the grief that Priam suffers at his loss is like the grief Achilles suffers at his:

> He took the old man's hand and pushed him
> gently away, and the two remembered, as Priam sat huddled
> at the feet of Achilleus and wept close for manslaughtering
>   Hektor
> and Achilleus wept now for his own father, now again
> for Patroklos. The sound of their mourning moved in the
>   house.[42]

Is this sort of sympathy for an enemy and recognition of our common humanity, not to mention the acknowledgment of the suffering and inhumanity of war, ever expressed by an Israelite for a Philistine, an Assyrian for a Babylonian, an Egyptian for a Hittite? Compare the inscription describing Ramesses' victory at Kadesh, where the enemy are mere anonymous, vile wretches to be slaughtered wholesale by Ramesses single-handed: "My majesty overpowered them, / I slew them without sparing them; / They sprawled before my horses, / And lay slain in heaps in their blood."[43] Or consider the beautiful Psalm 137, "By the rivers of Babylon," which ends, "A blessing on him who takes and dashes / your babies against the rock!" Such sentiments about an enemy represent a brutally simple and practical sensibility worlds apart from the complexity and psychological depth of Homer's characters, whose violence, equally cruel and destructive, is yet contained in a larger vision of the common suffering that all humans, even enemies, must endure.

Throughout Greek literature—the product of independent thought, in contrast to the statist propaganda of the autocratic East—we find thoughts about war that question its presumably justifying glory and honor. Some Greek poets scorned the ideal of death before dishonor, an ideal enshrined in the Spartan mother's injunction to her son to return home either with his shield or on it (i.e. dead), since the first thing a fleeing soldier did was abandon his heavy shield. The mercenary Archilochus, who died in a battle between the island city-states Naxos and Paros, felt no compunction in admitting that he saved his skin at the expense of his shield:

> Some barbarian is waving my shield, since I was obliged to leave that perfectly good piece of equipment behind under a bush. But I got away, so what does it matter? Let the shield go; I can buy another one equally good.[44]

Such a frank dismissal of martial sacrifice is perhaps what led to Archilochus' poetry being banned by the Spartans, one of whose marching songs proclaimed that sparing one's life was not the Spartan way. Alcaeus, the late-seventh-century poet from Lesbos, was likewise indifferent to losing his shield; he sent a herald to announce to his countrymen that the Athenians had hung up the discarded shield in the temple to Athena.[45]

Some disagreed with the idea that if a warrior dies in battle facing the enemy, with a wound in his chest testifying to his valor, his "glory is never forgotten," as Tyrtaeus says, "his name is remembered, / and he becomes an immortal."[46] Archilochus objects: "No man gains honour or glory of his countrymen once he be dead."[47] This cynicism is typically Greek, as is the recognition that human life is precious—perhaps too precious to be sacrificed for the glory of war.

IN ATHENIAN TRAGEDY AND COMEDY of the fifth century we find the most significant and searching examination of war and its human costs. "Now, in place of the young men / urns and ashes are carried home / to the house of the fighters," writes Aeschylus, for example, of the loss the Greeks incurred in fighting the Trojans.[48] Remember that Athenian dramas were civic performances in the public theater, reaching a large number of citizens. They testify that certain topics were matters of public interest and debate, and reveal much about the larger Athenian critical sensibility.

The Greeks even examined the suffering borne by their foes in war. Consider Aeschylus' *Persians,* produced in 472, eight years after the battle of Salamis. Before an audience including many who had fought the Persians or had lost loved ones, in a city that had been burned by the invaders, Aeschylus describes without rancor or gloating the battle's effects on the enemy, in the persons of Xerxes' wife and mother and the chorus of Persian elders, whose dread and anxiety and love are all sympathetically portrayed. "Woe upon woe," the chorus sings on learning of the disaster of Salamis, "of friends / The sea-dyed corpses whirl / Vagrant on cragged shores.... Recall how many / Persians widowed vain, / And mothers losing sons."[49] Through the play we come to regard Xerxes as a tragic hero. His daring and in some ways admirable reach for superhuman achievement have fostered an arrogant violence against the gods whose temples the Persian burn, and who consequently punish him with disaster—"payment / For his pride and godless arrogance," according to the ghost of his father, Darius.[50] At the end a battered Xerxes appears on stage to express his grief and guilt: "Here am I, alas, O woe: / To my native and ancestral land / Woe is the evil I've become."[51]

It is remarkable that a hated enemy could be made the exemplar of the tragic human condition, of the bold striving for grandeur and the susceptibility to failure and suffering, which Athenians could recognize in themselves. Pericles does so in his Funeral Oration when he says that the Athenians have "forced every sea and land to be the highway of our daring, and everywhere, whether for evil or for good, have left imperishable monuments behind us."[52]

In the tragedies of Euripides produced during the brutal Peloponnesian War we find the most searching criticism of violent conflict and a recognition of the senseless suffering, moral corruption, and dehumanizing passions that war unleashes. In *The Suppliant Women* (ca. 422) the fragility of peace, the ambiguity of violence even for a just cause, and the seeming inevitability of war given the destructive passions of men are all explored. The story concerns the war against Thebes (Athens' historical rival to the north) initiated by Oedipus' son Polyneices with the help of the king of Argos, Adrastus, and five other champions. After the "seven against Thebes" are defeated, the Athenian king Theseus attacks Thebes to recover the bodies of the slain that the city's king, Creon, refuses to surrender for burial. (Two years before the play was produced, after the battle of Delium the Thebans had left more than a thousand Athenian dead to rot for over two weeks.) Theseus defeats the Thebans but does not sack the city; yet this noble action is clouded by the speech of the children of the slain, who vow revenge, insuring that the cycle of violence will continue.

The speech of the Theban herald, who is trying to deter Theseus from doing the right thing in seeing to the burial of the dead, accurately describes the senselessness of war and its dangers in a democracy that makes decisions based on emotion (a point Thucydides would likewise make in his description of the Athenian deliberations leading to the disastrous Sicilian expedition of 415). The herald says:

> When the people vote on war, nobody reckons
> On his own death; it is too soon; he thinks
> Some other man will meet that wretched fate.
> But if death faced him when he cast his vote,
> Hellas would never perish from battle-madness.
> And yet we men all know which of two words
> Is better, and can weigh the good and bad
> they bring: how much better is peace than war!
>
> But evilly we throw all this [blessings of peace] away
> To start our wars and make the losers slaves—
> Man binding man and city chaining city.[53]

For the Athenians in the audience, such words would have struck painfully close to home, for they had indeed voted to enslave and subdue fellow Greek city-states for self-interested and base motives.

Equally pointed would have been the speeches of Adrastus on the overhasty recourse to violence and the folly of squandering opportunities for negotiation:

> O witless mortals! Richly you deserve
> Your many woes; you listen not to friends,
> But to your interests. Cities! You might use
> Reason to end your troubles, but with blood,
> Not words, you ruin your affairs.—Enough!
>
> O wretched mortals,
> Why do you slaughter each other with your spears?
> Leave off those struggles; let your towns take shelter
> In gentleness.[54]

Where else in the ancient world would a poet dare to offer such criticism of his city's policies and motives, and in a public forum like the open-air theater? And where else would be found a sensibility like Euripides' that, even while making that criticism, suggests as well the arguments for the other side? "I only think it just," Theseus announces to the Theban herald, "To bury their dead. I mean no harm to the city, / No man-destroying struggles; I uphold / The law of all the Greeks."[55] Euripides knows that sometimes war is necessary to ensure justice and prevent tyranny.

Another of Euripides' tragedies, the *Hecuba* (ca. 424), was produced near the time of the Athenian defeat at Delium. In the immediate aftermath of the sack of Troy, the aged queen, Hecuba, is driven into an insane desire for revenge by the treacherous murder of her last son, Polydorus, and the sacrifice of her daughter Polyxena to the shade of Achilles. She will go on brutally to blind her son's murderer, Polymestor, whose prophecy that she will turn into a dog underscores her loss of humanity. The play documents the moral corruption not just of the vanquished, who are dehumanized by suffering, but also of the victors, whose easy recourse to violence and treachery destroys their capacity for pity. That this corruption was historical as well as literary is shown by Thucydides' later description of the chilling Athenian rationale for destroying the Melians (416): it is simply an amoral law of nature that the strong rule the weak. Indeed, Odysseus' response to Hecuba when she begs for her daughter's life—"Nothing you do or say / can change the facts. Under the circumstances, / the logical course is resignation"—anticipates the words Thucydides puts in the mouth of the Athenians responding to the pleas of the Melians: "You know as well as we do that right, as the world goes, is only in question between equals in power, while the strong do what they can the weak suffer what they must."[56]

Most of Euripides' plays that were produced during the war touch on its brutality and the dehumanization of both conqueror and conquered. *The Trojan Women,* staged a mere nine months after the Athenian massacre of the Melians, tells the story of the Greeks' murder of Hector's infant son, Astyanax. In the character of the herald Talthybius, who must announce the sentence to Andromache, it highlights the psychological torture afflicting good but weak men who are ordered to commit evil in an unjust or worthless cause. "I am not the man to do this," Talthybius says as he hands the child to a guard. "Some other / without pity, not as I ashamed, / should be herald of messages like this."[57] How many Athenians thought of the Melians when they heard this speech?

The play touches on the waste of war, particularly one waged for base or selfish reasons. The Trojan princess Cassandra, destined to be Agamemnon's concubine and ultimately to be murdered by Clytaemestra, castigates the Greeks for the suffering they have inflicted not just on the Trojans but on their own families, all for the no-good Helen:

> Those the War God caught
> never saw their sons again, nor were they laid to rest
> decently in winding sheets by their wives' hands, but lie
> buried in alien ground; while all went wrong at home
> as the widows perished, and barren couples raised and
>   nursed
> the children of others, no survivor left to tend
> the tombs, and what is left there, with blood sacrificed.
> For such success as this congratulate the Greeks.[58]

Remember that the Athenians, driven by lust for power, territory, and wealth, were at that very moment planning the expedition to Syracuse, an adventure that would leave them as Cassandra describes the Greeks at Troy—except that the Athenians would be utterly defeated. Most of the army's forty thousand men were left dead in Syracuse, only a handful of survivors ever making it home to Athens. As Philip Vellacott notes, Euripides in his tragedies never forgets the "individual victim," never glosses over the sacrifice that is "always to be pitied and valued, never to be ignored."[59]

On the comic stage, war is typically the bitter fruit of the lust for power and pelf that drives corrupt politicians. In the *Acharnians* (425) Aristophanes gives us a burlesque origin for the war between Sparta and Athens. Certain men in Athens, "trouble-making excuses for men, misminted, worthless, brummagem [counterfeit], and foreign-made," railed against the Megarians, Athens' trading rival, for importing goods without paying duties. Then some drunken youths "went to Megara and kidnapped the whore Simaetha. And then the Megarians ... in retaliation stole a couple of Aspasia's whores [Aspasia being the politician Pericles' mistress], and from that the onset of war broke forth upon all the Greeks: from three sluts!"[60] In other words, greed for profit and sexual appetite are the causes of war, not lofty and noble sentiments, or policies intended to benefit the city. Hence it is mindless to squander lives and resources to gratify the lust and greed of crooked politicians, informers, arms manufacturers, ambassadors with bloated per diems, and careerist army officers.

A few years later, Aristophanes once again links the war to venal politicians in the *Peace* (421). The farmer Trygaios, having flown to heaven on a giant dung beetle to ask Zeus why he is allowing the Greeks to destroy each other, is told by Hermes that Pericles started the war out of fear that he would be implicated in the attack on the sculptor Pheidias, who was accused of pilfering some of the gold and ivory intended for his huge statue of Athena. In addition, the Spartans were bribed into war by the subject cities of the Athenian Empire, who feared an increase in their tribute. Once started, the war was kept blazing by crooked orators and the bribes of foreigners: "Thus the scoundrels throve and prospered: / whilst distracted Hellas came / unobserved to wrack and ruin."[61] So, Hermes continues, all the other gods have left Olympus out of disgust with mortals: "Here / Where they were dwelling, they've established War, / And given you up entirely to his will." When Trygaios asks why, Hermes responds, "Because, though they were oftentimes for Peace, / You always would have War," since each side begrudged the other any advantage, no matter how trivial.[62]

Hermes then, in a striking visual metaphor, indicates the huge mortar in which War intends to grind down the Greek city-states as soon as he finds the pestles—that is, the politicians and generals willing and eager to continue fighting to further their own ambitions. Fortunately, the real-life "pestles"—the Athenian Cleon and the Spartan king Brasidas—had both died in the recent battle at Amphipolis (422), thus giving each city's peace party an opportunity to negotiate. In the play Trygaios rescues a personified Peace from a cave and brings her back to Athens, and the comedy ends in a joyous outburst of song and dance, a festival of regeneration and fertility from which the arms manufacturers and traders are banned. To Aristophanes, war is a force of chaos exploited by the ambitious and greedy, a senseless calamity that destroys life's greatest pleasures and happiness.

By the time of the *Lysistrata* (411), Athens had suffered the calamity in Sicily, most of her allies were in revolt, and the Spartans were occupying nearby Deceleia, from which they could ravage at leisure the Athenian countryside. This twenty-year waste of lives and wealth is attributed by Lysistrata to nothing other than greed and ambition. That's why the women seize the Acropolis, to keep the warmongers away from the money needed to finance the war: "Peisander [a prominent politician] and all the other officials / just wanted a way to steal, so they always had some stew or other boiling."[63] Lysistrata goes on to suggest that eliminating the scheming, self-interested politicians and secret political organizations "who compress themselves into positions of power" would solve the city's problems.[64] Finally, she justifies the women's actions by reminding the men of the suffering that women must bear in war—the wives left alone, the maidens who will never marry, and the sons who will never return home. Given the terrible costs of war, men must be certain that their reasons and motives are just before inflicting such suffering on their societies.

Aristophanes was no pacifist. His frequent encomia to the hardy veterans of Marathon and Plataea, and his decrying of the corruption of character that has left the young men effeminate and worthless as soldiers, testify to his belief in the need always to be ready for war. Yet his comedies are highly critical of unjust wars, wars instigated and fought to enrich the purses and further the ambitions of corrupt leaders. Such public attacks on established political power are unheard of anywhere else in the ancient Mediterranean. No one questioned the Egyptian pharaoh or the Great King of Persia when he wasted his people's lives to increase his own power and glory.

THE ATTITUDES TOWARDS WAR WE HAVE BEEN TRACING, while never evolving into naked pacifism, nonetheless made armed conflict and violence an object of critical thought, and hence kept war from being completely accepted or taken for granted. Particularly important is the analysis of motive, the recognition that military violence is often the instrument of the venal and ambitious, and sometimes merely the reflection of a destructive human nature and passions otherwise kept in check by laws and customs—which war, in turn, disrupts. Certainly Thucydides' masterful history of the Peloponnesian War does not glorify war but rather sees it as a failure of our better natures, a manifest evil that brings out the worst in men. His description of the devastating breakdown of law and decency during the revolution on the island of Corcyra (427) should be required reading for every politician and general:

> The sufferings which revolution entailed upon the cities were many and terrible, such as have occurred and always will occur as long as the nature of mankind remains the same; though in a severer or milder form, and varying in their symptoms, according to the variety of the particular cases. In peace and prosperity states and individuals have better sentiments, because they do not find themselves suddenly confronted with imperious necessities; but war takes away the easy supply of daily wants and so proves a rough master that brings most men's characters to a level with their fortunes.[65]

As we contemplate the ethnic cleansing, genocide, and mass murder taking place all around us, we should remember this clear-eyed recognition of the destructiveness in human nature, an inclination to disorder requiring containment by strong social and cultural values—yet often, paradoxically, restrained only by a greater violent force wielded by the more righteous. If there is a lesson to be learned from the Greek analysis of war, it is that we have to be clear of the rightness of our motives before we unleash the terrible destructiveness of Ares, "lover of blood and death," who dances "in the dance that knows no music."[66]

Finally, we must remember that this insight into the horrible complexities of war and the price it exacts in human suffering is found nowhere else in the ancient world. The attitudes towards war that we today would consider civilized have their origins in Euripides and Aristophanes and Thucydides, not in the cruel boast of the pharaoh or of the Assyrian king. To illustrate this point, I close this chapter with an inscription from Assyria:

> I [Assurnasirpal] built a pillar over against his city gate, and I flayed all the chief men who had revolted, and I covered the pillar with their skins; some I walled up within the pillar, some I impaled upon the pillar on stakes, and others I bound to stakes round about the pillar; many within the border of my own land I flayed, and I spread their skins upon the walls; and I cut off the limbs of the officers, of the royal officers who had rebelled.[67]

This reminds us by contrast of what we owe to the unique sensibilities of the Greeks, who were not the bought spokesmen of the state. No Greek could ever have written such a thing.

Hence it is evident that the state is a creation of nature, and that man is by nature a political animal. And he who by nature and not by mere accident is without a state, is either a bad man or above humanity; he is like the "Tribeless, lawless, hearthless one," whom Homer denounces—the natural outcast is forthwith a lover of war; he may be compared to an isolated piece at draughts.

—*Aristotle*[1]

FIVE

The Birth of Political Man

FOR THE PAST TWO CENTURIES, after every presidential election in the United States a political miracle has taken place: A man who has commanded the nation's military force—in recent times the most deadly and destructive in the history of the planet—obeys both the will of the voters and constitutional statute by handing over all that power to a successor formally chosen by the electorate rather than by himself. We so take for granted that this transference not only will take place but will do so without violence or public disorder, that we forget how historically atypical such a peaceful surrender of power is.

That continuing miracle is the fruition of twenty-five centuries of political development that began with the Greeks. Consensual government—the idea that men should govern themselves according to laws, statutes, offices, and institutions, all belonging to the collective citizenry rather than to any individual or elite group—was rare, if not unknown, elsewhere in the ancient Mediterranean. Despite attempts to posit a primitive democracy among the third-millennium city-states of Sumer or those of the Phoenicians, only in the some thousand Greek city-states (the polis) do we find "politics": that is, the public business of the people, conducted by citizens. Only among the Greeks do we find explicitly articulated the idea that political power should reside in institutions and laws rather than resting on the frail reeds of flawed men, even those purportedly chosen or sanctioned by the gods.

Everywhere else in the Mediterranean world—in Egypt, Israel, Sumer, Babylon, Assyria—power remained in the hands of aristocratic or plutocratic elites, kings, priests and castes, with the mass of humanity denied any participation in the political direction of their communities. In these monarchies, government comprised hierarchical bureaucracies that were nothing more than an extension of the king's household, and military power was subservient to the ambitions and whims of kings and nobles. A typical view of governance appears in the inscription prepared by Xerxes when he succeeded to the throne of Persia: "I am Xerxes, the great king, king of kings, king of lands containing many men, king in this great earth far and wide. . . . I governed them, they brought tribute to me, they did that which was commanded them by me; the law which was mine, that held them firm."[2]

Autocratic rule was remarkably efficient at creating order and public works—the monumental architecture and the hydraulic organization of Egypt and Mesopotamia testify to what can be achieved when men are marshaled, directed to a goal and cowed by religious superstition or by force. Yet such men are neither free nor the choosers of their fate, and so in Aristotle's estimation—and our own—they are not fully human. As they did with women or slavery or war, the Greeks first made the problems of governance and public order and justice objects of debate and criticism. By doing so, they initiated a dialogue on human freedom that is still ongoing, and opened the way to creating forms of governance that are widely inclusive and respectful of the rights of all humans.

SOMETIME BETWEEN THE FALL OF THE MYCENEAN kingdoms and 650 B.C. the Greeks created the polis.[3] The great palace-centers of the Myceneans resembled other Near Eastern kingdoms: divinely sanctioned kings ruled from their palaces, and all political, legal, military, religious, and economic power and activity were centralized and organized by the king's household bureaucracy and retinue. After these palace-centers were destroyed by invading Sea Peoples around 1200 B.C., during the so-called Dark Age powerful noble clans ruled much smaller territories, supported by warriors attached to their service, and advised and sometimes checked by councils of aristocratic elders. The judicial and religious powers of these rulers were likewise more circumscribed than had been the case with the Mycenean kings. The Greeks of this "feudal" period seem to have learned the dangers and weaknesses of an overly centralized power, a lesson given mute testimony by the ruins of the great walls and tombs of the Mycenean kings.

The polis emerged from Dark Age households and alliances of aristocratic clans partly through the growth of a new class of men: those of the "middle," neither aristocratic big-men nor serfs dependent on the powerful landowners. Probably they were small farmers who cultivated vines, grains, and olives on marginal lands, earned enough of a surplus to create disposable income, and most likely developed the hoplite style of fighting.[4] As we have seen, the armored infantryman was neither a grandee on horseback, nor a serf who could not afford the bronze and iron panoply of the hoplite soldier. And the aristocratic notion of individual honor and heroism embodied in the figure of Homer's Achilles did not suit phalanx fighting, which depended on collective courage and group cohesion, each soldier performing his duty in the phalanx. It was these men of the "middle" who developed the government of the polis as a form of rule that protected their agrarian interests, ensured equality among land-holding citizens, fostered justice, and avoided the dangers of clan alliances and feuds, as well as the concentration of power and wealth in the hands of a man whose character was not always commensurate with his authority.

The interests of these small farmers—who worked roughly equal plots, occupied similar places in the phalanx during war, and enjoyed equal rights in the government—were not served by mounted elites who possessed large estates and immoderate wealth and who lorded over and exploited the volatile masses of the politically and economically dispossessed. Hence Greek literature contemporaneous with the rise of the polis reveals distrust of excessive wealth and disdain for the arrogance of elites who believed their money and privilege allowed them to subvert justice to further their private interests. The farmer-poet Hesiod, writing around 700 during the transition from rule by feudal kinglets to the constitutional order of the polis, upbraids the "gift-devouring kings" and their "reckless deeds and evil plans," their "slanted words" and "crooked ways" that pervert justice.[5] We see here a much different worldview from that shown in Homer when Thersites, a foul-mouthed commoner, accurately castigates Agamemnon and gets a beating for his willingness to speak truth to power. Hesiod represents the emergence of a new kind of consciousness, a recognition that justice and right are not the private possessions of the powerful, to be interpreted and administered according to their own interests and eccentricities.

To Hesiod, excessive wealth and power together corrupt man's character and create disorder and injustice in the state—a theme sounded later in the poetry of the Athenian statesman Solon. Around 600 he reformed the Athenian constitution, reined in the power of the nobles, and alleviated the discontent of the impoverished commons, who were always vulnerable to manipulation by unscrupulous leaders hungry for power. Solon decried *hubris,* the arrogant excess that blinds a man to the just limits of his actions and invites retribution from the gods. Frequently this arrogance grows from wealth. "Those among us," writes Solon, "who have already the biggest estates / try to get twice as much as they have. Who can satisfy all of them?" The insatiable desire for more riches breeds ruin—"disaster can grow out of money"—and the whole city will suffer: "But the citizens themselves in their wildness are bent on destruction / of their great city, and money is the compulsive cause." Exploiting the masses for their own gain, the wealthy elites foment civil disorder and factional strife: "The leaders of the people are evil-minded. The next stage / will be great suffering, recompense for their violent acts, / for they do not know enough to restrain their greed and apportion / orderly shares for all."[6] Civic disorder follows when justice is perverted to serve the greed of the powerful and the vengeance of the oppressed, who themselves are motivated by the desire for riches and retribution.

Solon's solution is a political order based on moderation—the ethic of the "middle"—and avoidance of extremes whether of wealth or of poverty, each of which in turn breeds tyranny and anarchy:

> I gave the people as much privilege as they have a right to.
> I neither degraded them from rank nor gave them free hand;
> and for those who already held the power and were envied
> for money
> I worked it out that they also should have no cause for
> complaint.
> Thus would the people be best off, with the leaders they
> follow:
> neither given excessive freedom nor put to restraint;
> for Glut gives birth to Greed [*hubrin*], when great prosperity
> suddenly
> befalls those people who do not have an orderly mind.[7]

Wealth cannot be the basis of power, for as Solon says, "Many bad men are rich, many good men poor."[8] Yet poverty breeds discontent and disorder as grievous as that spawned by the ambition of the rich; hence the middle way is best. "I stood as a mark in the midway between the two hosts" of nobles and commons, explains Solon.[9] Similarly, the poet Phocylides, writing a little later than Solon, remarks that "Many things are best in the mean; I desire to be of a middle condition in my city."[10]

The result of Solon's privileging the middle over the extremes of wealth and poverty would be civic order and justice for noble and common alike, predicated on laws and ordinances that were common to all and did not either favor or threaten the wealthy and noble. "I have made laws," Solon says, "for the good man and the bad [i.e. noble and commoner] alike, / and shaped a rule to suit each case, and set it down."[11] The result would be political order, for the extremes of tyranny and anarchy would be avoided. As the chorus in Aeschylus' *Eumenides* (458) sings, "Refuse the life of anarchy; / refuse the life devoted to / one master. / The in-between has the power / by God's grant always, / though his ordinances vary."[12]

We need again to emphasize how unusual in the ancient world was this championing of a citizenry midway between noble and serf. Everywhere else—Asia and the Americas included—it was taken for granted that aristocratic and wealthy elites ruled their societies in order to further their own power and privilege. The explicit contrast between Greek consensual government and elite rule elsewhere is a constant in Greek literature, as we shall have occasion to note. Perhaps the most succinct expression of this difference is found in Phocylides: "A little polis living orderly in a high place is stronger than block-headed Nineveh," the Assyrian capital destroyed in 612.[13] A city-state of middling citizens governing themselves through common, publicly available laws and institutions would outlive the larger, mightier cities controlled by kings and nobles who ruled through private whim and self-interest and who lorded it over impoverished, disgruntled masses. As Aristotle summarizes the idea,

> And this [the middle] is the class of citizens which is most secure in a state, for they do not, like the poor, covet other men's goods; nor do others covet theirs, as the poor covet the goods of the rich; and as they neither plot against others, nor are themselves plotted against, they pass through life safely. . . . Thus it is manifest that the best political community is formed by citizens of the middle class, and that those states are likely to be well-administered in which the middle class is large, and stronger if possible than both the other classes.[14]

The focus on moderation—the avoidance of extremes of wealth and poverty, and the restraint of irrational desire in governance—reflects the Greek recognition that all humans, including nobles and kings, are subject to powerful passions that threaten to overwhelm their sense of right and justice. That is why, throughout Greek literature, we find a distrust of power concentrated in one man's hands, thus magnifying the mischief that could grow from human passions, character flaws and susceptibility to chance.

To the Greeks, perhaps the best examples of the dangers of autocratic power were the Persian kings, quasi-divine absolute rulers who wielded a literal power of life and death over their subjects. The Greeks' defeat of two Persian invaders, first Darius and then Xerxes, offered them proof that giving excessive power to a mere mortal was to invite disaster. Aeschylus' treatment of Xerxes in the *Persians* repeatedly makes this point. The arrogance of the Persian king, which drives him to whip and fetter the Hellespont (bodies of water had gods associated with them) for wrecking his bridge, and then to burn the temples of the gods in Athens, blinds him to his mortal limitations, his subjection to time and chance and the higher powers of the gods. The herald who announces the disaster of Salamis to the Persian court repeats Xerxes' hubristic commands before the battle and then comments: "So he spoke in humored pride: of the god-given future / Nothing he knew." And later the ghost of Darius, Xerxes' father, will lament that "A great divinity / Deceived his sense," and mourn his son's "youthful pride" and "diseased sense."[15]

Our ignorance of the future, along with our blinding ambition and passionate pride, limits what we can accomplish; and too much power simply magnifies the destructive effects of our blind actions. This is the lesson Darius draws from his son's catastrophe: "Insolence [*hubris*], once blossoming, bears / Its fruit, a tasseled field of doom, from which / A weeping harvest's reaped, all tears."[16] In addition to this moral lesson, the Greeks drew a political one: that we should restrict the amount of power any one man or family or clan wields, and put power instead into institutions and offices regulated by custom and law. This reduces the mischief wrought by chance and the unavoidable weaknesses of human character.

Herodotus makes the same point by means of a debate among the Persians over the virtues and vices of monarchy, oligarchy, and democracy. The defender of democracy, Otanes, sets out succinctly the Greek view of monarchy's dangers:

> What right order is there to be found in monarchy, when the ruler can do what he will, nor be held to account for it? Give this power to the best man on earth, and it would stir him to unwonted thoughts. The advantage which he holds breeds insolence [*hubris*], and nature makes all men jealous. This double cause is the root of all evil in him; sated with power he will do many reckless deeds, some from insolence, some from jealousy. . . . But I have yet worse to say of him than that; he turns the laws of the land upside down, he rapes women, he puts high and low to death.[17]

Otanes recognizes that the passions inherent in all humans, volatile and destructive as they are, will necessarily lead to the abuse of power and subverting of custom to serve the king's selfish interests and appetites. In contrast, rule by citizens through magistracies and institutions whose officers are subject to oversight and whose decisions are submitted to public debate and deliberation has a better chance of avoiding these evils.

The Greeks could also find lessons about the dangers of absolute power in their own "tyrants," who ruled many Greek city-states in the seventh and sixth centuries. A *turannos* was frequently a disaffected noble who championed the cause of the commons and seized power through force. Many of them made needed improvements in their cities, breaking the power of the noble clans and promoting the arts and literature. Periander of Corinth was reckoned one of the Seven Sages, and was said to have received the semi-mythical poet Arion at his court. So too the Athenian tyrant Peisistratus beautified the city and subsidized the poets Simonides and Anacreon. But by the fifth century, after the tyrants had been expelled from most city-states, the *turannos* became the emblem of the dangers of excessive power residing in the hands of a mere mortal whose passions would necessarily lead to its abuse. Aristotle's definition of tyranny highlights the unjust and oppressive nature of the tyrant, who uses power to further his own rather than the citizens' interests: Tyranny is "that arbitrary power of an individual which is responsible to no one, and governs all alike, whether equals or betters, with a view to its own advantage, not to that of its subjects, and therefore against their will. No freeman willingly endures such a government."[18]

In Greek literature tyrants are consistently characterized as prone to using violence to acquire and protect their rule and to gratify their appetites. According to Herodotus, that same Periander who fostered poetry and culture also surpassed his father, the tyrant Cypselus, "in bloody-mindedness and savagery." In this he was following the advice of Thrasybulus, the tyrant of Miletus, who when asked by Periander's messenger what the best form of political constitution might be, merely walked through a wheat field cutting down the tallest ears. Periander understood perfectly: murder "all of the people in the city who were outstanding in influence or ability."[19] The irrational violence of the tyrant, his willingness to use force to further his private ambitions, became a familiar trope in Greek literature, a symbol of the dangers of putting too much power in the hands of any one human.

One of the best literary examples of this theme is found in the character of Creon in Sophocles' *Antigone* (441). Like most tyrants, Creon comes to power outside the normal procedures for choosing leaders: he is king by default, since the sons of Oedipus, his nephews, have killed each other in a duel for the throne. His order to leave the body of his nephew Polyneices unburied is an irrational decision that does not benefit the city but rather gratifies his selfish desire to humiliate and dishonor the traitor who led a foreign army against his own city. Likewise, Creon's harsh treatment of Antigone when she defies his order and gives her brother a token burial is a consequence of his private anger and humiliation at being defied by a mere girl. He buries her alive, an act that ultimately costs him the lives of his wife and son. His violent temper, his paranoid belief that he is being plotted against, his insecurity about his authority—stereotypical attributes of the tyrant—all signify the corruption that power brings to men whose character and reason are too weak for such enormous responsibility.

Creon's son Haemon tries to counsel his father to recognize the human weaknesses that compromise his deliberations: "For whoever think that they alone have sense, or have a power of speech or an intelligence that no other has, these people when they are laid open are found to be empty. It is not shameful for a man, even if he is wise, often to learn things and not to resist too much." Since our knowledge is limited by the human condition, we have to be open to revising the bases on which we act, and accept advice from those whose judgment is not clouded by anger: "Best by far if a man is altogether full of knowledge," says Haemon, "but . . . since things are not accustomed to go that way, it is also good to learn from those who give good counsel."

Haemon also reminds Creon that "there is no city that belongs to a single man," that the political sphere is larger than any one individual and so should not be governed in terms of any individual's private needs or desires.[20] But Creon angrily rejects his son's advice, which is later seconded by the priest Teiresias, who blames Creon for the divine displeasure polluting the city's altars, and who pleads with the king to relent and acknowledge the error of his decision. Yet Creon's anger, given scope by his power, blinds him to his disastrous behavior until it is too late—and Antigone, Haemon, and Creon's wife, Eurydice, are all dead. Creon's fate exemplifies the moral that excessive power in one man's hands will simply magnify the evil consequences of those blinding passions that inhabit all human beings, no matter how wealthy or well-born.

The Greek belief that no human escapes the limitations that define our nature undercuts as well the aristocratic view that an innate superiority transmitted by blood justifies a monopoly of government. Aristocrats, of course, remained influential in ancient Greece, even in democratic Athens, and much of the literature that has come down to us reflects their values and prejudices. Yet a definite anti-aristocratic strain can also be found in Greek thought: a recognition that our common humanity overrides the distinctions conferred by accidents of birth, and thus undercuts the notion that political power should reside solely in the hands of the noble elite. This questioning of aristocracy, an institution universal in the ancient world, is unique to the Greeks, and is especially significant for the development of Athenian radical democracy.

Throughout the poetry of the eighth to sixth centuries (the supposed heyday of aristocratic domination of the nascent city-states), questions are raised about the underlying assumptions of aristocratic rule—that those presumed to be by nature superior in virtue and wealth have a right to monopolize political power.[21] The mercenary Archilochus rejects the aristocratic belief in physical stature and beauty as markers of superiority: he disdains the long legs, long hair, and clean-shaven chin of the noble general, preferring the short but sturdy general of steadfast heart who will not move from his place in the phalanx.[22] Other poets too, even those who otherwise endorse an aristocratic ethic, challenge the traditional heroic ideal of individual glory and achievement. Tyrtaeus redefines martial honor in terms of the ability to stand fast in the ranks and achieve glory for the whole community rather than for the individual or clan, a sentiment found in Callinus as well.[23] The contrast between individual glory on the one hand and achievement for the community on the other is already apparent in Homer's Achilles, the aristocratic hero par excellence, whose rage at personal dishonor and thirst for revenge "put pains thousandfold upon the Achaians, / hurled in their multitudes to the house of Hades strong / souls of heroes."[24] Throughout the *Iliad* the costs to the community of seeking personal honor are emphasized and by implication criticized, most poignantly in the character of Hector who, as we saw in the last chapter, sacrifices a whole civilization, including his own family, to the epic quest for honor and glory.

Archilochus, Tyrtaeus, and Callinus challenge the individualistic martial values of the aristocrat partly because they compromise the effectiveness of the hoplite phalanx. But there are political implications also in the critique of aristocratic values. The high estimation placed on individual physical prowess, for example, is contrary to a system of government that depends on rational deliberation and persuasion rather than force. The poet-philosopher Xenophanes (ca. 650) criticizes the physical abilities on display in athletic events that were traditionally the purview of the nobility: "Better than brute strength / of men . . . is the wisdom that is mine." Men who have honed their physical skills alone will not produce civic virtue; "The city will not, on account of this man, have better government."[25]

Likewise, Phocylides rejects the idea that noble birth is inherently beneficial to the city. "What good does it do," he asks, "to be well born / for those whose words bring pleasure to none, nor their characters either?"[26] And Solon, as we have seen, consistently criticizes the powerful and wealthy whose arrogant excesses threaten the stability of the polis. The new standard is not what serves the private honor and glory of the aristocrat or his clan, but rather what serves the well-being of the community. By this measure, the values of the common people—"hard work, thrift, simplicity, cooperation, common sense, utility"[27]—provide the better basis for government.

Distrust of the aristocratic claim to innate superiority and to a rightful monopoly on power was most forcefully expressed in Athens, where the radical democracy gave power to the poor and non-noble. In Euripides' *Electra* (413) the main character's husband, an obscure but noble farmer, evokes from Orestes a remarkable speech asserting that true nobility and courage lie in character, not bloodline or wealth:

> Can you not come to understand, you empty-minded,
> opinion-stuffed people, a man is judged by grace
> among his fellows, manners are nobility's touchstone?
> Such men of manners can control our cities best,
> and homes, but the well-born sportsman, long on muscle,
> short
> on brains, is only good for a statue in the park,
> not even sterner in the shocks of war than weaker
> men, for courage is the gift of character.[28]

The claims of inherited worth are empty because no one is exempt from time and unforeseen change. Orestes says, "I have seen descendants of the noblest family / grow worthless though the cowards had courageous sons."[29] Even Plato, descended from one of the oldest aristocratic Athenian families, put little stock in blue blood. In the *Theaetetus,* Socrates contrasts the aristocrat who brags of his seven generations with the philosopher who knows that "every man has had thousands and ten thousands of progenitors, and among them have been rich and poor, kings and slaves, Hellenes and barbarians, innumerable."[30] Plato's elites are defined by the powers of their minds and their virtue rather than by lofty birth.

Whether these qualities are innate to only a few or can be taught to all was a fiercely debated question in Greek political philosophy. But all agreed that government cannot be the hereditary right of aristocratic or plutocratic elites, to be exercised through private protocols for selfish ends. "If any one gives too great a power to anything," writes Plato, "... and does not observe the mean, everything is overthrown, and, in the wantonness of excess runs in the one case to disorders, and in the other to injustice, which is the child of excess.... There is no soul of man, young and irresponsible, who will be able to sustain the temptation of arbitrary power."[31] Consensual government among the Greeks reflects in part a view of human identity as something bounded by time, chance, passions, and death. Since all, whether high- or low-born, are subject to these necessities, concentrating power in the hands of one man or a tiny elite is folly.

Political power must instead reside in institutions, offices, laws and procedures that transcend any one man or group of men, indeed time and space as well. These compose a "common thing" *(koinônia)* in which each citizen is a partner, and they function not through brute force but through reason and persuasion. The institutions of government must be available and beneficial to all citizens. Aristotle defines the good constitution in terms of equal justice and consideration for the interests of all citizens: "Governments which have a regard to the common interest are constituted in accordance with strict principles of justice, and are therefore true forms; but those which regard only the interest of the rulers are all defective and perverted forms, for they are despotic, whereas a state is a community [*koinônia*] of freemen."[32]

In short, a flourishing state needs a government of laws, not of men. "For that state in which the law is subject and has no authority, I perceive to be on the highway to ruin," says Plato in the *Laws;* "but I see that the state in which the law is above the rulers, and the rulers are the inferiors of the law, has salvation, and every blessing which the Gods can confer."[33] To live thus—in submission to law rather than to the force of men—is essential to being human. The Athenians who created democracy, Lysias writes in his early-fourth-century *Funeral Oration,* "deemed that it was the way of wild beasts to be held subject to one another by force, but the duty of men to delimit justice by law."[34]

THE THOUSAND OR SO GREEK CITY-STATES developed a whole range of governments, from narrow oligarchies to the radical democracy of Athens. In some sense all the governments were oligarchies, "government by the few," since citizenship was restricted to native free males and thus excluded the majority of the people living in the polis. Property qualifications in many city-states also limited who was given citizen rights. Yet more significant in the context of the ancient Mediterranean was the idea of citizenship *(politeia)* itself—a civic identity not dependent on birth or wealth or clan, with equal rights and responsibilities and control over public authority and military force. For Aristotle, participation in political and judicial office was the essence of the citizen.[35] Indeed, the citizens *were* the state, rather than mere subjects of various elites; as the Athenian general Nicias told his troops in Sicily, "Men make the city and not walls or ships without men in them."[36]

Human identity itself is consistently defined in Greek literature in political terms. True humanity involves a "political life," the participation in the governing of the city that insures freedom to direct one's life and not remain, like beasts, the mere playthings of nature and chance and powerful elites. Aristotle famously defined humans as "polis-dwelling life-forms," but even earlier, in Homer, we find this key idea. When Odysseus reaches the land of the Cyclopes, his description of their primitive society reinforces the inhuman savagery of their monstrous appearance and behavior. The Cyclopes "have no institutions, no meetings for counsels; / rather they make their habitations in caverns hollowed / among the peaks of the high mountains, and each one is the law / for his own wives and children, and cares nothing about the others."[37] The Cyclopes are literally inhuman because they live like animals, without politics or communal laws or fellow-feeling. When the Cyclops Polyphemus eats Odysseus' men raw, the Greeks recognize this act as the epitome of inhuman savagery.

Thucydides too saw the city's laws and customs as the forces that restrained the destructive passions. His description of the revolution in Corcyra and the savagery and brutality that followed the breakdown of law and justice attributes the disorder to "the lust for power arising from greed and ambition" and to the destructive nature of man when confronted by "imperious necessities."[38] This nature is constrained only by the laws, but "In the confusion into which life was now thrown in the cities, human nature, always rebelling against the law and now its master, gladly showed itself ungoverned in passion, above respect for justice, and the enemy of all superiority."[39] Only in city-states ordered and governed by law could people realize their common human potential, whether for good or for evil; only in the city-state could knowledge useful for human development flourish.[40]

The Greeks recognized that their conception of human flourishing—the achievement of virtue and the good life, which in turn create happiness—was dependent on living "politically." They saw too that this ideal set them apart from their Mediterranean neighbors. The famous conversation recorded in Herodotus between the wealthy Lydian king Croesus and the Athenian statesman Solon illustrates this contrast. When Croesus, after exhibiting his fabulous wealth to Solon, asks the Greek who is the happiest man he has ever seen, Solon names the Athenian Tellus. His explanation of his choice identifies the city as the context for human achievement: "He fought for his countrymen, routed the enemy, and died like a soldier; and the Athenians paid him the high honour of a public funeral on the spot where he fell."[41] As well as making the point that no one's happiness can be judged until he has died and escaped unforeseen change—a lesson Croesus will remember later when he loses his kingdom to the Persian Cyrus and is nearly burned at the stake—Solon defines human happiness in terms not of wealth and power but of service to the city and the city's recognition of that service.

In short, the city *makes* the man. Socrates argues this point when he refuses Crito's plea that he escape from prison. Imagining the "laws and the community of the city" standing before him, Socrates has them say, "Since you were brought into the world and nurtured and educated by us, can you deny in the first place that you are our child and slave, as your fathers were before you?"[42] As part of his birthright Socrates must obey the laws and institutions that have made his life possible, even if those laws unjustly condemn him to death. Herodotus has Demaratus, the exiled Spartan who accompanied the Persian king Xerxes, make a similar point about the power of law in free states. Explaining why Leonidas and his Spartans will not retreat even before the vast numbers of Xerxes' army at Thermopylae, Demaratus says, "They are free—yes—but not entirely free; for they have a master, and that master is Law, which they fear much more than your subjects fear you."[43] Freedom from the arbitrary whims of a flawed human being, and their own full humanity, derive from a life organized by common laws that transcend particular men.

"The goal of politics is the good for humans," writes Aristotle.[44] He begins the *Politics* by defining the polis as a community *(koinônia)* formed for the highest good of all its members. Later he explains that the state is a "community of families and aggregations of families in well-being, for the sake of a perfect and self-sufficing life," which will be a "happy and honourable life." The state exists for "noble actions," not just brute subsistence; hence "political excellence" trumps nobility of birth or wealth.[45]

Plato too sees the state as molder of men; his political utopias are designed to produce those few men who can achieve the highest fulfillment of human possibility. This accounts for his interest in public education, which is the "education in virtue from youth upwards, which makes a man eagerly pursue the ideal perfection of citizenship, and teaches him how rightly to rule and how to obey."[46] In the same vein, Socrates says the responsibility of the public speaker is "to implant justice in the souls of his citizens and take away injustice, to implant temperance and take away intemperance, to implant every virtue and take away every vice."[47]

This view of the state as a formative power, an arena for human fulfillment, and the ideal of virtue through political service were of fundamental importance in Western political thought. These Greek ideas animated the republicanism of the American Founders.

Of all the Greek city-states, democratic Athens of the fifth and fourth centuries is, of course, the most relevant for us today, for there the idea of citizenship was most inclusive. We must recognize, however, the significant differences between Athenian direct democracy and how "democracy" is commonly understood today. Athenian democracy was literally "rule by the mass," that is, all the citizens rich or poor.[48] But remember, too, that perhaps only one out of ten of all the residents of Athens—including slaves, women, and resident aliens—were citizens, free males over eighteen both of whose parents were Athenians.[49] The main instruments of government were the Assembly, the Council of Five Hundred, the law courts, and the magistrates.

The Assembly comprised all the citizens who made it to the meeting. By the end of the fifth century, they were probably paid to do so. In the Assembly the highest matters of state were debated and discussed, and motions approved or rejected. Any citizen could speak before the Assembly. "All the important decisions," David Stockton summarizes, "(and a great many minor decisions too) which were made by the Athenian state were determined, or at the very least had to be initiated, by a show of hands from as many adult male Athenians as had chosen to attend the meetings."[50]

The business put before the Assembly was determined by the Council: five hundred citizens, fifty from each of the ten Greek tribes, selected by lot to serve for a year with pay from public funds. While the Assembly tended to favor those who lived close by or had leisure to attend the meetings, the Council was representative of the whole citizenry. For one-tenth of the year each tribal contingent served as the standing committee (prytany) of the Council, living at state expense for the month. Every day one of the fifty was chosen by lot to be the chairman. The main function of the Council was to prepare the business, either motions or open questions, to be presented to the Assembly for a final decision. Councilmen, state officers, and any other citizen could propose business to the Council. In the fourth century the Council also acquired some executive and judicial powers, but always remained subordinate to the Assembly.

The law courts were likewise representative of all the citizens, and so in Athens the administration of justice was the responsibility of the people in a way unparalleled in human history. Every year six thousand citizens were enrolled as "dicasts," from which group were selected the men who would serve as both judges and jurors. They heard particular cases and decided guilt and innocence, interpreted the law and its applicability, determined what was fact and what not, and imposed penalties. There were no district attorneys, professional judges, or specially trained lawyers; with some exceptions, any citizen could charge another with a crime. Dicasts too were paid for their time. Once empanelled the dicasts heard both sides of the case and voted by secret ballot. There was no higher court of appeal. The dicasts provided as well the five hundred *nomothetai,* whose job was to decide whether a proposed law should be ratified or an existing one annulled.

Finally, most of the offices of state were also open to the majority of the citizenry. Some were filled by election, but nearly four hundred were chosen by lot. Virtually every function of public life—including the military, finance, public works and buildings, religious festivals and theatrical presentations—was filled by a citizen. For some offices every citizen, merely because he *was* a citizen, was assumed to be competent to perform adequately and so could be chosen at random. About one thousand offices had to be filled every year from a citizen population of thirty to forty thousand; this meant that, as Stockton puts it, "the proportion of citizens over the age of thirty who were actively involved in public duties and responsibilities was simply staggering."[51]

This remarkable system reflects not just an egalitarian view of competence but also an egalitarian view of human corruptibility, leading to a wariness of giving too much power to any one individual. The wide involvement of so many citizens, and the frequent cycling of different citizens through the various offices, juries, and the Council, made it difficult for any one individual or faction to gain dominance. Certainly, individual Athenians were remarkably influential, usually during times of military crisis; but nearly all the important politicians of the fifth century, from Themistocles to Alcibiades, ended up fined and/or exiled. The fear of individual ambition for power, kept alive by the threat of the tyrant, partly explains the strange institution of ostracism, a procedure in which a person suffered exile for ten years merely because six thousand citizens wrote his name on pottery shards.

This brief sketch of Athenian democracy reveals its central characteristic: the belief that all citizens, no matter what their economic or social standing, had the expertise and judgment to run the state, a belief obvious in the frequent use of the lot to fill offices. Thus Pericles in his famous Funeral Oration said of Athens, "Advancement in public life falls to reputation for capacity, class considerations not being allowed to interfere with merit; nor again does poverty bar the way, if a man is able to serve the state, he is not hindered by the obscurity of his condition."[52] So too Euripides' Theseus, in a famous encomium to Athenian democracy, links access to annual office with equality of opportunity: "This city is free, and ruled by no one man. / The people reign, in annual succession. / They do not yield the power to the rich; / The poor man has an equal share in it."[53] The power over their own lives that democracy conferred on its citizens was so valuable that Democritus could say, "Poverty under democracy is as much to be preferred to so-called prosperity under an autocracy as freedom to slavery."[54]

This form of democracy is obviously very different from what most of us today mean by that term. Yet although the actual workings of ancient democracy are not directly relevant to our own structures of government, some of Athenian democracy's core principles have influenced our thinking about the relationship of the citizen to the state. Pericles and Euripides touched on one: that as citizens, people despite their social class are deemed both competent and entitled to participate in the public business of the state, which is precisely the assumption behind our form of government today.

Several other of our ideas about government and citizenship derive from ancient Athens as well. The most important, freedom and autonomy, will be the focus of a later chapter. Another, already discussed, is that military force should be the responsibility of citizen-soldiers rather than the private concern of elites. Citizen-soldiers who freely vote on when and how the state goes to war make the best warriors, since they have chosen to fight for their own and their families' freedom and property.

At the same time, citizens exercised oversight of generals and war-making. In Athens, matters of war were in the hands of the *strategoi,* the ten citizens elected annually by popular vote to head the army and navy. "Their duties were to mobilise armies and fleets on the instructions of the assembly, and to command such armies and fleets with a view to achieving objectives laid down, in more or less detail, by the people."[55] These "generals" were subject to audit by the Council. Aristotle informs us that "the appointment of these officers is submitted for confirmation in each prytany [that is, ten times a year], when the question is put whether they are considered to be doing their duty. If any officer is rejected on this vote, he is tried in the law-court, and if he is found guilty the people decide what punishment or fine shall be inflicted on him."[56] After leaving office, the *strategos* was subject to a final audit of his tenure. The most notorious example of citizen discipline of the military followed the Athenian naval victory over the Spartans at Arginusae (406), when eight victorious generals were condemned to death and six executed (two of the generals wisely refusing to return to Athens) for not rescuing their crews even though they were prevented by bad weather. The tradition of civilian control of the military, virtually unheard of elsewhere in the ancient world, has been and remains vital to the democracies of the West.

Like the generals, the other Athenian magistrates were closely controlled by the citizens. The magistrates were "chosen for short terms of office, subjected to regular examination during their tenure, and put through the most rigorous and searching scrutiny when they rendered their accounts at the end of their term."[57] This oversight, rooted in a distrust of human character in possession of power, was explicitly contrasted with Eastern autocracies. When Aeschylus in the *Persians* describes the ominous dream of Xerxes' mother, he has her say, "My son, should he succeed, would be admired; / But if he fails, Persia cannot hold him / To account."[58] The Greek word "account" that Aeschylus uses *(hupeuthunos polei)* is the technical term used of the accounting the Athenian magistrates gave to the city. And in Herodotus, Otanes contrasts the magistrates who are audited in a democracy with the autocrat who answers to no one.[59]

In addition to the civilian audit of political and military officials, we have also inherited from the Athenians the assumption that decisions of public policy and action should follow reasoned debate, and that opponents should be persuaded rather than coerced. Lysias, in his *Funeral Oration,* says that the hallmark of humanity is not just submission to law but also the imperative "to convince by reason."[60] By his time the idea was old: half a century earlier Aeschylus, in his trilogy the *Oresteia* (458), made the transition from force to persuasion a characteristic of the democratic polis. The Furies, goddesses of blood vengeance, are enraged that an Athenian jury has acquitted Orestes of the charge of murdering his mother. Hence they threaten to use their primal powers to blight Athens' fertility, until they are convinced by Athena to accept a subordinate yet powerful place in the city's spiritual life. "I admire," says Athena, "the eyes / of Persuasion, who guided the speech of my mouth / toward these, when they were reluctant and wild. / Zeus, who guides men's speech in councils, was too / strong."[61] Indeed, the goddess Persuasion historically was worshiped in a temple on the southwest slope of the Acropolis, near the public buildings where all matters of state were discussed and debated.

In his Funeral Oration, Pericles makes rational deliberation and persuasion the foundation of right action: "Instead of looking on discussion as a stumbling-block in the way of action, we think it an indispensable preliminary to any wise action at all."[62] Reasoned debate, moreover, should take precedence over physical force. In the debate over the fate of the rebellious Mytileneans, Thucydides has Diodotus, opposing the blustering Cleon's drastic proposal to kill the men and enslave everybody else, argue that "The good citizen ought to triumph not by frightening his opponents but by beating them fairly in argument."[63] Elsewhere in Thucydides, the Syracusan Athenagoras defends democratic collective debate and decision-making because "none can hear and decide so well as the many."[64] To the fifth-century Sophist Gorgias, persuasion was the highest art of all, because it creates agreement by the individual's own choice rather than by compulsion.[65]

Again, the idea that decisions should arise from rational debate and free choice rather than being handed down from on high by an autocratic ruler differentiates the Greeks from the Persians and other monarchical states. Herodotus frequently contrasts the free and often contentious deliberations of the Greeks—such as the heated "skirmish of words" before the battle of Salamis—with the staged discussions of the Persians, where disagreement with the Great King is often dangerous.[66] The Spartan Demaratus indicates as much when in response to the Great King's solicitation of his opinion, he replies, "My lord, is it a true answer you would like, or merely an agreeable one?" Xerxes' answer—"Tell me the truth, and I promise that you will not suffer by it"—implies that severe consequences often did attend unpleasant advice.[67] A little later, before Salamis, when the Athenian exile Dicaeus confesses his fears that a disaster is about to overtake the Great King, Demaratus advises, "Do not breathe a word of this to anybody.... If it should reach the ears of the king, you would lose your head."[68]

One of the best examples of how ingrained the practice of deliberation and voting was among the Greeks can be found in Xenophon's account of the adventures of ten thousand Greek mercenaries who went to fight for the Persian pretender Cyrus in 401. After Cyrus' defeat and death and the treacherous murder of the Greeks' generals, Xenophon arose before the men and proposed a course of action that all the men assented to with a show of hands.[69] Even in times of great danger and military crisis—the mercenaries were hundreds of miles from any Greek cities, and were being hounded by the Persians—the Greeks depended on rational deliberation and consensus before acting.

Finally, the fundamental assumption behind Athenian democracy, the one most critical for Western political values today, is that equality of all citizens before the law is the best guarantor of justice. The Greeks called this *isonomia.* It is the term used for "democracy" in fifth-century writing. In Herodotus, Otanes uses *isonomia* to mean democracy and its principles of assigning offices by lot, holding magistrates accountable, and vesting power in the Assembly.

When Theseus defends democracy in *The Suppliant Women,* he contrasts the equality of law for rich and poor, which creates justice, with the private law of the tyrant, which breeds injustice: "With written laws, / People of small resources and the rich / Both have the same recourse to justice. . . . / And if the little man is right, he wins / Against the great."[70] The Syracusan Athenagoras, speaking out against oligarchic conspirators "who wish not to be on a legal equality with the many," rhetorically asks, "How can it be right that citizens of the same state should be held unworthy of the same privileges?"[71] The Sophist Protagoras predicates the political equality of all men on an innate capacity for justice and common sense; hence every citizen is capable of running the city, for each can learn the "political craft" *(politikê technê).*[72] Demosthenes, defining the differences between oligarchic and democratic attitudes towards the law, quotes the Athenian law that says any statute passed by the state must affect all citizens equally, and then comments that it is "an injunction conceived in the true spirit of democracy. As every man has an equal share in the constitution generally, so this statute asserts his equal share in the laws."[73] Aristotle likewise bases democracy "upon the recognized principle of democratic justice, that all should count equally."[74]

Examples could be multiplied, but clearly the essence of democracy for the Greeks was the creation of justice through the equality of all citizens before the law, based on their capacity for rational deliberation. Gregory Vlastos is worth quoting on the unique significance of this idea. In Athens, he writes, the common people derived from *isonomia*

> more than the common people had yet won for themselves anywhere else since the dawn of history. Hitherto material progress had normally been coeval with the concentration of both political and economic power in the hands of kings and nobles. *Isonomia* refused to countenance either the ancient monopoly of law in the hands of a hereditary aristocracy or the claims to political privilege of the new plutocracy whose social power rivaled that of the old nobility. It promised the poorest citizen an equal right in the law-making, law-administering, law-enforcing power of the state. It expressed the spirit of a constitution, hitherto undreamed of in civilized society, which declared that the poor man's share in law and political office was equal to that of the noble and the rich.[75]

Today this idea, expanded to include all humans regardless of sex or country or race, lies at the heart of all attempts to create a just and free society.

THE UNIQUE GENIUS OF THE GREEKS can be seen not just in their invention of democracy, but also in their searching criticisms of the same—what the Athenian aristocrat Alcibiades called a "patent absurdity."[76] Many of the attacks on democracy reflect an elitism that assumes some people are simply better than others, and thus deserve more political power. Understandably, aristocrats found the breakdown of class distinctions and privileges odious. The sixth-century reactionary Theognis of Megara, upset by the ascendancy of wealthy non-nobles, groused that "Those who before knew nothing of lawsuits, nothing of laws, / who lived on the ranges, far out from the town, like wild deer, / these are now the Great Men. . . . Our former nobles / are Rabble now." These commoners, Theognis sneers, have no innate wisdom or virtue; they have "only one virtue: / Money."[77]

The charge that democracy allows the "worse" (in birth and character) to tyrannize their betters crops up in a work about Athens once attributed to Xenophon. Despite a grudging admiration for some aspects of Athenian democracy, the author, usually called the Old Oligarch, dislikes it because the Athenians "have chosen to let the worst people be better off than the good," and "they everywhere assign more to the worst persons, to the poor, and to the popular types than to the good men." The Old Oligarch disapproves because among the common people "there is a maximum of ignorance, disorder, and wickedness."[78]

The elitist view that the wisdom and virtue needed to govern well are by nature the inherited qualities of a few—that, as Pindar puts it, "the splendor in the blood has much weight"[79]—while the common run of humanity not only lacks these qualities but is typified by vice and ignorance, underlies most of the attacks on Athenian democracy, even when "the few" are not defined by inherited aristocratic status. In Herodotus' debate about the best forms of government, the spokesman for oligarchy, Megabyzus, says, "The masses are a feckless lot—nowhere will you find more ignorance or irresponsibility or violence.... The masses have not a thought in their heads; all they can do is to rush blindly into politics and sweep all before them like a river in flood."[80] Thucydides, too, has little faith in the judgment of the masses; "as the mob is fond of doing" is his usual explanation for why the people has changed its collective mind.[81] The masses are fine when led by a brilliant leader like Pericles, but when they are indulged by unscrupulous leaders, disaster follows. By Euripides' day these criticisms of the people were stereotypical. Thus the Theban herald in *The Suppliant Women*, whom Theseus lectures about the superiority of democracy, responds with the usual calumnies against the people's intelligence and charges of their susceptibility to manipulation: "The town I come from is controlled / by one man, not a mob. And there is no one / To puff it up with words, for private gain, / Swaying it this way, that way."[82]

Socrates was famous for his denigration of the "opinion" of the many as mere belief unsupported by reasoned argument and by the "knowledge" available only to a few. In prison he asks Crito rhetorically, "Concerning the just and unjust and shameful and noble and good and bad things ... must we follow the opinion of the many and fear it rather than that of the one—if there is such an expert—whom we must be ashamed before and fear more than the others?"[83] Socrates' implied answer, of course, subverts the fundamental principle of Athenian democracy: that the many are intelligent enough to give advice and guidance to the state. Socrates frequently sneered at the Athenian Assembly, which in his view was filled with the "weakest and silliest" people: "fullers or the shoemakers or the carpenters or the smiths or the farmers or the merchants or the dealers in the agora, whose business it is to buy at a cheaper rate and sell at a dearer one."[84]

If the masses are incapable of rational deliberation, and, *contra* Protagoras, are impossible to educate in the *politikê technê,* the "political craft," then obviously the Athenian ideal of allowing all citizens to participate in the government, especially through debate and discussion in the Assembly, is folly. Anti-democrats who criticize the deliberations of the Assembly see the mass of citizens as driven by emotion rather than reason, and thus easily manipulated by the orators and demagogues who can "make the worse argument the better," obscuring the true and the just beneath clever rhetoric, all for their own gain.

Thucydides presents us with several reconstructions of debates in the Athenian Assembly, and ironically puts a scathing indictment of the people's vulnerability to rhetoric and their own passions into the mouth of one of the worst demagogues, Cleon. Angry at the Assembly for changing a decree of the previous day and passing a new one punishing the rebellious Mytileneans less severely, he tells the citizens, "[You] go to see an oration as you would to see a sight, take your facts on hearsay, judge of the practicability of a project by the wit of its advocates, and trust for the truth as to past events, not to the fact which you saw more than to the clever strictures which you heard; the easy victims of newfangled arguments, unwilling to follow received conclusions; slaves to every new paradox, despisers of the commonplace." The Athenians, Cleon concludes, are "very slaves to the pleasure of the ear."[85]

Though Thucydides obviously despises Cleon, the historian's own description of Athenian debate in the Assembly bears out the demagogue's evaluation, particularly when it ends up approving the disastrous Sicilian expedition. "Everyone fell in love with the enterprise," Thucydides writes, using the word *eros,* "sexual passion," to convey the irrational character of the people's decision based on self-interest, ambition, and greed.[86]

Various other mechanisms of democracy are also held up to scrutiny in Greek literature. The annual tenure of magistrates is criticized in Isocrates' defense of monarchy: "Men who enter upon office for an annual term are retired to private life before they have gained any insight into public affairs or any experience in handling them."[87] The institution of state pay for service in the government, intended to allow fuller participation by citizens who could not afford to take time off from work, is thought to have corrupted the people. Socrates says of Pericles, "He was the first who gave the people pay, and made them idle and cowardly, and encouraged them in the love of talk and of money."[88] The chorus of Aristophanes' *Women at Assembly* contrasts the rotten present with the good old days when "none would have dared to let himself be paid for the trouble he spent over public business.... [T]he citizen has become as mercenary as the stonemason."[89] Aristotle also censures Pericles for instituting payment for service on juries, "since it was always the common people who put themselves forward for selection as jurors, rather than the men of better position. Moreover, bribery came into existence after this."[90] Rather than serving out of a sense of duty or obligation to the greater good, Athenian citizens are accused of participating in government only to acquire wealth. Throughout Aristophanes' comedies the corruption of public officials is lambasted, and tied to the social and political disorder afflicting Athens.[91]

Perhaps the most significant criticism of the anti-democrats focused on the radical egalitarianism that democracy fostered through its assumption that every citizen had a right to participate in governing—an egalitarianism belied by the natural hierarchies of talent, virtues, and abilities that exist among people. Aristotle defines democracy in terms of radical egalitarianism: it arises "out of the notion that those who are equal in any respect are equal in all respects; because men are equally free, they claim to be absolutely equal."[92] In the *Republic,* Plato scorns democracy as "full of variety and disorder, and dispensing a sort of equality to equals and unequals alike."[93] Later, in the *Laws,* Plato explains the injustice of this sort of egalitarianism: "Servants and masters never can be friends, nor good and bad, merely because they are declared to have equal privileges. For to unequals equals become unequal, if they are not harmonised by measure." Plato goes on to contrast a crude quantitative equality, easy to institute, with a more just equality that recognizes the natural differences of talent and achievement. This superior sort of equality "gives to the greater more, and to the inferior less and in proportion to the nature of each; and, above all, greater honour always to the greater virtue, and to the less, less; and to either in proportion to their respective measure of virtue and education. And this is justice."[94] If Plato is right, it then follows that to award power and privilege to all regardless of merit, as the Athenian democracy presumably did, is unjust.

The results of enforced, unnatural equality are injustice and the corruption of public life to the lowest common denominator, the self and its appetites, for in the indulgence of appetite all are indeed equal. The mid-fourth-century orator Isocrates denounced democratic egalitarianism because it trained citizens "in such fashion that they looked upon insolence as democracy, lawlessness as liberty, impudence of speech as equality, and license to do what they pleased as happiness."[95] That radical egalitarianism leads to licentiousness and disorder is the same assumption behind Plato's savage portrait of democratic man in the *Republic:*

> He lives from day to day indulging the appetite of the hour; and sometimes he is lapped in drink and strains of the flute; then he becomes a water-drinker, and tries to get thin; then he takes a turn at gymnastics; sometimes idling and neglecting everything, then once more living the life of a philosopher; often he is busy with politics, and starts to his feet and says and does whatever comes into his head; and, if he is emulous of any one who is a warrior, off he is in that direction, or of men of business, once more in that. His life

> has neither law nor order; and this distracted existence he terms joy and bliss and freedom; and so he goes on.[96]

I leave it to the reader to judge how close this portrait of the superficial, fickle, narcissistic democratic man answers to our own age, which has exalted both egalitarianism and appetitive indulgence to levels of approbation that Plato would never have imagined.

THE GREEK CREATION OF POLITICS has influenced immeasurably not just the West but the whole world. The assumptions behind consensual government—that citizens should not be defined just by birth or wealth, that all citizens should participate in running the state, that power should rest in common laws and institutions and offices rather than in men—lie at the heart of the political ideals that at least for now represent the best chance people everywhere have for living lives free from tyranny and injustice. And though Athenian direct democracy influenced the American Founders primarily as a negative example to be avoided—John Adams asserted that Athens was characterized by "levity, gayety, inconstancy, dissipation, intemperance, debauchery, and dissolution of manners"[97]—nonetheless the principles behind the machinery of Athenian democracy still influence us powerfully. All citizens, merely by being citizens, are presumed competent to participate in government; civilians control the military; public officials are held to account and audit; reasoned debate, open to all citizens, is used to formulate policy and resolve differences; and all are equal before the law regardless of social status or wealth.

These ideals, which we in the West enjoy and to which most of the rest of the world aspires, have their roots not in ancient Egypt or Israel or Babylon, but in the tiny Greek city-states scattered across the Mediterranean:

> Rameses and Nebuchadnessar, Croesus the Lydian and Cyrus the Persian, ruled over great empires; but within their

> dominions there were no politics because there were no public affairs. There were only the private affairs of the sovereign and his ruling class. Government and all that pertained to it, from military service and taxation to the supply of women for the royal harem, was simply the expression of the power and desire of the ruler. The great advance made by Greece was to have recognized that public or common interests exist and to have provided, first for their management, and secondly for their study. In other words, the Greeks were the first to rescue the body politic from charlatans and to hand it over to physicians.[98]

The problems of governance that the Greeks identified—particularly the central question of who rules, the few or the many—are still with us today, and their solutions must start with the knowledge of what our intellectual forebears already learned.

Should we not assume that just as the eye, the hand, the foot, and in general each part of the body clearly has its own proper function, so man too has some function over and above the functions of his parts? What can this function possibly be? Simply living? He shares that even with plants, but we are now looking for something peculiar to man. Accordingly, the life of nutrition and growth must be excluded. Next in line there is a life of sense perception. But this, too, man has in common with the horse, the ox, and every animal. There remains then an active life of the rational element.... The proper function of man, then, consists in an activity of the soul in conformity with a rational principle or, at least, not without it.

—*Aristotle*[1]

SIX

The Birth of Rational Man

In April of 1970 the Apollo 13 moon mission went awry. A tank of liquid oxygen exploded, depriving the command module Odyssey of the oxygen needed for the fuel cells that powered the craft and for the air the astronauts breathed. A nightmarish succession of problems afflicted the crew and ground control in Houston, problems that had to be solved from two hundred thousand miles away under the intense time pressure caused by the dwindling oxygen and power. The biggest difficulty, of course, was working out the complex calculations and procedures that would safely get the crew back to earth in a crippled ship. As the popular film *Apollo 13* showed, each crisis was met and overcome by sheer innovative brilliance, extemporaneous engineering, and occasional luck. The crew made it back to earth alive, and what could have been a disaster for NASA was eventually recognized as one of its finest hours.

This triumph of nerve and skill over calamity has its ultimate origins in a new way of looking at the world that arose in ancient Greece. At one level, the science and technology that make space travel possible are obviously a culmination of the long, halting development of procedures for acquiring knowledge about nature and its laws. But more important perhaps is the *attitude* towards nature and humanity's relationship to it evidenced in NASA's reaction to unforeseen disaster. Let's consider what *didn't* happen when the crisis struck: there was no mass hysteria at Houston, no executions of NASA officials, no human sacrifice, no witch-doctors summoned to exorcise demons from the computers, no spells or horoscopes cast, and no animal entrails studied for information or solutions. These historically have been human society's more typical reactions to disaster: attempting to control and manipulate unknown supernatural forces through traditional rituals. But these—perhaps apart from private prayer—were never an option for the men trying to rescue Apollo 13's crew. That is because we moderns of the West believe that the natural world is ordered by laws we can know, rather than haunted by mysterious, supernatural forces; and we assume, moreover, that human minds can use their accumulated knowledge of these laws and their ingenuity to figure out rational solutions to crises.

In short, we believe humans are fundamentally rational, possessing the ability to understand and control a knowable world, rather than being the mere playthings of occult forces and capricious divinities. The intellectual dynamism that began with the Greeks has, for better *and* for worse, historically characterized the West, and partly explains its remarkable and often malign global influence.

All humans everywhere have developed some of the skills and procedures that constitute scientific activity. The species could not have survived had people not accurately observed their world and passed on that knowledge to others. Cooking, tool-making, pottery, metallurgy, building, sailing, and farming all demanded ingenuity, accuracy of observation, and an ability to learn from experience. Before the Greeks, great advances were made by the Egyptians and Mesopotamians, particularly in astronomy, engineering, and mathematics; and the Greeks learned much from their Near Eastern neighbors. Herodotus credited the Egyptians with the invention of geometry and the division of the year into twelve parts, for instance, and he acknowledged that the Greeks took from the Babylonians the sundial, the gnomon (a vertical rod used to measure shadows) and the division of the day into twelve hours.[2] Aristotle too attributed to the Egyptians the invention of the "mathematical arts," as did numerous other Greek scientists.[3]

Yet as critical and impressive as these achievements were, they did not result from a scientific attitude towards the world. For one thing, Egyptian and Mesopotamian learning was practical, limited to solving immediate problems and serving short-term, utilitarian interests. Egyptian geometry, for example, resulted according to Herodotus from the need of the pharaoh to survey the land after inundation by the Nile in order to calculate an accurate tax assessment. Babylonian astronomy was in some respects remarkably brilliant, yet it remained subordinated to the unscientific need to predict future events and discover omens.[4]

The Greeks, on the other hand, began thinking about the natural world from a more abstract and general perspective. As far as we know, they invented an explicit theoretical and abstract view of nature. Eventually this penchant for theorizing, coupled with an elitist disdain for grubby "mechanic" activities, would lead to the radical idealism of Plato, in which the knowledge of the material world gained by the senses is of no account, true wisdom residing in a disembodied reason contemplating the immaterial, permanent truths. The thinker who approaches most closely to pure knowledge, Socrates argues, is he "who has got rid, as far as he can, of eyes and ears and, so to speak, of the whole body, these being in his opinion distracting elements which when they infect the soul hinder her from acquiring truth and knowledge."[5]

Yet Greek philosophers, even those who disdained practical applications of knowledge, nonetheless demonstrated from time to time the everyday utility of their more abstract theorizing. The first philosopher, Thales (early sixth century), was mocked for falling into a well while gazing upward at the heavens; yet he answered critics of his impractical intellectualism by leasing all the olive presses because he predicted a big olive crop.[6] Three hundred years later the brilliant mathematician Archimedes was so engrossed in solving a problem while Syracuse fell to the Romans (212) that he ignored the orders of a Roman soldier, who ran him through. Yet although, according to Plutarch, Archimedes repudiated "as sordid and ignoble the whole trade of engineering, and every sort of art that lends itself to mere use and profit," he developed many useful inventions, including a screw named after him still in use today to raise water from one level to another. Indeed, the philosopher's military engines delayed the capture of Syracuse for two years.[7]

Despite the many practical applications of their science, however, the peculiar genius of the Greeks lay in viewing knowledge abstractly and theoretically, which led them to consider and demonstrate why and how something should be true, and to search for the underlying causes of phenomena. The theorem named after the sixth-century philosopher Pythagoras—that the square of the hypotenuse of a right-angled triangle is equal to the sum of the squares of the other two sides—was known to the Egyptians and Babylonians, but they never worked out a proof of it. The Greeks, however, did, as can be seen in Plato's *Meno,* where Socrates leads an illiterate slave-boy through a demonstration of the theorem.[8]

This concern with rational demonstration created as well a tradition of building on the work of previous thinkers and showing how one's own ideas improved on theirs or better answered the questions they raised. This willingness to acknowledge and grapple with other philosophers' ideas recurs throughout Greek philosophy, most famously in Aristotle's work. He begins his *Metaphysics* with a critical summary of previous philosophers' theories, including those of his one-time teacher Plato, and he is aware that he is part of a tradition of knowledge. "For in the case of all discoveries," Aristotle writes in the *Physics,* "the results of previous labours that have been handed down from others have been advanced bit by bit by those who have taken them on."[9]

G. E. R. Lloyd summarizes the importance of this Hellenic critical tradition: "The urge is towards finding the best explanation, the most adequate theory, and they [philosophers] are, then, forced to consider the grounds for their ideas, the evidence and arguments in their favour, as well as the weak points in their opponents' theories." And this critical debate is "the necessary precondition for progress in both philosophy and science."[10] Without it, knowledge languishes in thrall to utilitarian imperatives, religious coercion, accidents of time and place, and the dead hand of traditional superstition and institutional authority.

The more important characteristic of Greek intellectual activity, however, was its *context,* one very different from that which shaped the knowledge of their Near Eastern neighbors, who subordinated knowledge to myth, ritual, religion, and superstition. Benjamin Farrington, a champion of the scientific achievements of the Egyptians and Mesopotamians, describes this critical advance of the Greeks:

> The original thing in Greek science at its beginnings is that it offers us, for the first time in history, an attempt to supply a purely naturalist interpretation of the universe as a whole. Cosmology takes the place of myth. The ancient empires of the Near East had ... brought to a certain level of systematization and theoretical development a few officially approved sciences, such as astronomy, mathematics, and medicine. But there is no evidence of an attempt to give a naturalistic explanation of the universe as a whole. There is an official mythology, transmitted in priestly corporations and enshrined in elaborate ceremonial, telling how things came to be as they are. There are no individual thinkers offering a rational substitute for this doctrine over their own names.[11]

In contrast, the search for natural rather than supernatural explanations permeates all of Greek thought. It dominates the cosmologies of the natural scientists, where natural elements and consistent laws are postulated to account for the problem of material change and existence, in place of the grotesque gods and monsters of earlier myth. Although Herodotus occasionally admitted the gods into his analysis of historical events, he continually sought and recorded natural explanations. In his account, the three-day storm that wrecked Xerxes' fleet was brought to an end by the chants and spells and sacrifices of the Magi, the Persian priests—"or, of course, it may be that the wind just dropped naturally." His discussion of the Nile's flooding—a subject on which, tellingly, the Egyptian priests could give him no information—focuses on describing and critiquing various Greek theories, none of which posits supernatural causes.[12] His preference for rational explanation is partly what earned Herodotus his title as "father of history." To the Greeks, *historia* meant "exploration," "inquiry," not a recitation of received dogma.

An important consequence of liberating speculation from traditional religious notions was that knowledge could progress on its own terms, apart from the practical needs of priests or kings and the inertia of tradition and habit. Inquiry about nature could develop into an independent activity, limited only by the need to be as accurate as possible, and subject to the public protocols of rational deliberation and demonstration, which themselves became objects of systematic inquiry. "The Greeks," writes G. E. R. Lloyd, "preeminently bring into the open and discuss second-order questions concerning the nature of the inquiry itself. Much as the Egyptians and Babylonians contributed to the content of these studies, the investigations only acquire self-conscious methodologies for the first time with the Greeks."[13]

Removing the gods and occult forces from explanations of the world compelled humans to stand before nature with nothing but their own minds. As the philosopher-poet Xenophanes said, "Truly the gods have not revealed to mortals all things from the beginning; but mortals by long seeking discover what is better."[14] People became responsible for their understanding of the world. And that is a defining part of being fully human: the ability to think critically, to seek knowledge for its own sake, and to pursue the uniquely human pleasure of learning.

Greek writing affords many indications of this novel attitude, unparalleled anywhere else in the ancient Mediterranean. At the beginning of the fifth century Alcmaeon of Croton said, "Man differs from the other *(creatures)* in that he alone understands."[15] Aristotle famously declared, "All men by nature desire to know."[16]

Observing and learning are pleasurable because they express and fulfill a core aspect of our humanity. Anaxagoras, when asked why a man should prefer being born to nonexistence, answered, "For the sake of viewing the heavens and the whole order of the universe."[17] Human life has value because of our ability to learn about and appreciate our surroundings. So Aristotle defended his interest in lowly animals by saying, "If some [animals] have no graces to charm the sense, yet nature, which fashioned them, gives amazing pleasure in their study to all who can trace links of causation, and are inclined to philosophy.... Each and all will reveal to us something natural and something beautiful."[18]

Learning, then, is the most valuable activity for a human. The fifth-century philosopher Democritus claimed that he "would rather discover one cause than gain the kingdom of Persia."[19] Moreover, the pursuit of knowledge created an optimistic faith in humanity's ability to master its world and to progress. The comic poet Alexis, writing around the early fourth century, has a character voice this confidence:

> All that is sought, is found,
> Unless you leave the quest or shun its toils.
> For see how man's discovery has mastered
> Provinces of the heavenly world remote,
> The rising, setting, wheeling of the stars,
> The sun's eclipse! What then shall 'scape man's search
> In the related, kindred world below![20]

Given the topical nature of Greek comedy, the presentation of such a sentiment on the public stage suggests that this idea, whether generally approved or not, was of interest to the average Athenian.

We must not imagine here a sudden birth of scientific rationalism in which the divine played no part. Various mythic ideas about the gods and the divinity of nature influenced Greek philosophy. Hesiod's *Theogony* describes the creation of the world in terms of monsters and personified abstractions: "Chaos now first gave birth to Erebos and black Night; / and she in turn gave birth to Ether and Day," and so on through a succession of rapes, mutilations, incest, and cannibalism.[21] Superstition afflicted Greek life even during the fifth-century heyday of rationalism. The philosopher Anaxagoras, friend of Pericles, prudently left Athens after a decree was proposed that "anybody who did not believe in the gods or taught theories about celestial phenomena should be liable to prosecution." This legislation was aimed at all the "natural philosophers and visionaries" (literally, "chatterers about things in the sky") who, as Plutarch goes on to report, were accused of "belittl[ing] the power of the gods by explaining it away as nothing more than the operation of irrational causes and blind forces acting by necessity."[22] Another tradition has Anaxagoras prosecuted for impiety because "he maintained that the sun was a red-hot mass of metal" instead of a divinity.[23] The books of Protagoras were burned by the Athenians in the marketplace, according to one tradition.[24] Most famously, Socrates was charged with atheism and likewise accused, wrongly, of speculating about the heavens in naturalistic rather than divine terms.

Many Greek thinkers maintained religious dimensions in their work. Most famously, Pythagoras believed in reincarnation and established ascetic communities devoted to the study of mathematics in order to unlock the divine mystery of the universe and purify the soul. The early cosmologists, in the sixth and seventh centuries, viewed nature as a divine creative power. Plato's work is full of mystical speculations and metaphors. Often in Greek thought we also find the unscientific idea that humans are too limited by their physical bodies and unreliable senses to acquire true knowledge. Empedocles claimed to teach "not more than mortal intellect can attain," and prayed only for "such knowledge as divine law allows us creatures of a day to hear." And Socrates, who obeyed the advice of a private divine voice, was famous for his disavowal of any true knowledge, claiming only to expose false opinion, for "[g]od only is wise."[25]

Yet despite the prevalence of religious and mythological sensibilities, the critical spirit of Greek speculation was turned on religious ideas and practices in a way unique in the ancient Mediterranean. Heracleitus mocked the traditional practice of washing away blood-guilt by bathing in blood, "as if one were to step into mud in order to wash off mud," and he scorned those who "talk to these statues *(of theirs)* as one were to hold conversations with houses."[26] Xenophanes famously scorned the anthropomorphism of Homer and Hesiod, who "attributed to the gods all things that are shameful and a reproach among mankind: theft, adultery, and mutual deception." Xenophanes pointed out that Ethiopians had black gods and Thracians red-headed ones, and suggested that "if oxen (and horses) and lions had hands or could draw with hands ... horses would draw pictures of gods like horses."[27] The tragic stage frequently presented gods who were morally inferior to suffering mortals. Aeschylus' Zeus nailing Prometheus to a crag, Sophocles' Athena gloating over the broken Ajax, and Euripides' Aphrodite destroying an innocent Phaedra all reflect a culture-wide willingness to criticize traditional depictions of the gods.

Finally, explaining natural phenomena as an activity of gods came under fire as well. Dismissing the traditional explanation of thunder and lightning as Zeus' wielding of his weapons, for example, Anaximander gave instead a naturalistic account. Both "occur as a result of wind: for whenever it is shut up in a thick cloud and then bursts out forcibly, through its fineness and lightness, then the bursting makes the noise, while the rift against the blackness of the cloud makes the flash."[28] Plutarch relates an anecdote about the fifth-century statesman Pericles and his friend Anaxagoras that illustrates the way the light of reason was being turned onto superstition. Pericles had been sent the head of a one-horned ram from his estate. The soothsayer Lampon used the skull to make a prophecy about Pericles' political future; "Anaxagoras, on the other hand, had the skull dissected and proceeded to demonstrate that the brain had not filled its natural space, but had contracted into a point like an egg at that place in the cavity from which the horn grew."[29] Such public questioning of the gods and their powers was unthinkable in Egypt or Israel or Babylon.

Questioning of religious beliefs accelerated through the fifth and fourth centuries. The plays of Euripides refer repeatedly to the intellectual ferment and scepticism of his time, earning him the charge of atheism. Characters rationalize their wickedness by invoking the behavior of the gods. In a fragment from Euripides' lost play

Bellerophon, the existence of evil is offered as proof that the gods do not exist.[30] Often, the gods were described as indifferent to human behavior—"they took no care for man."[31] Protagoras voiced a sceptical view: "About the gods, I am not able to know whether they exist or do not exist." Critias, going further and anticipating Voltaire, attributed the invention of the gods to the need for a threat of supernatural retribution to promote justice and maintain social order: "A wise and clever man invented fear *(of the gods)* for mortals, that there might be some means of frightening the wicked."[32] Such views culminated in the materialist philosophy of Epicurus, who believed that even the gods were made of material atoms and were utterly unconcerned with human action—which earned him a spot in Dante's hell along with sodomites and usurers.

Criticism of traditional beliefs was possible because, unlike most of their Mediterranean neighbors, the Greeks had no state cults, official doctrines, or powerful priestly castes with an institutional stake in promoting sanctioned views and punishing heretics. Thus a climate of tolerance—sometimes violated, to be sure, as in the cases of Socrates and Anaxagoras—promoted critical inquiry into all issues pertaining to nature and human life. "Men who love wisdom," Heracleitus said, "must be inquirers into many things indeed."[33] This concern for independent pursuit of knowledge led to the creation of "schools" of learning, such as Plato's Academy and Aristotle's Lyceum, where programs of research were carried out, and to the great library of Alexandria, created in the third century to be not just a repository of books but also a state-subsidized center for research ranging from textual criticism to botany and analytic geometry. The desire for knowledge fostered as well an ongoing rational debate about the nature of things that progressed and, after many centuries of dormancy and retrogression, led to the world we live in today—a world in which, for better *and* for worse, science provides the dominant means of understanding and altering our environment and ourselves.

AN IMPORTANT DEVELOPMENT IN GREEK PHILOSOPHY was its identification of the problem of epistemology, or how we know what we know. Can we acquire knowledge through sense-perception, through the observation of phenomena and the passing on of data so that factual information increases and becomes more accurate through time? Or can pure intellection, a rational activity apart from the fallible data provided by the senses, reach truth? Or, as the Sceptics claimed, is any sort of true knowledge at all impossible? The debate between "rationalists" and "empiricists," still resonant in philosophy today, has been fundamental in Western thought, and it was begun by the Greeks.[34]

We have seen already that a class-inspired disdain for practical applications of knowledge, coupled with a distrust of the ceaselessly mutable material world and the fallible senses, culminated in the radical idealism of Plato. Such an attitude obviously would make irrelevant the sort of observation and experimentation that have made modern science so successful. Plato's idealist predecessor Parmenides—who paradoxically denied the existence of change and motion, thus rejecting completely the validity of "common sense"—believed that pure reason alone was the only way to apprehend the real truth. "You must debar your thought from this way of search," he said, "nor let ordinary experience in its variety force you along this way, *(namely, that of allowing)* the eye, sightless as it is, and the ear, full of sound, and the tongue, to rule; but *(you must)* judge by means of the Reason (*Logos*) the much-contested proof which is expounded by me."[35]

Later Democritus, who elaborated the atomic theory of matter, contrasted "two sorts of knowledge, one genuine, one bastard [or 'obscure']. To the latter belong all the following: sight, hearing, smell, taste, touch. The real is separated from this."[36] And we have already noted Plato's objection to the duplicitous knowledge gleaned by the senses. In the *Republic,* his thirty-year educational program for the elite Guardians is intended to foster in them nothing but abstract reasoning unsullied by sense-perception. "In my opinion," Socrates asserts, "that knowledge only which is of being and of the unseen can make the soul look upwards, and whether a man gapes at the heavens or blinks on the ground, seeking to learn some particular of sense, I would deny that he can learn, for nothing of that sort is matter of science [i.e. 'true knowledge']."[37] As G. E. R. Lloyd summarizes, "The idea of the untrustworthiness of the senses had powerful advocates in the ancient world."[38]

Yet champions of sense-perception as a valid means of acquiring knowledge appeared as well. Sometimes those who distrusted the senses nonetheless admitted that they could at least point the way toward true knowledge. Anaxagoras said that "through the weakness of the sense-perceptions, we cannot judge truth"; but he also admitted that "visible existences are a sight of the unseen."[39] Likewise Democritus scorned sense-perception as "bastard knowledge," but still had the senses chastise an imperious reason, saying, "Miserable Mind, you get your evidence from us, and do you try to overthrow us: The overthrow will be your downfall."[40] Heracleitus pointed to the root of the problem—not the senses per se, but the use to which the mind puts their information: "Evil witnesses are eyes and ears for men, if they have souls that do not understand their language."[41] The need to judge and discriminate correctly among all the bodily sources of information in order to acquire knowledge was also a concern for Empedocles: "But come, consider with all thy powers how each thing is manifest, neither holding sight in greater trust as compared with hearing, nor loud-sounding hearing above the clear evidence of thy tongue, nor withhold thy trust from any of the other limbs, wheresoever there is a path for understanding, but think on each thing in the way by which it is manifest."[42]

Contrary to the rational idealists, then, many other philosophers recognized that some topics of inquiry, unlike mathematics and geometry, demanded data provided by the senses, the raw material of which reason had to make sense. Perhaps the best statement about the relationship of theory to observation was made by the greatest observer and cataloguer in the ancient world, Aristotle. During a discussion about how bees reproduce he remarked, "Such appears to be the truth about the generation of bees, judging from theory and from what are believed to be the facts about them; the facts, however, have not yet been sufficiently grasped; if ever they are, then credit must be given rather to observation than to theories, and to theories only if what they affirm agrees with the observed facts."[43] Much intellectual mischief could have been avoided in later Western philosophy if these words of Aristotle had been heeded.

This faith in sense-perception encouraged the use of observation and even experimentation among many Greek thinkers, another corrective to the received wisdom of tradition and superstition. We saw above how Anaxagoras countered the soothsayer's interpretation of the one-horned ram skull by cutting it open and giving an explanation based on what the observers could see for themselves. Even the other-worldly Pythagoreans, by Plato's account, conducted experiments in order to test their theories of harmonics.[44] Anaxagoras reportedly proved the corporeality of air "by straining wineskins and showing the resistance of the air, and by cutting it off in clepsydras [water-clocks]."[45] Anaximenes pointed to the fact "that breath exhaled from compressed lips feels cooler than from an open mouth to support a theory that the hot and the cold are to be identified with the rare and the dense respectively," and Xenophanes used the fossils found on mountains and in quarries to support the idea that the land was once covered by water.[46] Of course, Aristotle was the ancient master of clear and precise observation and classification of natural phenomena, particularly in his works on animals, which refer to over five hundred species and show evidence of the use of dissection to gather data. The accuracy of some of his observations, such as the navel string that attaches the newborn dogfish to its mother, was not recognized until modern times.[47]

History, too, began to be liberated from traditional tales and legends, and moved beyond the mere chronicling of events; truth was argued on the basis of a rational analysis of evidence, including the individual's own observation and experience. The geographer and proto-historian Hecataeus (c. 500) prefaced his work by saying, "I am here writing what to me appears to be true: for the tales of the Greeks are diverse and in my opinion, ridiculous."[48] Herodotus continually recorded the varied, and sometimes contradictory, results of his researches, guided always by the need to present what seemed most likely to be true to a rational observer. After his report of the Egyptians' account of their land's creation by the Nile, he concluded, "I have little doubt that they were right in this; for it is clear to any intelligent observer, that the Egypt to which we sail nowadays is, as it were, the gift of the river."[49] Individuals had the ability to weigh and judge the evidence and use their minds to come to a conclusion about what is true or not.

Thucydides most explicitly set out a historical method predicated on the rational evaluation of evidence rather than on the fancies of myth and legend. Discounting those traditions that most people accepted "without applying any critical test whatever," Thucydides offered instead conclusions drawn from proofs, "having proceeded upon the clearest data, and having arrived at conclusions as exact as can be expected in matter of such antiquity." Regarding the subject of his history, the war between Athens and Sparta, he said, "Far from permitting myself to derive [the narrative] from the first source that came to hand, I did not even trust my own impressions, but it rests partly on what I saw myself, partly on what others saw for me, the accuracy of the report being always tried by the most severe and detailed tests possible."[50] A good example of Thucydides' method is his description of the plague that afflicted Athens in 430. His catalogue of the symptoms, his review of the plague's possible origins, and his detailing of the social and moral effects reveal a reliance on personal experience (Thucydides survived the disease himself) and rational explanation rather than on supernatural causes. The advantage of his method was that the knowledge so acquired could be useful to others in the future. "I shall simply set down [the plague's] nature," Thucydides wrote, "and explain the symptoms by which perhaps it may be recognized by the student, if it should ever break out again."[51]

It was in astronomy, however, that observation in the natural sciences was most extensively used in support of theory. Aristotle frequently referred to "what we have seen," mentioning for instance the eclipse of Mars by the moon, a comet that appeared in 341, a tail appearing on a star in the constellation Canis Major, and the conjunction of Jupiter with one of the stars in Gemini.[52] The more accurate estimates of the length of the seasons achieved in the fourth century resulted in part from direct observation, as did the work of Eudoxus (early fourth century) concerning the motion of the planets, and the catalogue of 850 stars compiled by the second-century astronomer Hipparchus, who also discovered the precession of the equinoxes.[53] Hipparchus particularly relied on his own observation of celestial phenomena as well as earlier records from the Near East, and reportedly invented or improved on optical instruments to aid in observation, including the dioptra, a "horizontal bar with fixed backsight and movable foresight used to measure, for example, the diameter of the sun."[54]

Surveying the Greeks' empirical research in history, geography, medicine, astronomy, and zoology, Lloyd concludes that the "notion of empirical research" is one of their most important legacies to modern science.[55] Obviously, reliance on observation was (and is) vulnerable to subjective distortion and other limitations, not the least being the impulse to skew observed data to fit a preconceived theory. Yet empirical research, when combined with the drive for a rationally coherent explanation of phenomena and with the application of mathematics to those explanations, has been indispensable in liberating knowledge from myth and superstition, thus allowing for intellectual progress through cumulative research.

The unique innovations of the Greeks sketched above—especially the search for rational rather than supernatural explanations, and the reliance on empirical observation—can be best appreciated by looking at ancient medicine, a field in which the Greeks made a quantum leap beyond the practices of their Near Eastern neighbors. Numerous medical writings from Egypt and Mesopotamia survive, showing that these civilizations had to some extent observed and organized various medical conditions, symptoms, and cures. Yet medical practice in these cultures remained in thrall to religion, superstition and magic. Mesopotamian medicine, Roy Porter suggests, "might be regarded as sorcery systematized."[56] So too the

Egyptians "held that all ... internal diseases ... were caused by supernatural agents (gods, goddesses, and dead enemies) who took 'possession' of the bodies of the living. Clearly, supernatural ailments could be exorcised only by supernatural remedies."[57]

In contrast, and despite the continued prevalence of religious and magical healing among the Greeks, a medical practice developed that eschewed supernatural causes and cures, being based instead on natural philosophy and empirical observation. The body of writings traditionally attributed to the late-fifth-century physician Hippocrates, and dating from the fifth to fourth centuries, is united, in Porter's description, by

> the conviction that, as with everything else, health and disease are capable of explanation by reasoning about nature, independently of supernatural interference. Man is governed by the same physical laws as the cosmos, hence medicine must be an understanding, empirical and rational, of the workings of the body in its natural environment. Appeal to reason, rather than to rules or to supernatural forces, gives Hippocratic medicine its distinctiveness.[58]

That is why our word "physician" derives from the Greek word for "nature."

A disdain for supernatural explanation of disease is most famously stated in a Hippocratic treatise about epilepsy, *On the Sacred Disease:* "It is not, in my opinion, any more divine or more sacred than other diseases, but has a natural cause, and its supposed divine origin is due to men's inexperience, and to their wonder at its peculiar character."[59] No demons or malign spirits cause the epileptic's fits, the writer continues, but rather a loss of vital air because the veins are blocked with phlegm. That this account is incorrect is not as important as the attempt, typical of the Greek medical writers, to find a cause for disease in the body and its diet and environment rather than in the supernatural ("from the things that come to and go from the body, from cold, sun, and from the changing restlessness of winds").[60] Also significant is the author's analysis of the motives and practices of those who claim to cure disease by purifications and rituals: they are covering up their ignorance and failure, and profiting from both to boot. Clearly we have here a naturalistic view of disease in which reason and experience, rather than magic and superstition, are the keys to treatment.

Next, the importance of careful observation and description appears throughout the Hippocratic corpus.[61] Close examination of the patient's symptoms and diet is continually stressed. In the *Prognostic,* the doctor is urged to examine carefully the patient's face, eyes, posture, breathing, sleeping habits, temperature, bowel movements, appetite, and the appearance of any and all bodily effluvia. Likewise in the *Epidemics,* the case histories "display a remarkable appreciation of the variety of points to be considered, and an acute sense of the need for thoroughness and attention to detail" well beyond the cursory descriptions in Egyptian medical writings.[62] According to *Airs, Waters, Places,* the environment of the patient must be taken into account as well: the effects of the seasons, the winds, the water, and exposure to the sun of any town, and how these shape what we would call the "lifestyle" and character and values of the inhabitants. "For if a physician know these things well, by preference all of them, but at any rate most," says the author, "he will not ... be ignorant of the local diseases, or of the nature of those that commonly prevail."[63]

This bias towards the observation of particular cases is especially strong in *The Ancient Medicine.* This polemic attacks medical theories that are based on a simplistic, preconceived notion or "postulate" impossible to verify through experience: "Wherefore I have deemed that it [medicine] has no need of an empty [or novel] postulate, as do insoluble mysteries, about which any exponent must use a postulate, for example, things in the sky or below the earth."[64] Because sickness and disease are concrete, serious and recurring phenomena, medicine must attend to what is observed in the patient and what has been learned in the past by others and handed down to the practitioner. Indeed, "medicine has long had all its means to hand, and has discovered both a principle and a method, through which the discoveries made during a long period are many and excellent, while full discovery will be made, if the inquirer be competent, conduct his researches with knowledge of the discoveries already made, and make them his starting point."[65] Rather than being slaves to a fossilized tradition, doctors should instead use received knowledge in tandem with what they see before them, so as "to bring practice into intelligent agreement with medical principles born of long reflection on past experience."[66] The emphasis on reason and research instead of rules and practices whose authority derives from religion is unique to the Greeks—and has led to our remarkably successful medical practice today.

THE ADVANCES IN INTELLECTUAL PRACTICE that we have been discussing were in part made possible by a broader, distinctively Hellenic view of the nature of man. As Aristotle puts it in the epigraph to this chapter, reason and its activity are the defining essence of human identity, and human purpose and fulfillment must involve the activity of the rational soul. "That which is proper to each thing," Aristotle says in the *Ethics,* "is by nature best and most pleasant for each thing; for man, therefore, the life according to intellect is best and pleasantest, since intellect more than anything else *is* man. This life therefore is also the happiest."[67] This definition of humans has been the engine driving Western intellectual history.

Aristotle and Plato were mainly concerned with reason per se as the defining attribute of humans and the creator of order and virtue in the individual soul. But elsewhere in Greek literature we find another dimension to this critical question of human identity, one equally influential on the development of the West. Not just reason, but the mind's projections out into the world—the order it can create out of the welter of chaotic forces and raw materials—make us what we are: creatures that radically transform their environment and harness the energies of nature for their own survival. We encountered an aspect of this idea in the last chapter, with Aristotle's view of humans as "political animals," social creatures whose identities are constituted by the shared laws and customs they live by. Culture, which encompasses politics and technology, is what makes us human. Our identity results from the way our culture interacts with, controls, and often collides with the forces of nature, including our own natural appetites and passions.

This theme abounds in Greek literature; indeed, the culture-nature contrast is a Greek discovery. Two literary examples illustrate this idea very well. In the *Odyssey,* the hero's battle with the savage Cyclops—a creature with no technology or culture or laws or political institutions—is at one level the battle between humans and raw nature. Odysseus is weaker physically than the Cyclops, but he has a mind that can think up a plan: get the Cyclops drunk, then blind him with a sharpened olive-wood stake. Homer's description of the stake being rammed into the Cyclops' eye makes the contrast between culture and nature explicit: Odysseus and his men twirl the stake "like a man with a brace-and-bit who bores into / a ship timber," and the monster's eyeball sizzles like hot iron plunged into cold water.[68] The two similes from the important technologies of ship-building and metallurgy suggest that the defeat of the Cyclops represents too humanity's conquest of nature through the power of the mind and the technologies it projects into the world. Homer anticipates this point when earlier he records Odysseus' survey of the uninhabited island near the Cyclopes' land. This site, rich in undeveloped natural resources, could be made into a "fair settlement" if the Cyclopes only had ships and the other civilizing technologies.[69]

Likewise the myth of Prometheus ("Forethought") defines humans in terms of the mind and technology. When all life on earth was created, gifts were given to each species by Prometheus' brother Epimetheus ("Afterthought")—strength, speed, claws, horns, flight—so that each species had a chance to survive. But he didn't save anything for humans, last in line.[70] Thus to ensure mankind's survival Prometheus gave us an energy source, fire, and more important, the mind that could think up skills, crafts, and technologies, from agriculture and ship-building to mathematics and language—all the things, in short, that animals don't have and gods don't need. "I found them witless," Aeschylus' Prometheus says, "and gave them the use of their wits and made them masters of their minds."[71] Humans can not only survive but dominate the planet because of the mind and its creations, the "unnatural" transformations of raw nature that compensate for humanity's physical puniness next to the vast, destructive powers of nature. Hence in the words of the *Antigone*'s chorus, nothing "is more wonderful [awesome, terrible] than what is man," a "cunning fellow" who "has a way against everything, / and he faces nothing that is to come / without contrivance."[72]

Plato created a powerful image of the human soul that illustrates the role of reason and culture in making us what we are. In the *Phaedrus* he describes the soul as a charioteer who controls a pair of winged horses, one noble, the other base. For the soul to reach the ends Plato believes to be suitable for a human—the intellectual apprehension of virtue and goodness and beauty, the true, immortal reality beyond this world of change and decay—the charioteer must, with the help of the good horse (a nonrational part of the soul amenable to reason), control the bad horse, which represents the animal passions and appetites that blindly pursue bestial ends.[73] Note that in Plato's image, human identity comprises: a natural energy source, the two horses; the chariot, an artifact of culture and technology; and the charioteer, the rational mind that must steer the chariot to its proper and suitable destination by exploiting the energy of the horses. If the charioteer fails and allows the bad horse to corrupt the good, then rather than fulfilling his destiny as a human, he will sink into the mere material world of the beasts, who live only for appetite. This view of human identity and its potential has had a remarkable—some would say malign—influence on Western thought, and has contributed immeasurably to the world we live in today, for it has legitimized the pursuit of knowledge and the radical transformation and exploitation of nature as the quintessential humanizing activities.

As WITH EVERYTHING ELSE THE GREEKS DISCOVERED, the definition of man as a rational animal was attended with sharp criticism of the idea that reason is the essence of human identity, or that the mind has the capacity to control the appetites and passions and thus create psychic and social order. Sophocles' *Oedipus* (431), for example, explores the limits of the rational mind. Its hero, Oedipus the riddle-solver, knows in the abstract what a human being is—human identity being the point of the Sphinx's famous riddle about the creature that walks on four feet in the morning, two at noon, and three in the evening. That is, a human is a natural creature limited by its organic body that has a beginning in space and time, enjoys a brief flourishing, and then descends into decay and death. Yet at the same time Oedipus doesn't know his own name or who his real parents are; he is abstractly wise, yet concretely ignorant. Moreover, his relentless and destructive pursuit of self-knowledge, at one level admirable, nonetheless chills us, who know where it will lead him: to knowing that he is guilty of murder and incest, the worst crimes of sex and violence, the passions of the body that compromise the power of the mind. All men, as Aristotle says, may by nature desire to know; but the content of that knowledge—the recognition of their own destructive natures—ultimately will horrify them.

It is Euripides, writing in the late fifth century during the high tide of Greek rationalism, who explores most searchingly the limits of reason and the power of passion. Medea, infuriated by the sexual dishonor inflicted on her by Jason and his new bride, murders her rival Glauke, King Creon, and her own two sons in order to exact revenge. As she agonizes over her decision to kill the children, she cries out, "Passion is mightier than my counsels, and this is the greatest cause of evils for mortals."[74] Similarly Phaedra, stricken with the disease of lust for her stepson Hippolytus, anticipates St. Paul when she says, "We know the good and recognize it, but we cannot accomplish it."[75] And in Euripides' lost play *Chrysippus*, about the rape of the boy Chrysippus by Oedipus' father, Laius, the latter explains that "nature drove me on, even though I had thought/judgment."[76] Clearly Euripides at least had little faith in Socrates' view that virtue is knowledge, that if we can rationally apprehend the good, we will do it. The power of our natural passions is simply too great, the power of reason too feeble.

The rationalist ideal in the West has always coexisted with the recognition, first given voice by Euripides, that thinking and calculating are not all there is to being human. Christianity subordinated reason to revelation, the truths of this material world ultimately significant only insofar as they confirm the grand truth of our true nature and destiny, a truth not discovered by our minds but freely revealed to us by God. Later, the Romantic movement also would reject the claims of an imperious reason and its powerful science, making the case for the greater truth and meaning residing in the imagination and in the heart, whose reasons, Pascal said, reason knows nothing of. An idealization of the capacity to feel, rather than to think, as the quintessential human trait is found in the German Romantic Herder, who rejected Descartes's rationalist equation of thinking with being when he cried, "I am not here to think, but to be, feel, live!"[77] The explosion of scientific knowledge and the transformations wrought by technology gave urgency to the criticism of what William Blake called "single vision and Newton's sleep," the view that the mystery of human life and action and value could be rationally known and calibrated and ultimately organized into the brave new world.

Today, however, a trite anti-rationalism has been institutionalized in our culture, blinding us to the very real improvements reason and science have made in our lives. The Romantic critique of reason, as valid as it was and still is, has degenerated into clichés and a sentimental obsession with feeling. The idea that we have somehow created an inhuman, "air-conditioned nightmare" where we are in thrall to a soul-killing science is perpetually recycled in our popular culture. The catastrophes of the twentieth century (and those we imagine will happen in the twenty-first) are often cited as evidence of the wrong turn the West took when, Faust-like, it sold its soul for knowledge and power; yet in fact they are typical of man's perennial inhumanity to man and his chronic irrationality. They represent not the culmination of reason and science, but a corruption of both by atavistic passions. Both Hitler and Stalin were enemies of reason, their nightmarish tyrannies built on myths and lies. A more balanced assessment of our century, moreover, would have to consider whether the lives saved by antibiotics and the modern agricultural revolution outnumber those lost to industrialized warfare.[78]

Worse than these popular remnants of Romantic antirationalism, however, is the epistemic nihilism fashionable among far too many intellectuals. The postmodernist claim that science does not acquire true knowledge but is rather a mere social construct validating the power of the political and economic establishment is mindlessly endorsed by people ignorant of how science works and blind to how thoroughly their lives are shaped and improved by this so-called fiction, which they presume to be no more efficacious than the dance of the shaman or the chants of the witch doctor. For no matter how much angst we in the West suffer from our complex, fast-paced, technologically dominated lives, no matter how much we pretend to bewail our "disenchanted world," none of us wants to return to the chronic pain, early death, malnutrition, disease, superstition, and everyday cruelty and suffering that were the common destiny of most human beings before the modern age, and unfortunately are still the fate of billions of people in the Third World. We fortunate Westerners have the Greeks to thank for our material comfort, for they were the first to stand intellectually on their own two feet, look both the gods and nature in the eye without flinching, and take responsibility for human life and its improvement.

Hydarnes, the advice you give us does not spring from a full knowledge of the situation. You know only one half of what is involved; the other half is a blank to you. You understand well enough what slavery is, but freedom you have never experienced, so you do not know if it tastes sweet or bitter. If you ever did come to experience it, you would advise us to fight for it not with spears only, but with axes too.

—*Herodotus*[1]

SEVEN

The Birth of Freedom

WHEN CHINESE DISSIDENTS IN MAY 1989 gathered in Beijing's Tiananmen Square to demand a freer society and a more inclusive government, they constructed a powerful symbol, one that descended not from their own ethnic or national traditions, but solely from those of the West: the Goddess of Democracy, a figure obviously modeled on the classically inspired Statue of Liberty. These Chinese freedom-fighters understood something too many Western intellectuals have forgotten: that political freedom is dependent on consensual government, a link forged in ancient Greece. There the concept of political freedom itself was first created and recognized as a value worth dying for—as the Spartans made clear in their answer to the Persian Hydarnes' suggestion that they submit to the Great King Xerxes.

In speaking of freedom, however, we must distinguish between a de facto freedom—a condition arising accidentally—and freedom based on principle, growing from a conscious ideal actively pursued. Many peoples have enjoyed de facto freedom, mainly because their societies are not organized and complex enough to enforce any limitations on males who can use weapons. In this sense the Scythians were freer than the Greeks, and the Germanic tribes freer than the Romans. But this is a freedom dependent on violence—the kind of freedom we find in Homer, where a warrior like Achilles is willing to use force against Agamemnon when the king attempts to impose his will and take away Achilles' prize, the girl Briseis, and is prevented from killing him only by the intervention of a god. We also find this sort of freedom behind Hector's concern that the "day of freedom" will be taken from his wife, Andromache, after he and the other Trojan warriors are dead and can no longer defend them. Freedom is simply the community's independence from others, but is monopolized by those elites willing and able to use violence to protect their families and property, or to take the lives and property of others.

Freedom in this sense is defined in opposition to the condition of slavery. Orlando Patterson and others are right to note that the beginnings of freedom in the West are intimately bound up with the institution of chattel slavery. But as Patterson also points out, "Valuing the status of being a freeman did not necessarily entail valuing freedom as an ideal to be *actively* pursued. And it was a far cry from identifying it with the right to participate in the running of one's community."[2] That many people enjoyed de facto freedom and even fought to keep it is an unexceptional fact: even animals will fight for their freedom, as the Greek historian Diodorus said. What is more important is what the Greeks alone invented: the *idea* of freedom, a *value* that survived the accidents of time and chance and hence entered the Western tradition, where it has developed to the point that the inhabitants of Western countries today enjoy a level of political and personal freedom unprecedented in history.

The peculiar genius of the Greeks, however, can be seen not only in their unique invention of freedom as an ideal, but also in their analysis of the concept in its various dimensions, not to mention the criticism of some kinds of freedom that can be found in their writings. When discussing freedom, however, we must distinguish between "personal" freedom, the freedom of the individual to live as he pleases with a minimum of external restraint; "civic" freedom, the freedom of citizens to participate in public life and political institutions; and "philosophical" freedom, freedom as an ideal condition of the soul rightly directed towards the ends suitable for a rational human being.[3]

Personal freedom is the natural freedom that can exist wherever political organization is rudimentary; it is enjoyed by those—almost always elite male warriors—who monopolize force and violence. "Civic" freedom is the invention of the Greeks alone, who first made civic participation an expression of freedom underwritten by political institutions, particularly in Athens, where civic and personal freedom conjoined and were enjoyed by the greatest number of citizens. So too freedom as a philosophical ideal and a conscious object of thought is found only among the ancient Greeks. Finally, we find in the ancient Hellenic sources as well a recognition of freedom's potential destructive consequences, a typical result of the Greek critical spirit.

ELSEWHERE IN THE ANCIENT MEDITERRANEAN, freedom was the possession mainly of elites arranged in pyramidal hierarchies, at the apex of which was the pharaoh or king, who alone enjoyed complete freedom. As Orlando Patterson notes, "Since only the king-god was free, the only freedom worth having was that which came vicariously in enslavement to him, unless one could replicate this godlike experience with another, a replication possible only with slaves."[4] In this regard the Greeks themselves realized that they were very different from their neighbors. "For the man of Hellas there is nothing greater than freedom," reads a third-century inscription.[5] Our discussion of slavery showed how the Greeks defined themselves as a people in terms of their political freedom, contrasting their free lives with those of barbarians, who were politically enslaved. Euripides' Iphigenia evokes this cultural stereotype when she chooses to be sacrificed so that the Greek fleet can sail to Troy: "It is / a right thing that Greeks rule barbarians. . . . They are bondsmen and slaves, and we, / Mother, are Greeks and free."[6]

The crucial historical event for the Greeks' consciousness of themselves as uniquely free was the Persian Wars. When the independent Greek city-states twice turned back an autocratic Persian Great King, they proved the practical as well as moral advantages of a freedom predicated on civic participation over subjection to autocratic rule.

In both Herodotus' *History* and Aeschylus' *Persians*, the struggle with the Persians is explicitly cast as a struggle between freedom and slavery. The Persian "great king, king of kings, king of the countries possessing many kinds of people, king of this great earth far and wide,"[7] as he is styled in one inscription, had the power of life and death over his subjects. Herodotus tells the story of the unfortunate Pythius, a Lydian who made bold to ask Xerxes to release from military service just one of his five sons. The enraged Xerxes responded, "*You,* my slave" dare such a request, "whose duty it was to come with me with every member of your house, including your wife?" He then had the son cut in two and marched the whole army between the halves.[8]

Given the absolute power of the king, the Persians are consistently depicted as his "slaves," and the Great King as their "Master" before whom even the wealthiest and noblest must grovel in obeisance (*proskunêsis*). The Spartan envoys, whose reply to Hydarnes' suggestion that they submit to the Great King provides the epigraph to this chapter, refused to bow down to Xerxes when they were shown into his presence, even when the Persian royal guards tried to force them physically. "It was not, they said, the custom in Sparta to worship a mere man like themselves."[9] Aristotle in his definition of honor treats this form of obeisance as something that characterizes barbarians, and perforce differentiates them from Greeks.[10]

Another way Herodotus illustrates Persian slavishness is in his frequent references to the polyglot Persian soldiers having to be whipped into battle, since they were unwillingly risking their lives for the aggrandizement and power of a despotic conqueror. In contrast, the Greeks were citizen-soldiers who at Marathon ran into battle and at Thermopylae chose to remain at their post even though they knew that they would die. In his description of the final battle at Thermopylae, Herodotus contrasts the outmanned Spartans, making one last charge beyond the defensive wall, with the Persian soldiers whose captains, "armed with whips, urged their men forward with continual blows."[11]

The moral drawn by Herodotus and the other Greeks is clear: free men make better warriors, for they are citizen-soldiers fighting for themselves and their families and property rather than to further the schemes of big-men or elites. In the fourth century Isocrates attributed Persian military failure to the engrained slavishness created by autocracy: "Because they are subject to one man's power, they keep their souls in a state of abject and cringing fear, parading themselves at the door of the royal palace, prostrating themselves, and in every way schooling themselves to humility of spirit." Consequently, the Persians have become a "mob" that has "lost all stamina for war and has been trained more effectively for servitude than are the slaves in our country."[12] The Greeks, on the other hand, have been bred by their political freedom for independence and self-reliance. Herodotus connects the Athenians' military prowess to their freedom, a "noble thing," for "while they [the Athenians] were oppressed under a despotic government, they had no better success at war than any of their neighbours, yet, once the yoke was flung off, they proved the finest fighters in the world."[13]

The military success of the Greeks, then, was attributed to their fierce love of freedom, which defined their ethnic uniqueness. The Athenians particularly were esteemed in this regard, since they bore the brunt of the fighting at Marathon, and ten years later, during Xerxes' invasion, suffered the most when they had to evacuate their city and watch it go up in flames. Herodotus concludes that "Greece was saved by the Athenians ... who, having chosen that Greece should live and preserve her freedom, roused to battle the other Greek states which had not yet submitted."[14] This view of the Athenian achievement in fighting for the freedom of all the Greeks reappears throughout the fifth century, turning up even in some fragments of a song by Pindar, who was from oligarchic Thebes, Athens' traditional enemy. His apostrophizing of Athens as the "bulwark of Hellas" that "laid the bright foundation of Liberty" earned him ten thousand drachmae from the Athenians—and a thousand-drachmae fine from his peeved native city.[15] Decades later Isocrates, indulging what by then was a cliché, would likewise commend the Athenians, who "chose to see their city ravaged rather than enslaved"; hence they left "their own country and adopt[ed] Freedom as their fatherland."[16]

While Athenians were often singled out, the *Persians* of Aeschylus stresses that *all* the Greeks fought the Persians to preserve their civic freedom. Here, Xerxes' mother tells the chorus of a troubling dream in which her son yokes and bridles two women, one Persian, the other Greek, to a chariot. "And one [the Persian], so arrayed, towers / Proud, her mouth obedient to the reins; / But the other stamps, annoyed, and rends apart / Her trappings in her hands; unbridled, seizes / The car and snaps its yoke in two; / My son falls."[17] When the messenger describes to Xerxes the naval battle at Salamis, he sends his captains into battle with the threat that if the Greeks slip away, "all your heads / Will roll. I warrant it." In contrast, the Greeks row into battle with the cry "O Greek / Sons, advance! Free your fathers' land, / Free your sons, your wives, the sanctuaries / Of paternal gods."[18] By the late fifth century, their definition of themselves as uniquely free in contrast to the enslaved barbarians had become a piece of received wisdom, repeated even by Persians. When Cyrus, pretender to the Persian throne, addressed the Greek mercenaries before the battle of Cunaxa (401), he asked them to "show yourselves worthy of the freedom which you have won and which I think you happy in possessing."[19]

THE GREEKS DERIVED THEIR FREEDOM from consensual government—the laws, institutions and offices that protected the individual citizen's autonomy, whether citizenship was narrowly defined, as in Sparta, or broadly, as in Athens. In Herodotus, Demaratus identifies law as the condition of Sparta's freedom. "For they [the Spartans] are free, yes," he explains to Xerxes, "but not entirely free; for they have a master, and that master is Law, which they fear much more than your subjects fear you."[20] Aeschylus in the *Suppliant*

Maidens (470) connects freedom to the Assembly's right to vote on decrees. The refusal of Pelasgus, King of Argos, to give the daughters of Danaus back to their Egyptian husbands has been ratified by the citizens who debated the question openly and voted. "You hear [the decision] announced by the tongue of freedom's voice," the king tells the Egyptian herald.[21] Similarly, Theseus' encomium to Athenian democracy in Euripides' *Suppliant Women* links freedom to the right to hold office: "This city is free, and ruled by no one man. / The people reign, in annual succession."[22] Whether in the Spartan oligarchy or the Athenian democracy, "civic" freedom derived from laws and the "constitution" that set out the procedures and protocols of governance by citizens, in contrast to the autocracies in which a king or a tiny elite ruled in their own interests. Thus Plato in the *Laws* says that one of the lawgiver's goals should be "that the city for which he legislates should be free."[23]

Aristotle defines the state as a "community of freemen.[24] And throughout Greek thought, freedom is joined to democracy. "The end [goal, purpose] of democracy is freedom," says Aristotle.[25] Democratic freedom in turn is linked to equality, specifically an equal right to rule. "For if liberty and equality are chiefly to be found in democracy," Aristotle writes in the *Politics,* "they will be best attained when all persons alike share in the government to the utmost."[26] Later he elaborates: "Democracy ... arises out of the notion that those who are equal in any respect are equal in all respects; because men are equally free, they claim to be absolutely equal."[27] As we shall see, the critics of democracy make its obsession with personal freedom and absolute equality the starting point of their attacks.

The polis most identified with freedom was democratic Athens, which gave its triremes names like *Dêmokratia* and *Eleutheria* (freedom) and *Parrhêsia* (free speech), and whose citizens worshipped a deified Democracy and Freedom, the latter as part of the cult of Zeus Eleutherios (Zeus the Liberator).[28] Freedom in Athens included not only the citizen's freedom to participate in governing, but also personal freedom, the liberty to live as one likes. Aristotle's description of democracy lists, after equality and majority rule, the principle that "a man should live as he likes. This, they say, is the mark of liberty, since, on the other hand, not to live as a man likes is the mark of a slave."[29] The most famous expression of this ideal is found in Pericles' funeral speech as recorded by Thucydides. "The freedom which we enjoy in our government extends also to our ordinary life," says Pericles. "There, far from exercising a jealous surveillance over each other, we do not feel called upon to be angry with our neighbor for doing what he likes." At Athens, he adds, "we live exactly as we please."[30] That this personal freedom was a cherished ideal of the Athenians is suggested by the fact that the general Nicias, when exhorting his men before a critical naval encounter during the doomed Athenian expedition to Syracuse, "reminded them of their country, the freest of the free, and of the unfettered discretion allowed to all in it to live as they pleased."[31] Freedom in private life became a stock attribute of democracy; as Demosthenes reminds his audience in his orations, they prefer to live in a democracy because life there is more "easy-going" and the "private station is more secure and free from risk."[32]

An important freedom that pertained both to personal and to political life was freedom of speech. "Free men have free tongues," as Sophocles puts it.[33] Politically, this meant *isêgoria,* the right of a citizen to address the Assembly. Theseus' praise of Athenian democracy in *The Suppliant Women* quotes the formula that opened the Assembly, the invitation to any citizen to speak before his fellows: "This is the call of freedom: / 'What man has good advice to give the city, / And wishes to make it known?' "[34] Indeed, when Herodotus links Athenian military prowess to political freedom, the word he uses is *isêgoria,* for political equality and freedom of speech are two sides of the same democratic coin.

Throughout Greek literature, democratic freedom and equality are linked to the equal right to engage in political speech, particularly in Athens. In a fragment from his lost play *The Golden Race* (420), the comic poet Eupolis praises Athens as the first city to institute equality of speech as a political ideal.[35] Demosthenes warns his audience to beware any attempt to subvert a citizen's right to justice, any action "robbing us of our liberties and of our right of free speech."[36] Clearly, in Athens the right of free and equal political speech lay at the heart of political freedom and justice, and constituted one of the essential attributes of citizenship. That is why Aeschylus has the Persian chorus, after they hear of Xerxes' defeat at Salamis, comment that "No longer is the tongue / imprisoned kept, but loose are men, / When loose the yoke of power's bound, / To bawl their liberty."[37]

In addition to political free speech, the Athenians prized freedom of expression in general, what they called *parrhêsia.* Several passages in Euripides celebrate this freedom as an aspect of Athenian democracy. Phaedra in the *Hippolytus* wishes for her husband and children a "rich and glorious life in Athens ... [and] freedom in word and deed."[38] Ion, a foundling who learns that his father is Athenian, hopes his mother is Athenian too so that he will be an Athenian citizen and "have rights of speech."[39] As these passages from Euripides suggest, *parrhêsia* shades into the political right to address the city and contribute to its deliberations. In Aristophanes' fantasy *Women at the Thesmophoria,* the all-female political organization proclaims that all freeborn women have the right to make speeches *(parrhêsia).*[40] Given that so much of Athenian life was much more public, literally "political," than we are used to, it is understandable that the terms *parrhêsia* and *isêgoria* would overlap.

Another remarkable example of the Athenian devotion to free expression is the incredible liberty granted to the dramatists, particularly the writers of comedy, who were free to criticize, often quite viciously, every aspect of public life, from politics to philosophy to drama itself. The productions of tragedy and comedy were public affairs subsidized by the state, overseen by state officers, and judged by fellow citizens, who awarded prizes to plays that in most ancient (and many modern) societies would have landed their authors in jail or on the gallows. Yet despite the city's control over production, the dramatist was free not just to address sensitive political issues but to criticize the city and its policies. As we have already seen, several of Euripides' plays produced during the Peloponnesian War contain obvious critical commentaries on the actions of Athens in the war. *The Trojan Women,* a powerful indictment of the cruelty of war and the amoral opportunism of the politicians who benefit from war's suffering, was produced in 415, a mere few months after the Athenians punished the recalcitrant island of Melos by putting all the grown males to death and selling the women and children into slavery.

It is in comedy, however, that we see the most pointed and brutal attacks on corrupt politicians. Many were depicted or mentioned by name on stage and excoriated with any and every charge the playwright could think up, including the most vulgar and obscene accusations. As K. J. Dover notes,

> Of all the men whom we know from historical sources to have achieved political prominence at Athens during the period 445–385, there is not one who is not attacked and ridiculed either in the extant plays of Aristophanes or in the extant citations from the numerous lost plays of the period.... All these leading men, and many minor politicians besides, are uniformly treated by the comic poets as vain, greedy, dishonest and self-seeking; and ... they are represented also as ugly, diseased, prostituted perverts, the sons of whores by foreigners who bribed their way into citizenship.[41]

Any public figure was fair game for caricature and abuse. Socrates was flayed on stage by Aristophanes in the *Clouds* (423), but he just sat and laughed, and even stood up so the audience could see how accurately the mask-maker (actors wore masks) had captured his ugly features. But a certain Poliagros, according to Aelian, hanged himself when given similar treatment.[42]

A favorite target of Aristophanes was Cleon, an ambitious demagogue who arose from humble origins—he was a tanner—to dominate Athens for several years after Pericles died, until his own death at the battle of Amphipolis in 422. According to Thucydides, he was "the most violent man at Athens, and at that time [427] by far the most powerful with The People."[43] The *Constitution of Athens*, usually attributed to Aristotle, makes Cleon the innovator of a new style of blustering oratory, as well as accusing him of harming the state: "[Cleon] seems, more than any one else, to have been the cause of the corruption of the democracy by his wild undertakings; and he was the first to use unseemly shouting and coarse abuse on the Bema [the speaker's platform]."[44] Whether Cleon was in fact as evil as some of our sources suggest, the point is that he was a powerful and influential politician whom Aristophanes mercilessly attacked.

Aristophanes' most sustained attack on Cleon occurs in the *Knights* (424). In this play, produced right after his stunning (and perhaps lucky) success at capturing three hundred Spartan soldiers on the island of Sphacteria, Cleon appears as Paphlagon, the slave of Demos, which is a personification of democracy. This Paphlagon, a name meant to suggest a blustering foreigner, is "a tanner, an arch criminal, and a slanderer" who "crouched before the master [Demos] and started flattering and fawning and toadying and swindling him with odd tidbits of waste leather."[45] The play goes to develop a whole litany of charges against Cleon: he opposed peace in order to continue profiting from the war; he took credit for the victory at Pylos, which was as much or even more the achievement of the other general, Demosthenes; he raised taxes on the rich to buy the political support of the poor; he raised the tribute on the Athenians' allies and accepted bribes from them; he blackmailed citizens by threatening them with litigation. In addition to leveling these and other charges at Cleon, Aristophanes pokes fun at his trade, his oratorical style, and his flattery of the people, with the occasional stock implication of homosexual improprieties thrown in for good measure.[46]

Even more remarkable, perhaps, than the dramatist's public attacks on a powerful politician—something unprecedented in the ancient Mediterranean, and in most of the world today—is Cleon's failure to silence Aristophanes. Apparently Aristophanes attacked Cleon in the lost play the *Babylonians* (426). According to the playwright in the *Acharnians,* produced the next year, "He [Cleon] hauled me before the Council, and slandered me, and tongue-lashed me with lies."[47] The Council, however, did nothing, and Aristophanes was free to go on denouncing Cleon and bragging about it to boot. In the *Acharnians* he said defiantly, "Let Cleon hatch his plots and build his traps against me to his utmost, for Good and Right will be my allies, and never will I be caught behaving toward the city as he does, a coward and a punk-arse."[48] The very next year he wrote the *Knights,* a brutal demolition of Cleon for which he won first prize. The year after that he bragged in the *Clouds,* "I'm the one who hit Cleon in the belly when he was at the height of his power." He then chastised the people for electing Cleon general and advised them to "convict that vulture Cleon of bribery and theft, then clamp his neck in the pillory" so that "everything will turn out better for the city, in spite of your mistake."[49]

It is hard for us, who take for granted a broad latitude in artistic expression enshrined in the First Amendment, to recognize how unusual such freedom was in the ancient world. For a citizen publicly to humiliate and castigate a powerful leader with impunity was literally unheard of, perhaps aside from the Old Testament prophets. Moreover, the abuse was not just coarse humor but pointed political speech, as Aristophanes himself makes clear in the *Acharnians.* "But listen," his chorus leader advised the audience, "don't you ever let him [Aristophanes] go, for he'll keep on making comedy of what's right. He promises to give you plenty of fine direction, so that you'll enjoy good fortune, and not to flatter or dangle bribes or bamboozle you, nor play the villain or butter you up, but to give you only the best direction."[50] Not, perhaps, until the eighteenth-century American constitutional debates would the role of free speech in protecting democratic freedom be more clearly articulated. No wonder the Cynic Diogenes, when asked what the most beautiful thing in the world was, answered "freedom of speech."[51]

In addition to civic and personal freedom, the Greeks developed an idea of "philosophical" freedom, an "internal" freedom that characterizes the rational, well-ordered soul and is not dependent on the status of the body. We have already touched on this ideal of personal autonomy in the discussion of slavery. There, bondage was a metaphor for the soul ruled by passion and appetite, while true freedom was the condition of the soul ruled by reason. If the passions and pleasures of the body are "slavish," as many philosophers say, then the rational control of passion creates the only true freedom; for rather than being driven blindly by the never-ending demands of appetite, reason freely chooses what is best for the soul. "Do you think," Xenophon's Socrates asks his interlocutor Euthydemus, "that the man is free who is ruled by bodily pleasures and is unable to do what is best because of them?" Euthydemus replies correctly, "By no means."[52] True freedom lies not in doing as one likes, or even in enjoying political rights, but in living a temperate, autonomous life that avoids the pain and disorder of the irrational.

In the Hellenistic philosophies of the fourth century and later, the focus on the individual's freedom was sharpened by the decline of the polis and the decreasing value of "civic" freedom, culminating in the Macedonian hegemony over the Greek city-states.

Epicureanism was a materialist philosophy that reduced all existence to the random movement of atoms. Pleasure was good, pain evil, and happiness resulted from a rational calculation of the proportionate quanta of pain and pleasure in any action or choice. The good life was one of self-sufficiency and rational activity fostered by withdrawal from a random world of pain and disorder. "The greatest fruit of self-sufficiency," Epicurus states, "is freedom."[53] To be free is to avoid politics and business and anything that compromises one's self-sufficiency and autonomy or subjects one to a material world whose blind laws and indifferent gods care nothing for human happiness. According to Epicurus, "We must liberate ourselves from the prison of routine business and politics."[54] Psychic calm and self-sufficiency make the soul free, not participation in government or civic life, and this mental autonomy depends on the cultivation of reason. Hence, as Epicurus says, "You must be a slave to philosophy in order to achieve true liberty."[55]

In contrast to Epicurus' doctrine of withdrawal, Stoic freedom was found in conformity to a nature ordered by and expressive of a divine reason in which humans share as rational creatures. Since each man is a part of this great whole, he is designed to fit in with it and fulfill his role in that providential order. If he can consciously understand that he is subordinated to this larger moral and rational order, he can make rational choices and perform actions appropriate to his position and in accordance with "nature." In the words of Diogenes Laertius, "When reason by way of more perfect leadership has been bestowed on the beings we call rational, for them life according to reason rightly becomes the natural life."[56] This is what it means "to live virtuously," which is the "proper function" of a human being. He will thus engage the world socially and politically, since his attitude toward that engagement, rather than the vagaries of his experience, is what counts. He will then enjoy true freedom, a freedom that cannot be compromised by shifts in fortune, since all these are mere parts of the greater divine plan that aims at the good of the whole—"the right reason which pervades all things."[57]

The person, then, who can achieve this unity of choice with "nature," including both the providentially ordered cosmos and his own true identity, will be "wise" and free. According to Diogenes Laertius, Stoics "declare that he [the wise man] alone is free and bad men are slaves, freedom being power of independent action, whereas slavery is privation of the same."[58] Freedom comes from choices made in accord with a cosmic rational and moral order and conducive to their goal, which is good. The idea that freedom for the individual derives from his subordination to a greater good, particularly after it was Christianized, would have a powerful impact on Western thought.

Finally, a radical idea of personal freedom was advanced by the Cynics, who predicated happiness and freedom on a return to a simple nature that an artificial and arbitrary human social and political organization had distorted. One should "live like a dog"—hence the name Cynic, from the Greek word for "dog." The most famous Cynic, Diogenes, was a contemporary of Plato and Alexander. Diogenes Laertius summarizes Diogenes the Cynic's life and philosophy thus: "He allow[ed] convention no such authority as he allowed natural right, and assert[ed] that the manner of life he lived was the same as that of Heracles when he preferred liberty to everything."[59] Thus Diogenes lived in a tub, wore only a loin-cloth, and threw away his cup and bowl when he noticed one child drinking from cupped hands and another using bread to scoop up lentils.[60] To the Cynics, only by stripping away all the artificial demands and customs and goods of social and political life could one achieve true freedom and self-sufficiency. Even the important virtue of shame was rejected as conventional and artificial; Diogenes advocated not just eating and urinating in public, but sex and masturbation as well; and when someone once chastised him for masturbating in public, he replied that he wished hunger could be as easily relieved by rubbing one's stomach.[61]

The philosophical concern with freedom as a good of the individual's soul rather than of the body contributed enormously to the growth of individualism and humanism. Once the freedom of the individual and his mind apart from government and society became a good, and once all humans were universally defined as capable and worthy of freedom because of their rationality and natural affinity with one another, the door was open to the development of the ideal we embrace and perhaps abuse today: that all people should be free from external constraints that shape or limit how they think and develop as human beings.

As remarkable as the Greeks' discovery of freedom was, perhaps equally significant is their criticism of its excesses and limitations. The fifth-century transformation of the Athenians from the saviors to the enslavers of their fellow Greeks through the creation of the Athenian Empire, followed by Athens' defeat at the hands of oligarchic Sparta, seemed to offer proof to some writers that the freedom and equality promoted by democracy could only degenerate into a self-destructive greed and self-aggrandizement. The irrational appetites of the many, validated and given political scope by democratic institutions, appeared to trump the more sober wisdom of the few.

The idea of personal freedom, the liberty to live as one likes, came under attack for validating egocentric license and indulgence of appetites to the detriment of the body politic. Plato was the severest critic of such freedom, which he examined under a harsh light in the *Republic*. The essence of democratic man, Socrates says, is freedom. "Are they not free," he rhetorically asks of men in democracies, "and is not the city full of freedom and frankness [*parrhêsias*]—a man may say and do what he likes ... [and] the individual is clearly able to order for himself his own life as he pleases?" The result of such freedom, however, is social and political confusion, as all manner of men, even criminals, are equally free, no matter how sorry their character is. What Plato calls the "forgiving spirit" of democracy, its unconcern with ability or talent or character, means that any sort of man can acquire power. Democracy "never giv[es] a thought to the pursuits which make a statesman, and promot[es] to honour any one who professes to be the people's friend." The result is "variety and disorder," along with a "sort of equality to equals and unequals alike."[62]

Socrates then details the impact of such a regime on the character of its citizens. They will be fickle and shallow, dominated by their appetites and whims. Untrained in self-control and temperance—since democracy's ideal of "doing as one likes," legitimized and exploited by demagogues, militates against such restraints on the individual's desires—democratic man's soul will be filled with evils rechristened as goods: "Insolence they term breeding, and anarchy liberty, and waste magnificence, and impudence courage." The result will be a man given over to "the freedom and libertinism of useless and unnecessary pleasures."[63]

This spirit of license will intensify, Socrates continues, and corrupt all authority and break down distinctions between citizen and resident alien, father and son, husband and wife, free and slave, until even the "horses and asses have a way of marching along with all the rights and dignities of freemen; and they will run at any body who comes in their way if he does not leave the road clear for them: and all things are just ready to burst with liberty." The ultimate, and paradoxical, result of such anarchic freedom will be the slavery of tyranny, after the people, drunk on the "strong wine of freedom" and scornful of the good advice of their betters, sell their political birthright to whatever demagogue promises to suppress the better men and leave the people's appetites and passions unfettered.[64]

Plato's analysis is based on a conservative, even pessimistic view of human nature as subject to overpowering appetites and passions in need of constant vigilance and external social and political constraints. These limitations, moreover, must be enforced by men of proven superior moral character and values, both of which are necessarily confined to an elite who possess them either by birth or, as Plato argues, by superior education. Aristotle agrees that absolute freedom for the masses is dangerous: "Where absolute freedom is allowed there is nothing to restrain the evil which is inherent in every man."[65] Other critics of democracy make much the same point. The so-called Old Oligarch notes that Athens favors the "poor, the popular, and the base," even though "among the people there is a maximum of ignorance, disorder, and wickedness." This paradox, however, actually makes sense, since the people "do not want a good government under which they themselves are slaves; they want to be free and to rule. Bad government is of little concern to them."[66]

Isocrates likewise criticizes Athenian radical democracy for encouraging license and undermining traditional values. Praising the more limited democracy of Solon and Cleisthenes, he contrasts it with the radical democracy of the late fifth century, which led to the terrorism of the Thirty Tyrants, the rightist junta installed by Sparta after Athens' defeat in 404. In the radical democracy the citizens "looked upon insolence as democracy, lawlessness as liberty, impudence of speech as equality, and license to do what they pleased as happiness."[67] Isocrates attributes this degeneration to the principle of mere arithmetical equality and the filling of office by lot, which ignore the differences in character and talent and virtue that actually exist among people.

To its critics, democracy at its most extreme promotes radical individualism, which in turn fosters an amoral relativism with power and pleasure the only goods, to be pursued and acquired by any means possible. Plato has left us several portraits of men who took the ethical pluralism of the moderate Sophists to an extreme of relativism: good and evil are meaningless, arbitrary cultural conventions which can be ignored by the superman, who obeys the law of nature that says the strong deserve to rule and exploit the weak.

Callicles in the *Gorgias* is perhaps Plato's best portrait of this sort of man. Scorning Socrates' contention that doing evil and getting away with it is worse than suffering evil, Callicles counters that since everybody is naturally driven by self-interest, the weaker band together and make laws and enforce conventions like "shame" and "justice" in order to "terrify the stronger sort of men, and those who are able to get the better of them, in order that they may not get the better of them." Thus the many say "dishonesty is shameful and unjust" to keep the stronger from acquiring more power:

> And therefore the endeavour to have more than the many, is conventionally said to be shameful and unjust, and is called injustice, whereas nature herself intimates that it is just for the better to have more than the worse, the more powerful than the weaker; and in many ways she shows, among men as well as among animals, and indeed among whole cities and races, that justice consists in the superior ruling over and having more than the inferior.[68]

To Plato, writing in the aftermath of the Thirty Tyrants and Socrates' execution in 399, Athenian democracy necessarily leads to this sort of frightening ethic, which celebrates what Callicles calls the man "with a nature of sufficient force" who "tramples underfoot our codes and juggleries, our charms and 'laws,' which are all against nature."[69] Democracy's ideal of individual freedom and absolute equality runs counter to the fact of human inequality and inherent depravity. Radical egalitarianism can be realized only at the level of appetite, which is amoral and insatiable and sees no good other than its own fulfillment. Thus Callicles represents the logical end of the democratic ideal: a return to the law of the jungle, and the destruction of democracy itself in tyranny.

Thucydides seems to agree with Plato that radical democracy must lend itself to the ethic of "might makes right," as shown in his stark representation of the Athenians' behavior toward the Melians. When in 416 B.C. the Athenians attacked the Spartans' ally Melos, their ambassadors curtly dismissed any talk of principle, "since you know as well as we do that right, as the world goes, is only in question between equals in power, while the strong do what they can and the weak suffer what they must." Even the gods approved of this "necessary law." Thus the only course for the Melians was to submit and lose their independence, becoming subjects of Athens—which they refused to do. A short time later, however, they capitulated, and the Athenians "put to death all the grown men whom they took, and sold the women and children for slaves."[70]

The democratic ideal of free speech likewise came under attack. When Plato described the democratic city as full of "frankness," he exploited the double meaning of *parrhêsia* as both "free speech" and "outspokenness." Much of the criticism focused on the debates in the Assembly, where all citizens had the right to speak. We have seen the denunciation of political deliberation that Thucydides puts in the mouth of Cleon: the idea that free speech degenerates into an emotional spectacle or a contest in which the clever manipulator of rhetoric can gull the ignorant masses, who lack the intellectual ability to judge the content of a speech adequately. To the Old Oligarch, the principle of free and equal speech even for the "worst people" is vital to democracy's goal of absolute freedom and equality for the masses; "For if the good men were to speak and make policy, it would be splendid for the likes of themselves but not so for the men of the people." Thus even a bad man can address the Assembly, for the people know that "this man's ignorance, baseness, and favour are more profitable than the good man's virtue, wisdom, and ill will."[71]

Isocrates complains that free speech, or rather "impudence of speech" (*parrhêsia*), has been glorified as "equality." In various orations he spotlights the abuse of free political speech. In *On the Peace* (mid-fourth century) he tells the Athenians, "There exists no 'free speech,' except that which is enjoyed in the assembly by the most reckless orators, who care nothing for your welfare."[72] Obviously he exaggerates, since by making this statement he refutes it. However, his point is that genuine free speech, which is useful and honest, is unlikely to please the masses. In his earlier, frankly pro-monarchical *Nicocles,* he criticizes the wrangling that takes place in the Assembly because of the orators. And in the *Panatheniacus,* he laments the self-serving verbal contests of the orators, the majority of whom "have the audacity to harangue the people, not for the good of the state, but for what they themselves expect to gain."[73]

To democracy's critics, free speech is useless if those speaking and listening do not have the intelligence or virtue or education to know what to say and when to say it—qualities considered the possessions of the few, not the many. As the philosopher Democritus says, "Freedom of speech is the sign of freedom; but the danger lies in discerning the right occasion."[74] Lacking that intelligence and discernment, the many will be dupes of the clever speakers who exploit their ignorance and passions. Plato makes this point when the character of Gorgias, a radical Sophist like Callicles, praises the power of rhetoric. "What is there greater than the word which persuades the judges in the courts or the senators in the council, or the citizens in the assembly, or at any other political meeting?—if you have the power of uttering this word," says Gorgias, you can make your fellow citizen your "slave" who will "gather treasures, not for himself, but for you who are able to speak and to persuade the multitude."[75] The dependence of a democracy on free and open speech among citizens leaves it vulnerable to the clever speakers who can bend the masses to their will.

DESPITE OUR DEBT TO THE GREEKS for our ideals of freedom, we should recognize the significant differences between their view of freedom and our own. For one thing, the political freedom praised by the Greeks, whether Spartan oligarchs or Athenian democrats, was not considered a good that all people deserved. Greeks owned other Greeks as slaves, and political freedom was limited to the minority of males who were citizens. Sparta kept perhaps a quarter of a million fellow Greeks relentlessly subordinated as helots, serfs forced to labor in order to support the small number of Spartan "similars" *(homoioi)*. And Spartan citizens themselves, their lives regulated in every detail by the state and its laws, had little of the personal freedom the Athenians enjoyed.

Even the greatest champions of political and personal freedom, the Athenians, had no compunctions about taking away the liberty of the various city-states they subjected. Indeed, the rhetoric of freedom and slavery used to describe the Greek struggle against the Persians was later employed by Spartans to describe their own fight with the Athenians. And even the Athenians frankly admitted that their empire was a "tyranny," which to the Greeks was the epitome of political slavery.[76] The speech of the Melian ambassadors in Thucydides when they refused to submit to the Athenians recalls the Athenian response to the Persians in Herodotus. "We will not," the Melians reply, "deprive of freedom a city that has been inhabited these seven hundred years."[77] After Athens' defeat, the Spartans were proclaimed the liberators of their fellow Greeks, much as the Athenians had been celebrated for delivering all the Greeks from the Persians.[78]

Whereas we define freedom as an inalienable right of *all* humans, the Greeks more parochially linked freedom to particular kinds of political organization, usually their own city-state's. Spartan freedom was not the same thing as Athenian, though both starkly contrasted with barbarian enslavement to despots.

We moderns have also defined freedom in individualistic terms, as the personal freedom to "do as we like" without limit or check. We seek absolute personal liberation from everything that might limit our desires and compromise our happiness, even including the mortal limitations—sickness, hunger, failure, the consequences of our bad decisions, time, old age and death—that have always circumscribed human life. In contrast, the tragic vision of the Greeks recognized that these natural constraints were the non-negotiable bounds of our freedom.

Greek literature is famous for its memorable expressions of the tragic vision. "As is the generation of leaves, so is that of humanity," wrote Homer.[79] "The dream of a shadow is man, no more,"

Pindar sang.[80] The early-fifth-century poet Simonides wrote that "Men's strength is slight, their plans impossible; within their brief lifetime toil upon toil; and death hangs inescapable over all alike; of death an equal portion is allotted to good men and to bad."[81] In tragedy especially, the aspirations and free choices of heroes lead ultimately to their suffering and death. Prometheus, Antigone, Oedipus, Ajax, Hippolytus, Pentheus all find their plans and actions colliding with the vagaries of time and chance, fate, the caprice of the gods, the restrictions of society, and the disorder of their own and others' passions. We admire their courage in the face of these limits and their willingness freely to defy them, exercising the most fundamental human freedom: to choose to die in service to their vision. But in the end we shudder at the spectacle of the suffering they leave in their wake. In tragedy, our freedom, however admirable and precious, is usually the freedom to fail gloriously, to suffer, and to die.

More practically, political freedom among the Greeks was both supported and circumscribed by the view that humans are "political animals." Human identity was dependent on participation in a particular political community, in contrast to the modern belief that private individuals develop their identities in opposition to society, insulated from the power of government. Aristotle gives a good summary of the importance of the state in constituting people's identity: "Neither must we suppose that anyone of the citizens belongs to himself, for they all belong to the state, and are each of them a part of the state, and the care of each part is inseparable from the care of the whole."[82] Plato is more extreme on this topic: "He who imagines that he can give laws for the public conduct of states, while he leaves the private life of citizens wholly to take care of itself; who thinks that individuals may pass the day as they please, and that there is no necessity of order in all things . . . who gives up the control of their private lives, and supposes that they will conform to law in their common and public life, is making a great mistake."[83] Thus Plato's utopias posit a nearly totalitarian control over every aspect of private life, in order that citizens be molded to serve the interests and the good of the state, upon which the flourishing of each person depends.

Both Plato and Aristotle admired Sparta for precisely this detailed organization of private life to further the virtue and good of the state. Demaratus said the Spartans were free only because they were subject to the law. But even in Athens, where personal freedom was most exalted, an active political life was seen as a necessary good for human fulfillment. In lauding Athenian personal freedom, Pericles points out nonetheless that "unlike any other nation, we regard the citizen who takes no part in these [political] duties not as unambitious but as useless."[84]

Indeed, Athens exerted control over its citizens' lives in ways that we today would consider to be intolerable encroachments on private life. All citizen males were liable for two years of military service when they turned eighteen. Rich people were subjected to "liturgies," that is, compulsory financing of a ship, a lyric or dramatic chorus, or religious festivals. All religious festivals and rituals, as well as athletic games, musical contests, and dramatic performances, were managed, supervised, and judged by state officers. Legitimate marriage was limited to Athenian citizens, and only children of legitimate marriages could inherit property, become citizens, and enjoy all the rights and privileges attendant on that status, including participation in religious festivals. Complex rules governed who should marry an "heiress," a girl whose family had no legitimate male heir to inherit the property. Laws against adultery prescribed public punishments for the adulterous woman and the husband who refused to divorce her. As Cynthia Patterson says, in a recent survey of the polis' interest in private life, "All these regulations emphasize the public and political interest in the integrity—economic, moral, sexual—of the polis' constituent households as essential to the stability of the polis as a whole."[85]

Citizens who participated in political life were particularly subjected to public civic control and oversight. The politically active were easy targets. Demosthenes, in the passage quoted above praising the tranquillity of private life, contrasts it with that of the politician, "precarious, open to attack, and full of trials and misfortunes every day."[86] So too Isocrates, no doubt exaggerating, claims that "no one may rely on the honesty of his life as a guarantee that he will be able to live securely in Athens."[87] As we saw earlier, public officials underwent extensive auditing, not just by the Council but also by private citizens who "may lay an information against any magistrate they please for not obeying the laws."[88] Politically active citizens were subject to other sorts of control, the strangest perhaps being ostracism, the exile for ten years of any citizen whose only offense was to have been unpopular with at least six thousand of his fellow citizens who wrote his name on pottery shards.

There were other, less drastic restrictions. Areopagites—magistrates responsible for trying cases of deliberate homicide, wounding, and arson—were forbidden to write comedies and eat in taverns.[89] Male citizens who had sold their bodies to other men for sex, who had beaten or neglected their parents, who had avoided military service or had run away in battle, or who had squandered their patrimony were all forbidden to address fellow citizens and perforce denied any political life.[90] Given the high level of citizen participation in Athenian politics, this level of oversight meant that many people in Athens were subjected to governmental intrusions in their lives well beyond the scrutiny of candidates and officials we practice and bemoan today.

The much-praised Athenian love of free speech was also limited by formal and informal restrictions. The mid-fourth-century orator Aeschines, besides referring to laws regulating who could address the Assembly, quotes other statutes that controlled speaking: evading the subject at issue, speaking on several propositions simultaneously, speaking twice on the same subject on the same day, being abusive or slanderous, speaking out of turn, interrupting others, shouting approval—all earned a hefty fine.[91] More informal methods for controlling debate seem to have existed as well. Speaking ineptly could get one dragged physically from the platform. Xenophon mentions Glaucon, an aspiring orator who, though not even twenty years old, attempted to address the Assembly, "and none of his friends or relations could check him, though he would get himself dragged from the platform and make himself a laughing-stock."[92] Plato's Socrates refers to the same rough treatment: if anyone tries to advise the Assembly on matters of which he knows nothing, the citizens "will not listen to him, but laugh and hoot at him, until either he is clamoured down and retires himself; or if he persist, he is dragged away or put out by the constables."[93]

Despite these restrictions of political speech, however, the Athenians still enjoyed a freedom of individual expression remarkable for their time, even among the free Greek city-states. Drama, especially comedy, continued to be relatively unrestricted. Even Jacob Burckhardt—who in his nineteenth-century lectures on the Greeks asserted implausibly that in Athens "the absence of individual freedom went hand in hand with the omnipotence of the State in every context"—nonetheless was compelled to admit that the freedom of the comic poets was "astonishing."[94] When Isocrates says that free speech does not exist at Athens, he excepts demagogues—and comic poets.[95] Intellectual freedom particularly remained unfettered, as long as inquiry did not directly threaten the state.

Even given that restriction, the cases of persecution of intellectuals were few.[96] Socrates is the most famous example, of course, but the historical circumstances of his trial were singular: Athens had just lost a long, bitter war against an enemy with whom many right-wing Athenians sympathized. A junta of anti-democratic thugs—the so-called Thirty Tyrants—had just recently been violently expelled. Several of the Thirty had been followers of Socrates, who was, moreover, frankly anti-democratic, and who had stayed behind in Athens when the democrats went into exile during the reign of the Thirty. Moreover, even in Plato's sympathetic reconstruction of Socrates' defense speech it is clear that the philosopher goes out of his way to bait the several hundred jurymen into first convicting him and then imposing the death penalty. Even so, had a mere 30 of the 501 jurymen voted the other way, Socrates would have been acquitted. Finally, the Athenians quickly regretted this violation of their civic ethics; according to Diogenes Laertius, they closed down the wrestling schools and gymnasia, put up a statue to Socrates, banished the accusers, and put one of them, Meletus, to death.[97] Socrates, who publicly examined and humiliated his fellow citizens for decades, turns out to be the exception that proves the rule of Athenian tolerance for intellectual activity.

DESPITE THESE DIFFERENCES, HOWEVER, the freedom we enjoy and prize today, a freedom underwritten and legitimized by the state and its laws, has its distant roots among the Greek city-states. As Richard Mulgan notes, in an essay careful to detail the differences between ancient Greek freedom and modern conceptions, "In the final sum, perhaps the similarities [between ancient and modern conceptions of freedom] are more important and more in need of historical explanation; the original emergence of any recognizable conception of freedom remains an overwhelming and mysterious event in the history of ideas."[98] Whatever the reasons for the appearance of liberty in ancient Greece, all who today aspire to personal and political freedom—and all of us who take both for granted—owe a debt of gratitude to the Greeks, especially the Athenians who, when reminded of the immense power the Persian king had arrayed against them, answered with words similar to those of the Spartans who would soon become their enemies: "Such is our love of freedom, that we will defend ourselves in whatever way we can."[99]

> What [the Greeks] did and suffered, they appear to have done and suffered *freely*, and thus differently from earlier races. They seem original, spontaneous and conscious, in circumstances in which all others were ruled by a more or less mindless necessity. This is why in their creativeness and their potentialities they seem the representatives of genius on earth, with all the failings and sufferings that this entails. In the life of the mind they reached frontiers which the rest of mankind cannot permit themselves to fall short of, at least in their attempts to acknowledge and to profit, even when they are inferior to the Greeks in the capacity for achievement. It is for this reason that posterity needs to study the Greeks; if we ignore them we are simply accepting our own decline.
>
> —*Jacob Burckhardt*[1]

CONCLUSION

The Critical Spirit

THROUGHOUT THIS BOOK, we have returned over and over to one unique characteristic of the Greeks that more than anything else explains their innovative brilliance: the "critical spirit," the way they made everything they encountered an object of thought to be discussed and analyzed free from the constraints of religion and government. This self-consciousness about human life, this power of abstraction is at best only implicit elsewhere in the ancient world. Only the Greeks made rational discrimination and "criticism" explicit. Their curiosity, their relentless questioning, their drive to explain human existence rationally and coherently and to find meaning in experience, are the starting point for all the other intellectual achievements we attribute to them: logic, physics, criticism, history, philosophy, rhetoric, dialectic, dialogue, tragedy, analysis, the "ologies" that so distressed Dickens' Mrs. Grandgrind—all are Greek words, all are formalized expressions of this fundamental quality we can call "critical self-consciousness." Without it, humans remain the slaves of "necessity": nature, supernatural forces, the dead hand of tradition, and the brute power of various elites.

This critical curiosity in Greek culture is related to what Jean Pierre Vernant calls the "extraordinary preeminence of speech over all other instruments of power."[2] Most of Greek intellectual life, including politics, was carried on verbally in the open, sunlit spaces of the city: in the market, the amphitheater, the porticoes, the gymnasia, and the Pnyx, the hill where the Assembly met. Open dialogue, debate, argumentation—all were critical in carrying on the search for truth and value and meaning. We see the high value placed on public discussion in the words of the Cynic philosopher Antisthenes, who praises leisure because "I can go and see whatever is worth seeing, and hear whatever is worth hearing."[3] Antisthenes' mentor Socrates preferred speech to the beauties of nature that many of us now consider a source of enlightenment. "I am a lover of knowledge," he said, "and the men who dwell in cities are my teachers, and not the trees or the country."[4]

Discussion—the word in Greek suggests more strongly the idea of analytic "sorting"—is vital for critical consciousness. In discussion, ideas are worked over and subjected to criticism and analysis, compelling their advocates to make a public and coherent defense. Thus Socrates says to Euthydemus, "The very word 'discussion' [*dialegesthai*] . . . owes its name to the practice of meeting together for common deliberation, *sorting, discussing* things after their kind: and therefore one should be ready and prepared for this and be zealous for it."[5]

Critical consciousness and its public expression were what most differentiated the Greeks from their neighbors, even when their own actual behavior was typical of other ancient peoples. All humans are sexual, but only the Greeks thought through so completely the meaning and implications of our sexuality. All societies in the ancient world kept slaves, but only a Greek said, "Nature created no one a slave"—or, like Aristotle, attempted to construct a theory justifying the institution. All ancients subjected women to subordinate roles and limited their lives, but only the Greeks put on the public stage intelligent, courageous, magnificent women who more often than not morally dwarfed the petty men around them, and who made trenchant commentaries on their unfair treatment, thus making possible a critical review of masculine assumptions and prejudices. Most ancient peoples made war against their neighbors, but only the Greeks publicly sympathized with the suffering of their enemies, as Aeschylus did in the *Persians,* before an audience including many who had fought the Persians or had lost loved ones to them.

Moreover, the distinctive creations of the Greeks—politics, rationalism, and the idea of freedom—were dividends of their critical consciousness. It began by examining human capacities and weaknesses, and then tried to make sense of the world from the context of what Thucydides called "the human thing," all the while respecting the full complexity of our identity, and accepting our own responsibility for life and its meaning instead of cowering before social or natural or supernatural forces. The Greeks, as Matthew Arnold said of Sophocles, "saw life steadily, and saw it whole"; they stood man on his feet, and ever since the world has not looked the same.

Critical consciousness permeates the literature and culture and history of the Greeks, but one man exemplifies it better than any other. Socrates is the prototype of the genuine Western intellectual: the passionately rational seeker of virtue and the Good, of the best life for a human being, at the expense of everything else including his own life.

Socrates lived in Athens during the later fifth century, when the Greek intellectual ferment was concentrated there, the city drawing like a magnet the teachers and philosophers of the whole Greek world. All questions were freely posed and answers freely debated. Plato in his *Protagoras* has left us a charming vignette of the excitement stirred by the arrival of a philosopher, in this instance the Sophist Protagoras; the eager Hippocrates waking Socrates before daybreak to tell him the news and ask him "to speak with him [Protagoras] on my behalf"; and the scene greeting the two when they arrived at the house where Protagoras was staying. As Protagoras and his entourage strolled through the courtyard, Socrates reports with tongue in cheek, "Nothing delighted me more than the precision of their movements: they never got into his way at all; but when he and those who were with him turned back, then the band of listeners parted regularly on either side; he was always in front, and they wheeled round and took their places behind him in perfect order."[6] Socrates immediately engaged the famous Sophist in a discussion, much to the delight of the rapt audience.

Public discussion, debate, and questioning were the essence of Socrates' famous "method." The search for the truth about virtue and goodness had to proceed through a methodical stripping away of all the false opinions a person might have randomly and thoughtlessly picked up from his environment. This procedure was called "dialectic," from the word for "discuss." As we see in the early dialogues of Plato—those most likely recording the historical Socrates' philosophy—dialectic was a dynamic process of question-and-answer in which received wisdom was challenged and analyzed to arrive at the truth of a concept and render an "account" of it, a logically coherent definition that could withstand scrutiny. "Have you ever supposed," Socrates asks in the *Republic,* "that men who could not render and exact an account of opinions in discussion would ever know anything of the things we say must be known?"[7]

Unlike his disciple Plato, however, Socrates did not believe that he could use this process to arrive at the truth; his method usually ended in an *aporia,* a "dead end," at which point Socrates confessed his own ignorance. But dialectic was nonetheless useful for exposing false opinions and muddled thinking, the received wisdom people automatically repeat because that is all they have heard growing up. If we cannot discover what is true, at least we can expose falsehood, and at least we can learn our own limitations and thus heed the injunction of Apollo to "know thyself."

What is significant about Socrates' method, however, is that it looked not to tradition or culture or even the gods, but to rational discussion for the true definition of an idea—even if Socrates in the end claimed he could never arrive at it, and that true wisdom was the purview of the gods alone. In this pursuit he embodies the Greek enlightenment, which made unfettered rational inquiry, rather than the pronouncements of religion or tradition, the royal road to truth.

The objects of the Socratic search for knowledge, moreover, were not the physical world and its laws, though these appear to have interested Socrates in his youth. Rather, he was interested in ethics and politics: how men and cities should live. What is the good for a man or a polis? By what activity do humans, as humans, fulfill themselves and find the happiness suitable for a rational creature? What should be our goals or ends, what should we pursue or shun, what should guide our every action and decision? While he may have heeded the "signs" given by his own "daimon" or private divinity at critical moments, Socrates nonetheless believed that the answers to these questions must be rational, the fruit of an intellectual process, rather than something bestowed by the revelations of mystics or seers or gods.

In the *Apology,* Plato's reconstruction of Socrates' speech defending himself before the jury of Athenian citizens, Socrates summarized his "mission," both its method and its goals:

> While I have life and strength I shall never cease from the practice and teaching of philosophy, exhorting any one whom I meet and saying to him after my manner: You, my friend,—a citizen of the great and mighty and wise city of Athens,—are you not ashamed of heaping up the greatest amount of money and honour and reputation, and caring so little about wisdom and truth and the greatest improvement of the soul, which you never regard or heed at all? And if the person with whom I am arguing, says: Yes, but I do care; then I do not leave him or let him go at once: but I proceed to interrogate and examine and cross-examine him, and if I think that he has no virtue in him, but only says that he has, I reproach him with undervaluing the greater, and overvaluing the less.[8]

The good of human life must be found in those activities unique to humans: actions guided by a rational virtue that fulfills the soul, rather than by the bestial appetites and passions that gratify the body. This search for the Good comprised for Socrates the well-examined and therefore truly human life. "The unexamined life," he famously said, "is not a life worth living for a human being."[9]

Socrates represents as well another unique characteristic of the Western tradition: the individual as dissident who "speaks truth to power" and suffers for it. Implicit in everything we have said about the Greeks is the idea of individualism: the unique, free person whose rational powers of observation and critical inquiry, whose self-consciousness and perception define him as a human being and give his life value. To be sure, as we noted earlier, humans to the Greeks were "political animals," products of and integrated into their particular cultures in ways we modern radical individualists reject. Yet in ancient Greece, for the first time in history and literature we see *individuals:* persons of a psychological depth, complexity, and particularity not to be found anywhere else in the writings of the ancient world. Where else does one find an Achilles, a Themistocles, a Pericles, an Alcibiades, a Sappho, a Lysistrata, an Archilochus, a Medea, a Cleon? And especially a Socrates: a snub-nosed, thick-lipped, bug-eyed, paunchy, usually dirty, somewhat shabby busybody with remarkable charisma and self-possession, who openly scorns the democracy and its tinkers and tanners blustering in the Assembly, and yet who fights bravely in her wars and accepts with equanimity her sentence of death.

The paradox of human identity—the clash of the individual with the society that forms him—though implicit in nearly all of Greek literature from Homer on, is perhaps best embodied in Socrates, the "gadfly" that devotes his life to stinging his beloved but flawed city of Athens into aspirations worthy of her. The intellectual history—and remarkable intellectual dynamism—of the West has in part been the story of all the "opposing selves," to borrow Lionel Trilling's phrase, who stake the claim for the dignity and worth of the free individual despite all the forces—societal, religious, and political—that would suppress him. And Socrates is their patron saint.

TRUE TO THE CRITICAL SPIRIT, THE GREEKS recognized the limits of human reason's power to discover truth and meaning. As we saw earlier, tragedy in particular, with its steady acceptance of all the forces that constrain human aspiration and knowledge, presented on the public stage characters whose human limitations compromised their attempts to know the truth about the world and themselves, or to impose order on the welter of passions as much a part of human identity as the rational mind. Oedipus, the riddle-solver who does not know even his true name; Phaedra, the believer in rational virtue and shame who is consumed with illicit lust; and many other tragic characters all depict in their suffering and passion the limits of reason and critical consciousness.

Euripides' last play, the *Bacchae* (405), gives us a brilliant analysis of just how limited humans are in their desire for knowledge and rational control over themselves and the world. The god Dionysus, who embodies the sheer creative and destructive, yet necessary power of nature, has returned to Thebes, his mortal mother Semele's home, to wreak vengeance on those who reject his worship, particularly the young ruler Pentheus. The king is enraged at the disorder created in the city by the god, and particularly at the women who have abandoned their looms in the household to celebrate the god's mysteries on the mountain.

At the start of the play, the old prophet Teiresias makes a claim for traditional wisdom and customs, which in the audience's home of Athens were right then being scrutinized by the new philosophy:

> We do trifle with divinity.
> No, we are the heirs of customs and traditions
> hallowed by age and handed down to us
> by our fathers. No quibbling logic can topple *them,*
> whatever subtleties this clever age invents.[10]

This speech evokes the fifth century's new intellectuals, the Sophists, who in public discussion and debate used a novel cleverness with language and quibbling logic to undermine traditional wisdom. In response to Pentheus' accusations against him, Teiresias explicitly condemns the "clever speaking" typical of the fifth-century Sophists: "You are glib; your phrases come rolling out / smoothly on the tongue, as though your words were wise / instead of foolish."[11]

After Pentheus goes off to try to capture the god and the women who worship him, the chorus seconds Teiresias' condemnation of the intellectual's knowledge: "And what passes for wisdom is not; / unwise are those who aspire, who outrange the limits of man."[12] Given the brevity of life and the limits on human knowledge, critical consciousness will necessarily learn little of true significance for human life, breeding only an arrogance that will bring on disaster. Pentheus is the case in point: his attempts to control the god, to impose limits on the amoral power of nature, are pathetic failures—the iron chains he puts on the god drop off of their own accord, and the bolted prison door magically swings open. Worse, Pentheus quickly becomes the plaything of the god, who liberates the dark desires lurking deep within the youth. His morbid curiosity about the women's sexual practices as they worship the god is exploited by Dionysus, who so befuddles Pentheus that the youth willingly dresses as a woman and follows the god to the forest. As the god tells Pentheus, "You do not know / the limits of your strength. You do not know / what you do. You do not know who you are."[13]

Like Oedipus, Pentheus is ignorant of what he truly is: not a rational creature who is the product of a civilized social and political order, but rather a welter of chaotic, destructive passions—"Inhuman," as the chorus says, "a rabid beast, / a giant in wildness raging."[14] Pentheus' destruction is suitably, horribly uncivilized: he is dismembered by the women of his own household, including his sisters, his aunt, and his mother, who returns in triumph to Thebes, cradling her son's severed head.

Euripides saw that the Greek enlightenment and the penchant for questioning everything were arrogant and dangerous. Humans as natural beings are bound by necessities—chance, passions, suffering, death—that limit what they can know. I do not believe Euripides suggests that a return to traditional religion is the answer; Pentheus' grandfather Cadmus eagerly welcomes Dionysus yet still suffers in the end along with everybody else. But this tragedy clearly warns us against the presumptions of an arrogant reason that trivializes the irrational and believes the mind has the power to control or ultimately even know anything truly about the world and ourselves—where we came from and where we are to go.

THE CRITICAL CONSCIOUSNESS INHERITED from the Greeks has been the key to the remarkable ascendancy of the West. Science, technology, individualism, liberal democracy, natural rights—no matter what these gained from other traditions, all are ultimately the precious cargo of the Greek way of looking at the world. At this point some readers may be wondering about the Hebraic contribution to the West. After all, is not our own culture usually called Judaeo-Christian? Indeed, what Matthew Arnold famously called the "Hebraic pole" of Western culture, the other being the "Hellenic," has contributed immeasurably to the spiritual development of the West. The ideal of Hebraism, as Arnold defined it, was "conduct and obedience," and "strictness of conscience." Hebraism is concerned with "becoming conscious of sin, of awakening to a sense of sin."[15] In short, the religious identity of Western man with its drive toward moral improvement is in part the fruit of Hebraism. We owe as much to Jerusalem as we do to Athens.

Yet granting that, we must mention some qualifications. The West has been predominantly Christian, and Christianity is a Hellenized Hebraism, "neither a cancellation of nor a declension from Hellenism but a development and completion of it," as R. W. Livingstone put it.[16] For all the early church's anxiety about mingling Athens and Jerusalem, the medieval church easily incorporated the Greco-Roman heritage and Christianized it, a fact obvious on every page of Augustine or Boethius or Dante or Thomas Aquinas. More important, however, is the reality that at the beginning of a new millennium, religion is simply not a significant part of our popular, political, or public culture. This process of, to use Nietzsche's famous metaphor, "killing" God began in the nineteenth century. Even Matthew Arnold, who argued eloquently for the preeminence and importance of the Hebraic influence on Western culture, lamented in his poem "Dover Beach" (1867) that "The Sea of Faith / Was once, too, at the full," but now the poet hears only "Its melancholy, long, withdrawing roar." Half a century later, R. W. Livingstone said prosaically, "This is not a great religious age."[17] How much less religious, then, is our own, in which a materialist science provides the dominant worldview, in which religion has been banished from our political life, and materialism has replaced spiritualism as the engine of the individual's quest for personal happiness.[18]

I say this simply as a fact, certainly not as something to celebrate, though many do. Man cannot live by bread alone, and we have created a world in which the very real spiritual needs of human beings have been trivialized into New Age fads and therapeutic narcissism. Moreover, a materialist science, for all its spectacular triumphs over nature, has been singularly unsuccessful at providing an alternative morality. For that unhappy development we must hold the Hellenic tradition partially to account: the Greek philosophers first created the ideal of a rational virtue, the belief that if we but know the good, we can accomplish the good. But that fact also means that in our public and political lives, the part of our culture informed by the sensibility of the Greeks—what Arnold called "the most unprejudiced and intelligent observation of human affairs"—will necessarily predominate.[19]

Anyone can easily test this assertion for himself. Read at random a passage from Plato or Thucydides, and then one from the Bible. The mental outlook and the sensibility of the former will be more familiar and comfortable to most of us than that of the latter. In Greece we will find, as Livingstone says, "people who think as we do."[20] And if we are honest, we will admit as Livingstone does that "Most men would prefer to have been Greeks of the age of Pericles, rather than Jews in the prosperous days of their monarchy or under the Hasmoneans."[21] For better or worse, the world we live in today prizes personal freedom, individual rights, material comfort, and a rational organization of life over obedience to the divine.

THE TRADITION OF CRITICISM BESTOWED by the Greeks and enshrined in the West has been the engine of change and progress, driving the improvement of at least the material side of human life.

Yet the dynamism of the West has also been at times appallingly destructive, magnifying the powers of the evil inherent in all human beings. Science and technology freed from moral constraints—constraints once provided by religion—will be the slaves of the irrational, as we have seen frequently this century. At the start of a new millennium we face an important quandary: the science and rationalism descended from the Greeks have put into our hands an immense power, both to improve and to destroy. A political ethic that bestows dignity and worth on the individual and values his freedom, also derived ultimately from the Greeks, has led to freedom for more people than at any other time in history. Yet at the same time, that very freedom and material prosperity, now uncoupled from the counterforce once provided by Christianity, have created a public and popular culture of trivial mediocrity, in which humans are reduced to the lowest common denominator: appetite and its gratification.

This, too, is ground the Greeks trod before us—Sophocles' Oedipus, Euripides' Pentheus, Plato's Democratic Man all reflect an awareness of the limits and destructive implications of rationalism and freedom. That is why today we must once more listen to that brilliant, fractious discussion started by the Greeks, learn again to speak with their phrases and to see with their eyes. We must listen to the Greeks not because they will give us the answers, but because they first formulated the questions and problems, and they first identified whence we too believe the answers are likely to come: not from the revelations of the priest but from the minds of free, rational human beings. To do otherwise, as Jacob Burckhardt says, is to accept our own decline.

Acknowledgments

This book is the fruit of many conversations about the Greeks I have experienced over the years. My students at the California State University in Fresno are practical realists who demand to know clearly why they should bother about a civilization dead for twenty-five hundred years. Meeting their demand has made me think hard about why anyone *should* care. Likewise with the Elderhostlers to whom I lecture at the St. Nicholas Ranch in Dunlap, California. They too want the straight dope without any professional obfuscation or faddishness. I'm grateful for both audiences.

I have long thought about this book, but the support and enthusiasm of Peter Collier, publisher of Encounter Books, gave me a push at the right time. My friend and colleague Victor Davis Hanson has over the years generously allowed me to plunder from his vast store of knowledge about all things Hellenic. He also read the manuscript and saved me from numerous infelicities of fact and style. My wife and best friend Jacalyn also read the manuscript and made many valuable suggestions. I am grateful to her and my sons Isaac and Cole, who cheerfully put up with my long absences among the Greeks, and who always know how to bring me back.

Notes

Introduction: Seeing With Greek Eyes

1. Jacob Burckhardt, *The Greeks and Greek Civilization*, trans. Sheila Stern, ed. Oswyn Murray (New York, 1998), 12.
2. Edith Hamilton, *The Greek Way* (New York, 1943), 8. The 1942 edition was called *The Great Age of Greek Literature.*
3. Jacques Ellul, *The Betrayal of the West*, trans. Matthew J. O'Connell (New York, 1978), 21.
4. Hamilton, *The Greek Way*, 19.
5. Hamilton, *The Greek Way*, 18.
6. Gary Wills, "Loving the Unlovable Greeks," *New York Times Book Review* 103 (15 November 1998).
7. Josiah Ober, *Political Dissent in Democratic Athens: Intellectual Critics of Popular Rule* (Princeton, 1998), 4.
8. Gilbert Murray, "The Value of Greece to the Future of the World," in *The Legacy of Greece*, ed. R. W. Livingstone (Oxford, 1921), 14.
9. Quoted by Bernard Knox, "The Oldest Dead White European Males," in *The Oldest Dead White European Males* (New York, 1993), 30. Knox's essay is highly recommended.
10. Knox, "The Oldest Dead White European Males," 21.
11. Peter McLaren, "White Terror and Oppositional Agency: Towards a Critical Multiculturalism," in *Multiculturalism: A Critical Reader*, ed. David Theo Goldberg (Cambridge, Mass., 1994), 51.
12. See the essays in *Black Athena Revisited*, ed. Mary R. Lefkowitz and Guy MacLean Rogers (Chapel Hill, 1996).
13. Gary Wills, "There's Nothing Conservative about the Classics Revival," *New York Times Magazine*, 16 February 1997, 42.
14. Victor Hanson and John Heath, "Who Killed Homer?" *Arion* 5.2 (1997), 117. See too the authors' book *Who Killed Homer: The Demise of Classical Education* (New York, 1998).
15. Unless otherwise noted, all dates are B.C.

16. Martha Nussbaum, *Cultivating Humanity: A Classical Defense of Reform in Liberal Education* (Cambridge, Mass., 1997), 139–43.
17. For a more extended critique of Nussbaum's position see my "Cultivating Sophistry," *Arion* 6.2 (1998), 189–91.
18. Paul Cartledge, *The Greeks: A Portrait of Self and Others* (Oxford and New York, 1993), 12–13.
19. In *The Malice of Herodotus,* quoted by Knox, in *The Oldest Dead White European Males,* 20. Knox makes the same point about Herodotus.
20. Plato, *Timaeus* 22a, in *The Dialogues of Plato,* trans. Benjamin Jowett (Oxford, 1953).
21. Pindar Fragment 169, in Sir John Sandys, *The Odes of Pindar* (Cambridge, Mass. and London, 1919).
22. Cartledge, *The Greeks,* 182.
23. Cartledge, 17. Cartledge fudges with the phrase "essentially like us"; I would like examples of any earlier thinker who made such a claim rather than emphasizing the continuity of key ideals. And Cartledge seems oblivious to the possibility that two thousand years of Western culture's estimation of Greek influence could be right, and he wrong.
24. David M. Halperin, *One Hundred Years of Homosexuality and Other Essays on Greek Love* (London, 1990), 32. See my review of Halperin in "Idolon Theatri: Foucault and the Classicists," *Classical and Modern Literature* 12.1 (1991), 81–100.
25. Eva Keuls, *The Reign of the Phallus: Sexual Politics in Ancient Athens* (Berkeley and Los Angeles, 1985), 1.
26. Keuls builds an argument for the starvation of women on a line in Aristotle; see *Reign of the Phallus,* 146.
27. Diogenes Laertius 6.63.
28. Hanson and Heath, "Who Killed Homer?" 120.
29. Murray, "The Value of Greece," 15.
30. Murray, "The Value of Greece," 23.
31. In R. W. Livingstone, *Greek Ideals and Modern Life* (1935; reprint, New York, 1969), 43.
32. Cf. Charles Burton Gulick, *Modern Traits in Old Greek Life* (New York, 1963), 7: "To understand our relation and debt to Greece we must distinguish between the actual copying of Greek life and thought

on the one hand, and that unconscious possession of habits and thoughts which go back historically to Greece."

33. See Hanson and Heath's discussion in *Who Killed Homer?* 23–28.
34. James J. O'Donnell, *Avatars of the Word: From Papyrus to Cyberspace* (Cambridge, Mass., 1998), 114.

Chapter One: Eros the Killer

1. Apollonius, *Argonautica* 4.445–47, trans. Richard Hunter, *Jason and the Golden Fleece* (Oxford, 1993), 109. For Greek sexuality see my study *Eros: The Myth of Ancient Greek Sexuality* (Boulder, 1997), from which this chapter is adapted.
2. Richard Jenkyns, *The Victorians and Ancient Greece* (Cambridge, Mass., 1980), 169.
3. Marilyn B. Skinner, "*Quod Multo Fit Aliter in Graecia*," introduction to *Roman Sexualities*, ed. Judith P. Hallett and Marilyn B. Skinner (Princeton, 1997), 3.
4. Plato, *Republic* 588c–589b, trans. Francis Macdonald Cornford, *The Republic of Plato* (Oxford, 1941), 316–17.
5. Archilochus Fragment 84 Edmonds [J. M. Edmonds, *Greek Elegy and Iambus* (London and Cambridge, Mass., 1931)].
6. Archilochus Fr. 103 Edmonds.
7. Hesiod, *Theogony* 120–22.
8. Fragment 130 Campbell [D. A. Campbell, *Greek Lyric* (London and Cambridge, Mass., 1982–1993).
9. Sappho Fr. 31.9–10 Campbell.
10. Apollonius, *Argonautica* 3.296–97.
11. Euripides, *Hippolytus* 1, 133, 232–33, trans. David Grene, in *Euripides I*, ed. David Grene and Richmond Lattimore (Chicago, 1955).
12. In Plato, *Republic* 329c.
13. David Halperin, *One Hundred Years of Homosexuality and Other Essays on Greek Loves* (London, 1990), 33.
14. Plato, *Symposium* 189c–193e.
15. *Problemata* 879b–880a.
16. Aristotle, *Nicomachean Ethics* 1148b.
17. Euripides Fr. 920 Nauck [August Nauck, *Tragicorum Graecorum Fragmenta* (Hildesheim, 1964)].
18. In Xenophon, *Memorabilia* 2.1.30.
19. Itch metaphor in Plato, *Gorgias* 491e–92a; also in Xenophon, *Memorabilia* 1.2.29–30.

20. In Diogenes Laertius, *Lives of the Philosophers* 6.4.
21. Aristophanes, *Clouds* 1085–1100.
22. For examples and further discussion see Jeffrey Henderson, *The Maculate Muse: Obscene Language in Attic Comedy,* 2nd ed. (Oxford, 1991), 204–22.
23. Plato, *Laws* 836d.
24. Aristophanes, *Frogs* 423–24.
25. Aristophanes, *Thesmophoriazusae* 97–205.
26. Plato, *Phaedrus* 239c–d.
27. Thornton, *Eros,* 116.
28. Aristophanes, *Knights* 426, trans. Douglas M. MacDowell, in *Aristophanes and Athens: An Introduction to the Plays* (Oxford, 1995), 98.
29. Aristophanes, *Knights* 423–26, 1242, 78, 875–80, 736–40.
30. Aeschines, *Against Timarchos* 1.3, 1.42, 1.46, 1.85, 1.95, 1.54, 1.160, 1.185, 1.85–86.
31. Plato, *Phaedrus* 251a.
32. Xenophon, *Symposium* 8.27–28.
33. Aristotle, *Rhetoric* 1383b, trans. W. R. Roberts, in *The Complete Works of Aristotle,* ed. Jonathan Barnes (Princeton, 1984).
34. Plato, *Symposium* 183d.
35. Plato, *Laws* 836b–c, 841d.
36. James Davidson, *Courtesans and Fishcakes: The Consuming Passions of Classical Athens* (London, 1997), 176.
37. Mimnermus Fr. 1.1 Edmonds
38. *Iliad* 14.215–17.
39. Hesiod, *Theogony* 206.
40. Euripides *Hippolytus* 380–81; see too Fr. 920 Nauck and *Medea* 1079–80.
41. Plato, *Philebus* 31a.
42. Plato, *Gorgias* 493a–494a.
43. Plato, *Timaeus* 86b; *Laws* 714a.
44. Aristotle, *Nichomachean Ethics* 1118a–b.
45. Plato, *Phaedrus* 247c.
46. Plato, *Republic* 389d–e, *Gorgias* 491d.
47. Aristotle, *Nicomachean Ethics* 1118a–b.
48. Plato, *Symposium* 219d–221b.
49. Aristotle, *Politics* 1252a–1253b, trans. Benjamin Jowett, in *The Complete Works of Aristotle,* ed. Barnes.

50. For examples see my *Eros,* 239 n. 18.
51. Aeschylus, *Seven against Thebes* 754; Sophocles, *Oedipus Turannos* 1210–11.
52. Euripides, *The Phoenician Women* 21–22.
53. Plato, *Menexenus* 238a.
54. Aeschylus, *Eumenides* 557–61.
55. Fr. 583 in *Sophocles: Fragments,* ed. and trans. Hugh Lloyd-Jones (Cambrige, Mass. and London, 1996).
56. Sappho Fr. 105a Campbell.
57. For brief descriptions of the Thesmophoria see Walter Burkert, *Greek Religion,* trans. John Raffan (Cambridge, Mass., 1985), 242–46; H. W. Parke, *Festivals of the Athenians* (Ithaca, N.Y., 1977), 82–88; and Thornton, *Eros,* 146–50.
58. Aristophanes, *Wasps* 1066–70.
59. Let me remind the reader that I am not describing actual behavior but rather an ideal as evidenced by the fragmentary literary remains. What physical acts really took place is ultimately unknowable.
60. Euripides Fr. 897 Nauck.
61. See Aeschines 1.9–11.
62. Plato, *Symposium* 183c–d.
63. Xenophon, *Symposium* 8.8–10, also 1.26.
64. Plato, *Phaedrus* 253d–256a.
65. Plato, *Symposium* 209c–211b.
66. Plato, *Symposium* 211e–212a.

Chapter Two: The Best and Worst Thing

1. Hesiod, *Works and Days* 703–5. For a more detailed discussion of the issues in this chapter see my *Eros: The Myth of Ancient Greek Sexuality,* 69–98, 161–92. See too Mary R. Lefkowitz's valuable *Women in Greek Myth* (Baltimore, 1986).
2. For female genital mutilation see Cesar Chelala, "Egypt Takes Decisive Stance against Female Genital Mutilation," *The Lancet* 351.9096 (10 January 1998), 120. For difficulties in childbirth and the resultant medical complications see Raymond Tallis's account of his experiences in Africa in *The Enemies of Hope: A Critique of Contemporary Pessimism* (New York, 1997), 117–19.
3. Robbie E. Davis-Floyd and Carolyn F. Sargent, introduction to *Childbirth and Authoritative Knowledge: Cross-Cultural Perspectives,* ed. Davis-Floyd and Sargent (Berkeley and Los Angeles, 1998), 11.

4. Eva Cantarella, *Pandora's Daughters: The Role and Status of Women in Greek and Roman Antiquity,* trans. Maureen B. Fant (1981; reprint, Baltimore, 1987), 46, 177. For the seclusion issue in more detail and for bibliography see my *Eros: The Myth of Ancient Greek Sexuality,* 251–53.
5. F. A. Wright, *Feminism in Greek Literature: From Homer to Aristotle* (1923; reprint, Port Washington, N.Y. and London, 1969), 1, 57–58.
6. Sarah Pomeroy, *Goddesses, Whores, Wives, and Slaves* (New York, 1975), 79. Eva Keuls, *The Reign of the Phallus,* 34, 97.
7. For adultery see J. Roy, "An Alternative Sexual Morality for Classical Athens," *Greece and Rome* 64.1 (1997), 11–22. For "men's quarters" see Michael Jameson, "Private Space and the Greek City," in *The Greek City: From Homer to Alexander,* ed. Oswyn Murray and Simon Price (Oxford, 1990), 171–95.
8. In H. W. F. Saggs, *Civilization before Greece and Rome* (New Haven, 1989), 169.
9. Deuteronomy 22.21.
10. See Lefkowitz, *Women in Greek Myth,* 39.
11. Sophocles Fr. 855 Nauck.
12. Hesiod, *Theogony* 570–613; *Works and Days* 54–89.
13. *Theogony* 604.
14. Semonides Fr. 7 Edmonds, trans. Hugh Lloyd-Jones, in Mary R. Lefkowitz and Maureen B. Fant, *Women's Life in Greece and Rome,* 2nd ed. (Baltimore, 1992).
15. For the ancient gynecological writers see Lefkowitz and Fant, *Women's Life in Greece and Rome.*
16. *Peri Gonônes* 4, in Robert Garland, *The Greek Way of Life: From Conception to Old Age* (Ithaca, N.Y., 1990), 17.
17. See Plato's description in *Timaeus* 91c.
18. *Iliad* 3.158, trans. Richmond Lattimore, *The Iliad of Homer* (Chicago, 1951).
19. *Eoiae* Fr. 68.5, in Hugh G. Evelyn-White, *Hesiod, the Homeric Hymns, and Homerica* (Cambridge, Mass. and London, 1914).
20. Ibycus Fr. 296 Campbell.
21. Steisichorus Fr. 201 Campbell.
22. *Little Iliad,* Fr. 1 Evelyn-White.
23. Lycophron 142–43.
24. Plutarch, *Life of Theseus* 31–34; *Cypria* Fr. 11 Evelyn-White.

25. *Cypria* Fr. 1 Evelyn-White; Helen and Achilles: Pausanias 3.19.13.
26. *Odyssey* 14.69.
27. *Odyssey* 11.438–39.
28. Alcaeus Fr. 42 Campbell; Aeschylus, *Agamemnon* 689.
29. *Iliad* 3.39–40.
30. Euripides, *Andromache* 298; Lycophron 102, 1143.
31. See the *Agamemnon* of Aeschylus.
32. Athenaeus, *Deipnosophistae* (The Scholars at Banquet) 512e, 556f.
33. The story is told in Sophocles' play *The Women of Trachis.*
34. Euripides, *Hippolytus* 79–81.
35. Euripides, *Bacchae* 221–25.
36. Euripides, *Medea* 231–51.
37. Pindar, *Olympian Ode* 15.53–54.
38. *Medea* 252–54, trans. Rex Warner, in *Euripides I,* ed. David Grene and Richmond Lattimore (Chicago, 1955).
39. Lysias 1.33.
40. *Against Neaira* 59.34, 41, 113.
41. *Against Neaira* 59.122.
42. Aristotle, *Politics* 1252a.
43. Aristotle, *Economics* 1343b, trans. E. S. Foster, in *The Complete Works of Aristotle,* ed, Barnes.
44. Aristotle, *Nicomachean Ethics* 1162a; *Politics* 1264b.
45. Xenophon, *Oeconomicus* 3.12, 3.15, 7.13, 7.15.
46. Diane Ackerman, *A Natural History of Love* (New York, 1994), 24.
47. In Lefkowitz and Fant, *Women's Life in Greece and Rome,* 12.
48. *Odyssey* 1.429–33, 15.356–58, trans. Lattimore.
49. Hesiod, *Works and Days* 702; Semonides Fr. 6 Edmonds; Theognis 1225–26.
50. Sophocles Fr. 942 Lloyd-Jones, trans. Lloyd-Jones.
51. Euripides, *Alcestis* 277–79, 329–30, 336–37.
52. Xenophon, *Symposium* 9.7.
53. Aristotle, *Prior Analytics* 68b.
54. Aristophanes, *Lysistrata* 165–66.
55. *Odyssey* 11.445–46; cf. too 2.117–18, 121, also 24.194.
56. Aristophanes, *Women at the Thesmophoria* 548.
57. *Odyssey* 6.181–84.
58. See Thornton, *Eros,* 184–85 and 241 n. 58.
59. *Odyssey* 5.207–10.

60. Readers who see a "double standard" in Odysseus' having sex with Calypso and Circe should remember that they are goddesses, whom it doesn't do to slight. Back in Ithaka, Odysseus tells Penelope all about the goddesses, but wisely leaves out Nausicaa—the virgin human he doesn't touch represents more of a threat than do the two goddesses.
61. *Odyssey* 19.582–87.
62. Sophocles Fr. 583 Lloyd-Jones, trans. Lloyd-Jones.
63. Plutarch, *Moralia* 347f–348a; the story may be a later fabrication.
64. Plutarch, *Moralia* 245c–f; Pausanias 2.20.8–10. Plutarch has the women actually fight and defeat the Spartans; Pausanias has the Spartans withdraw because win or lose, they'd look bad.
65. Sophocles, *Antigone* 677–80, trans. Elizabeth Wyckoff, in *Greek Tragedies,* vol. I, ed. David Grene and Richmond Lattimore (Chicago, 1960).
66. *Antigone* 502–3, trans. Wyckoff.
67. Aristophanes, *Lysistrata* 527–28, trans. Matt Neuberg (Arlington Heights, Va., 1992).
68. *Lysistrata* 573–586, trans. Neuberg.
69. *Lysistrata* 638–41, 648, trans. Neuberg.
70. Both passages in Lefkowitz and Fant, *Women's Life in Greece and Rome,* 67, 73; passage from the *Laws* translated by T. J. Saunders.
71. Diogenes Laertius 7.175. For other sources see Malcolm Schofield, *The Stoic Idea of the City* (Cambridge, 1991), 43.
72. See the comments by Hanson and Heath, *Who Killed Homer?* 109.

Chapter Three: The Roots of Emancipation

1. In Peter Garnsey, *Ideas of Slavery from Aristotle to Augustine* (Cambridge, 1996), 75.
2. See Orlando Patterson, *Freedom,* vol. 1, *Freedom in the Making of Western Culture* (New York, 1991), 11–12.
3. CSI website is at www.csi-int.ch/; go to press releases or trip reports. See also *National Catholic Reporter* 35.15 (12 February 1999), 9.
4. R. W. Livingstone, *Greek Ideals and Modern Life* (1935; reprint, New York, 1969), 7.
5. M. I. Finley, "Ancient Slavery and Modern Ideology," in *Ancient Slavery and Modern Ideology* (New York, 1980), 64. See too Hanson and Heath, *Who Killed Homer?* 111–16.

6. Plato, *Republic* 469b–c.
7. *Odyssey* 15.415–84.
8. See M. I. Finley, "Debt-Bondage and Slavery," in *Economy and Society in Ancient Greece* (New York, 1981), 15–66.
9. In Athenaeus, *Deipnosophistae* 236c–d.
10. Heracleitus Fr. 53 Diels, in *Ancilla to the Presocratic Philosophers,* ed. Kathleen Freeman (Cambridge, Mass., 1957).
11. *Iliad* 6.450–55, trans. Richmond Lattimore (Chicago, 1951).
12. *Odyssey* 8.528–30, trans. Richmond Lattimore (New York, 1967).
13. See Xenophon, *Memorabilia* 2.3.3; Yvon Garlan, *Slavery in Ancient Greece,* rev. ed., trans. Janet Lloyd (Ithaca, N.Y., 1988), 65.
14. Plutarch, *Life of Theseus* 4; cf. Robert Garland, *The Greek Way of Life: From Conception to Old Age* (Ithaca, N.Y., 1990), 124.
15. Herodotus 8.75.
16. For others see Aulus Gellius, *Attic Nights* 2.18.
17. After 1800, private manumission was more or less restricted by state legislatures; see Peter Kolchin, *American Slavery, 1619–1877* (New York, 1993), 89–90.
18. Pausanias 1.32.3, 7.15.7. Other examples in Garlan, 171.
19. Mentioned by Aristophanes in *Frogs* 190, 693ff.
20. See Garlan, 75–77.
21. Pseudo-Demosthenes 59.29–31.
22. In Thomas Wiedemann, *Greek and Roman Slavery* (Baltimore, 1981), 46–47. An idea of what these laws may have been like can be gleaned from Plato's utopian legislation regarding freedmen in the *Laws* 915a–c.
23. Lysias 30.
24. See A. R. W. Harrison, *The Law of Athens: The Family and Property* (Oxford, 1968), 181–86.
25. In Athenaeus 263c, in Wiedemann, *Greek and Roman Slavery,* 81.
26. Aristophanes, *Ecclesiazusae* 721–24.
27. Gorgias Fr. 8a Diels-Kranz, in *The Older Sophists,* ed. Rosamond Kent Sprague (Columbia, S.C., 1972).
28. Aristophanes, *Thesmophoriazusae,* 491. Cf. also Fr. 695 Nauck.
29. *Mime* 5.20–34, trans. I. C. Cunningham, in *Theophrastus: Characters; Herodas: Mimes; Circidas and the Coliambic Poets* (Cambridge, Mass. and London, 1993).
30. Dio Chrysostom 15, in Wiedemann, 225.

31. Garlan, 157.
32. This law is mentioned by Aeschines, *Against Timarchos* 1.17. See Harrison, 166–80; Garlan, 41.
33. *The Constitution of the Athenians* 1.10, trans. G. W. Bowerstock, in *Xenophon: Scripta Minora* (Cambridge, Mass. and London, 1968).
34. Diodorus Siculus 34.2.25–6, in *Diodorus of Sicily*, trans. C. H. Oldfather (Cambridge, Mass. and London, 1935). See also Garnsey, 54–55.
35. Garlan, 41.
36. Galen, *The Diseases of the Mind* 4, in Wiedemann, 180.
37. Victor Ehrenberg, *The People of Aristophanes: The Sociology of Ancient Comedy* (New York, 1961), 187.
38. For examples see K. J. Dover. ed., *Aristophanes: Frogs* (Oxford, 1993), 43–44.
39. Xenophon, *Memorabilia* 2.1.17, in Wiedemann, 173.
40. Diodorus Siculus 3.13; see also 38.1, on the mines in Spain.
41. *Odyssey* 17.322–3, trans. Lattimore; Plato quotes the line at *Laws* 777a. Cf. Theognis 535–38 Edmonds.
42. *Hecuba* 356–64, trans. William Arrowsmith, in *Euripides III*, ed. David Grene and Richmond Lattimore (Chicago, 1958).
43. Athenaeus 265c–f, 264c, in Wiedemann; Herodotus 6.137.
44. Athenaeus, 267e, trans. Charles Burton Gulick (Cambridge, Mass. and London, 1929).
45. Athenaeus 268d, trans. Gulick, adapted.
46. Athenaeus 263c.
47. See Garlan, 132–33.
48. Lucian, *Saturnalia* 7; *Cronosolon* 13; in Arthur O. Lovejoy and George Boas, *Primitivism and Related Ideas in Antiquity* (Baltimore and London, 1935), 66.
49. Macrobius, *Saturnalia* 1.7.37, in Lovejoy and Boas, 67.
50. Athenaeus 639b–640a.
51. Joseph Vogt, *Ancient Slavery and the Ideal of Man*, trans. Thomas Wiedemann (Cambridge, Mass., 1975), 7–8.
52. Aristophanes, *Frogs* 741–53.
53. *Frogs* 1–5, trans. Richmond Lattimore, *Aristophanes: The Frogs* (Ann Arbor, 1962).
54. In K. J. Dover, ed., *Frogs*, 45.

55. *Frogs* 605–73.
56. See K. J. Dover, *Aristophanic Comedy* (Berkeley and Los Angeles, 1972), 204–8.
57. For Arginusae and its effects on attitudes towards slaves see Dover, ed. *Frogs*, 49–50. For another Aristophanic slave characterized with complexity and humanity see Carion in the *Wealth* (388 B.C.).
58. Euripides, *Orestes* 1115–16, 1369–79, 1506–26, trans. William Arrowsmith, in *Euripides IV*, ed. David Grene and Richmond Lattimore (Chicago, 1958).
59. Euripides, *Hecuba* 332–34, 480–83, trans. Arrowsmith, in *Euripides III*, ed. David Grene and Richmond Lattimore (Chicago, 1958).
60. Euripides, *Andromache* 141–44, trans. John Frederick Nims, in *Euripides III*.
61. *Andromache* 89–90, trans. Nims.
62. Euripides, *Helen* 1627–41, trans. Richmond Lattimore, in *Euripides II*, ed. David Grene and Richmond Lattimore (Chicago, 1956).
63. Philip Vellacott, *Ironic Drama: A Study of Euripides* (Cambridge, 1975), 219.
64. Plato, *Laws* 776b, in Wiedemann, 83.
65. *Laws* 757a, in Garlan, 149.
66. *Laws* 778a, translated in Garnsey, 54.
67. Aristotle, *Politics* 1254a–1260a, translated in Garnsey; cf. 107–27 for a more detailed discussion of Aristotle's theory.
68. Aristotle, *Eudemian Ethics* 1241b, translated in Garnsey, 120.
69. *Politics* 1255a, trans. Benjamin Jowett, in *The Complete Works of Aristotle*, ed. Barnes.
70. Garnsey, 124.
71. *Politics* 1253b, in Garnsey, 75.
72. *Politics* 1255a, trans. Jowett.
73. Euripides, *Iphigenia in Aulis* 1400–1, trans. Charles R. Walker, in *Euripides IV*.
74. Euripides, *Ion* 854–56, trans. Ronald Frederick Willetts, in *Euripides III*.
75. Euripides, *Helen* 728–31, trans. Lattimore.
76. Euripides Fr. 511, in Garlan, 124. See too Fr. 831.
77. Euripides Frs. 33, 38, 40 Snell, trans. in Vogt, *Ancient Slavery*, 22.
78. Sophocles Fr. 591, trans. Hugh Lloyd Jones, in *Sophocles*, vol 3, *Fragments* (Cambridge, Mass. and London, 1996).
79. Sophocles Fr. 854, in Garnsey, 65.

80. Bion, in Garnsey, 65.
81. Diogenes Laertius 7.121–22, in Garnsey, 130; see also 128–52 for a discussion of Stoicism and slavery.
82. Philemon Fr. 95 Kock, in Robert Schlaifer, "Greek Theories of Slavery from Homer to Aristotle," in *Slavery in Classical Antiquity,* ed. M. I. Finley (Cambridge, 1960), 128; my translation.
83. Cicero, *De Finibus* 3.62–63, in Garnsey, 143.
84. Antiphon, in Garlan, 123. Cf. too Plato, *Statesman* 262d.
85. Isocrates, *Panegyricus* 50, trans. George Norlin, *Isocrates* (Cambridge, Mass. and London, 1928).
86. Plutarch, *De Alexandri Magni Fortuna aut Virtute,* in H. C. Baldry, *The Unity of Mankind in Greek Thought* (Cambridge, 1965), 159.
87. Epictetus 1.9.1–6, in Garnsey, 142.
88. Epictetus 1.13, in Garnsey, 143.
89. Seneca, *Epistulae* 47, trans. Moses Hadas, *The Stoic Philosophy of Seneca* (New York, 1958). See too Seneca's *On Benefits,* in which the philosopher argues for the possibility that a slave can act nobly and virtuously.
90. M. I. Finley, "Was Greek Civilization Based on Slave Labour?" in *Slavery in Classical Antiquity,* 70.

Chapter Four: The Father of All

1. Heracleitus Fr. 53 Diels, in Kathleen Freeman, *Ancilla to the Pre-Socratic Philosophers* (Cambridge, Mass., 1957).
2. Herodotus 6.113, trans. Aubrey de Sélincourt (Harmondsworth, 1954).
3. Herodotus 7.227, trans. de Sélincourt.
4. For the Greeks and war I am indebted to the work of Victor Davis Hanson; see *Who Killed Homer? The Demise of Classical Education* (New York, 1998), 58–75; *The Western Way of War* (New York, 1989); *The Other Greeks: The Family Farm and the Agrarian Roots of Western Civilization* (New York, 1995), especially 221–323; and *The Wars of the Ancient Greeks and Their Invention of Western Military Culture* (London, 1999).
5. See Victor Davis Hanson, "No Glory That Was Greece," in *What If?* ed. Robert Cowley (New York, 1999).
6. Arther Ferrill, *The Origins of War: From the Stone Age to Alexander the Great* (London, 1985), 37–38.
7. *Iliad* 16.215–17, trans. Lattimore. All subsequent quotations of

Homer will be from Lattimore's translation. For Mycenean and Dark Age fighting see Hanson, *The Wars of the Ancient Greeks,* 29–45.

8. *Iliad* 3.446–49.
9. For the hoplite and phalanx see Hanson, *The Western Way of War,* 55–88.
10. Alcaeus Fr. 140 Campbell, his translation.
11. Anacreon Fr. 382 Campbell.
12. Plutarch, *Aristides* 18, trans. Ian Scott-Kilvert, in *The Rise and Fall of Athens: Nine Greek Lives* (Harmondsworth, 1960).
13. Tyrtaeus 11.21–26, trans. Richmond Lattimore, *Greek Lyric* (Chicago, 1955), 16.
14. Tyrtaeus 11.31–34, trans. Lattimore.
15. Tyrtaeus 10.25, in Hanson, *The Western Way of War,* 212.
16. Tyrtaeus 11.20, trans. Lattimore.
17. Xenophon, *Agesilaus* 2.14–15, trans. E. C. Marchant, in *Xenophon: Scripta Minora.*
18. Tyrtaeus 12.11–12, and Callinus 1.9–11, trans. Lattimore, *Greek Lyric.*
19. Simonides, Epigram 2 Campbell.
20. Sophocles, *Antigone* 670.
21. Callinus 1.7 Edmonds.
22. Xenophon, *Agesilaus* 2.7, trans. Marchant.
23. Herodotus 7.209.
24. For this transformation see Hanson, *The Other Greeks,* 329–55, 369–75.
25. As argued by Hanson in *The Other Greeks.*
26. Hanson and Heath, *Who Killed Homer?* 62–70.
27. Plato, *Laws* 626a, trans. Benjamin Jowett, *The Dialogues of Plato.*
28. Plato, *Laches* 181a, trans. Jowett.
29. In Introduction to *Aeschylus I: Oresteia,* trans. Richmond Lattimore (Chicago, 1953), 1.
30. Iliad 5.890. For a survey of war in Greek literature see Nathan Spiegel, *War and Peace in Classical Greek Literature,* trans. Amiel Ungar (Jerusalem, 1990).
31. Pindar Fr. 110 Bergk.
32. Herodotus 1.87, trans. de Sélincourt.
33. Sophocles, *Ajax* 1192–94, trans. John Moore, in *Sophocles II* (Chicago, 1992).

34. *Iliad* 5.73–76, 144–47, 290–93.
35. In *The Ancient Egyptians: A Sourcebook of Their Writings*, ed. Adolf Erman, trans. Aylward M. Blackman (New York, 1966), 259.
36. Deuteronomy 20.10–14.
37. In *Ancient Records of Assyria and Babylonia*, vol. 1, trans. Daniel David Luckenbill (1926; reprint, New York, 1968), 140–42.
38. *Iliad* 5.70–71, 149–51.
39. *Iliad* 6.429–32.
40. *Iliad* 6.466–75.
41. *Iliad* 22.70, 79–89, 303–5.
42. *Iliad* 24.508–12.
43. In Gérard Chailand, *The Art of War in World History* (Berkeley and Los Angeles, 1994), 57.
44. Archilochus Fr. 6 Campbell, trans. Lattimore, *Greek Lyric.*
45. Alcaeus Fr. 428a Campbell. Anacreon, of the late sixth century, perhaps wrote a poem about the loss of his shield too. Anacreon Fr. 381b Campbell.
46. Tyrtaeus 12.31–32, trans. Lattimore.
47. Archilochus Fr. 63 Edmonds, translation adapted.
48. *Agamemnon* 434–36, trans. Richmond Lattimore, in *Aeschylus I* (Chicago, 1953).
49. *Persians* 275–77, 286–89, trans. Seth G. Bernadete, in *Aeschylus II,* ed. David Grene and Richmond Lattimore (Chicago, 1956).
50. *Persians* 806–7, trans. Bernadete.
51. *Persians* 931–33, trans. Bernadete.
52. Thucydides 2.41, trans. Richard Crawley, in *The Landmark Thucydides,* ed. Robert B. Strassler (New York, 1996).
53. *The Suppliant Women* 481–88, 492–94, trans. by Frank William Jones, in *Euripides IV* (Chicago, 1958).
54. *The Suppliant Women* 745–50, 949–52, trans. Jones.
55. *The Suppliant Women* 524–26, trans. Jones.
56. *Hecuba* 228–30, trans. Arrowsmith; Thucydides 5.89, trans. Crawley.
57. *The Trojan Women* 786–89, trans. Lattimore.
58. *The Trojan Women* 376–83, trans. Lattimore. Cf. *Andromache* 611–13.
59. Philip Vellacott, *Ironic Drama,* 177.
60. *Acharnians* 517–29, trans. Jeffrey Henderson (Cambridge, Mass. and London, 1998).

61. Aristophanes, *Peace* 646–47, trans. B. B. Rogers (Cambridge, Mass. and London, 1924).
62. *Peace* 204–7, trans. Rogers.
63. *Lysistrata* 490–91, trans. Neuberg.
64. *Lysistrata* 577, trans. Neuberg.
65. Thucydides 3.82.2, trans. Crawley.
66. *The Phoenician Women,* trans. Elizabeth Wyckoff, in *Euripides V* (Chicago, 1959).
67. Luckenbill, *Ancient Records of Assyria and Babylonia,* 145.

Chapter Five: The Birth of Political Man

1. Aristotle, *Politics* 1253a, trans. Benjamin Jowett, in *Complete Works,* ed. Barnes.
2. In A. T. Olmstead, *History of the Persian Empire* (Chicago, 1948), 231.
3. See Donald Kagan, *The Great Dialogue: History of Greek Political Thought from Homer to Polybius* (New York, 1965), 1–32.
4. See Victor Davis Hanson, *The Other Greeks,* 181–219.
5. Hesiod, *Works and Days* 261–64, trans. Athanassakis.
6. Solon Frs. 1.71–73 Diehl, 1.75 Diehl, 3.5–10 Diehl, trans. Lattimore, *Greek Lyric.*
7. Solon Fr. 5.1–4, 7–10 Diehl, trans. Lattimore.
8. Solon Fr. 15 Edmonds.
9. Solon Fr. 37 Edmonds.
10. In Aristotle, *Politics* 1295b, trans. Jowett.
11. Solon Fr. 24 Diehl, trans. Lattimore.
12. Aeschylus, *Eumenides* 526–31, trans. Lattimore, in *Aeschylus I: Oresteia.*
13. Phocylides Fr. 5 Edmonds.
14. *Politics* 1295b, trans. Jowett.
15. Aeschylus, *Persians* 372–4, 725–6, 745, 750, trans. Seth Benardete, in *Aeschylus II.*
16. *Persians* 821–23, trans. Benardete.
17. Herodotus 3.80, trans. A. D. Godley (Cambridge, Mass. and London, 1921).
18. *Politics* 1295a, trans. Jowett.
19. Herodotus 5.92, trans. de Sélincourt. See too Euripides, *The Suppliant Women* 444–55.

20. Sophocles, *Antigone* 707–11, 721–23, 737, trans. Hugh Lloyd-Jones (Cambridge, Mass. and London, 1994).
21. See Walter Donlan, "The Tradition of Anti-Aristocratic Thought in Early Greek Poetry," *Historia* 22.2 (1973), 145–54. Donlan conveniently lists all the passages.
22. Archilochus Fr. 60 Diehl.
23. Tyrtaeus 9; Callinus 1.
24. *Iliad* 1.2–4, trans. Lattimore.
25. Xenophanes 2.11–12, 19, trans. Lattimore, in *Greek Lyric.*
26. Phocylides Fr. 3, trans. Lattimore, in *Greek Lyric.*
27. Donlan, 150.
28. Euripides, *Electra* 383–90, trans. Emily Townsend Vermeule, in *Euripides V.*
29. *Electra* 369–70, trans. Vermeule.
30. Plato, *Theaetetus* 175a, trans. Jowett.
31. Plato, *Laws* 691b, trans. Jowett.
32. *Politics* 1279a, trans. Jowett.
33. *Laws* 715d, trans. Jowett.
34. Lysias, *Funeral Oration* 19, trans. W. R. M. Lamb (Cambridge, Mass. and London, 1930).
35. *Politics* 1275a.
36. Thucydides *The Peloponnesian War* 7.77, trans. Richard Crawley, in *The Landmark Thucydides,* ed. Robert B. Strassler (New York, 1996).
37. *Odyssey* 9.112–15, trans. Lattimore.
38. Thucydides 3.82, trans. Crawley.
39. Thucydides 3.84, trans. Crawley.
40. Cf. Plato, *Laws* 678a; *Phaedrus* 230b.
41. Herodotus 1.31, trans. de Sélincourt.
42. Plato, *Crito* 50d, trans. Jowett.
43. Herodotus 7.104, trans. de Sélincourt.
44. *Nicomachean Ethics* 1094b.
45. *Politics* 1252a, 1280b–81a, trans. Jowett.
46. *Laws* 643b–644a, trans. Jowett.
47. Plato, *Gorgias* 504e, trans. Jowett.
48. For the working of Athenian democracy see David Stockton, *The Classical Athenian Democracy* (Oxford, 1990), 57–116. The important ancient source is Aristotle's *Constitution of Athens.* My sketch

of these workings that follows is intended to be general and ignores problems of chronology or the evolution of function.

49. See the *Oxford Companion to Classical Civilization,* ed. Simon Hornblower and Anthony Spawforth (Oxford, 1998), 220–21.
50. Stockton, *Classical Athenian Democracy,* 83.
51. Stockton, 112.
52. Thucydides 2.37, trans. Crawley.
53. *The Suppliant Women* 405–8, trans. Frank William Jones, in *Euripides IV* (Chicago, 1958).
54. Democritus Fr. 251 Diels, trans. Freeman.
55. A. H. M. Jones, *Athenian Democracy* (1957; reprint, Baltimore, 1977), 124.
56. *Constitution of Athens,* 61, trans. F. G. Kenyon.
57. Donald Kagan, *The Great Dialogue,* 88.
58. Aeschylus, *Persians* 211–13, trans. Benardete. See too Aeschylus' *Prometheus Bound* 324.
59. Herodotus 3.80.
60. Lysias, *Funeral Oration* 19, trans. Lamb.
61. Aeschylus, *Eumenides* 970–74, trans. Lattimore.
62. Thucydides 2.40, trans. Crawley.
63. Thucydides 3.42, trans. Crawley.
64. Thucydides 6.39, trans. Crawley.
65. Plato, *Philebus* 58a.
66. Herodotus 8.64, trans. de Sélincourt.
67. Herodotus 7.102, trans. de Sélincourt.
68. Herodotus 8.65, trans. de Sélincourt.
69. See Xenophon, *Anabasis* 2.3.33.
70. Euripides, *The Suppliant Women* 432–37, trans. Jones.
71. Thucydides 6.38, trans. Crawley.
72. Plato, *Protagoras* 322d–323a.
73. Demosthenes, *Against Timocrates* 59, in *Demosthenes,* trans. J. H. Vince (Cambridge, Mass. and London, 1935).
74. *Politics* 1318a, trans. Jowett.
75. Gregory Vlastos, "Isonomia," 1953, reprint in *Studies in Greek Philosophy,* vol. 1, *The Presocratics* (Princeton, 1995), 103.
76. Thucydides 6.89, trans. Crawley.
77. Theognis 54–57, 699–700, trans. Lattimore, *Greek Lyric.*

78. *The Constitution of the Athenians* 1.1, 4, 5, trans. Bowerstock, in *Xenophon: Scripta Minora.*
79. Pindar, *Nemean* 3.40, trans. Richmond Lattimore, *The Odes of Pindar* (Chicago, 1947).
80. Herodotus 3.81, trans. de Sélincourt.
81. Thucydides 2.65, 4.28, in Jennifer Tolbert Roberts, *Athens on Trial: The Antidemocratic Tradition in Western Thought* (Princeton, 1994), 55.
82. *The Suppliant Women* 410–13, trans. Jones.
83. Plato, *Crito* 47c–d, trans. Thomas G. West and Grace Starry West, in *Four Texts on Socrates* (Ithaca and London, 1984).
84. Xenophon, *Memorabilia* 3.7.5–6, trans. Hugh Tredennick and Robin Waterfield (Harmondsworth, England, 1990). See too *Protagoras* 319b.
85. Thucydides 3.38, trans. Crawley.
86. Thucydides 6.24, trans. Crawley. See too the satirical depiction of a debate in Euripides' *Orestes* 866–956, where the noblest speaker is voted down.
87. Isocrates, *Nicocles* 17, trans. George Norlin, *Isocrates* (Cambridge, Mass. and London, 1928).
88. Plato, *Gorgias* 515d, trans. Jowett.
89. Aristophanes, *The Women at Assembly* 304–6, 308–10, trans. in *The Complete Greek Drama* (New York, 1938). For other passages from comedy regarding democratic corruption and bribery see Ehrenberg, *The People of Aristophanes,* 341–43.
90. *Constitution of Athens* 27, trans. Kenyon.
91. See especially the *Knights,* with its satiric portrait of the politician Cleon.
92. *Politics* 1301a, trans. Jowett.
93. *Republic* 558c, trans. Jowett.
94. *Laws* 757a–b, trans. Jowett.
95. Isocrates, *Areopagiticus* 20, trans. George Norlin (Cambridge, Mass. and London, 1929).
96. *Republic* 561d, trans. Jowett.
97. In Roberts, *Athens on Trial,* 183; Adams' emphases omitted.
98. A. E. Zimmern, "Political Thought," in *The Legacy of Greece,* ed. R. W. Livingstone (Oxford, 1921).

Chapter Six: The Birth of Rational Man

1. Aristotle, *Nicomachean Ethics* 1097b–1098a, trans. Martin Ostwald (New York, 1962).
2. Herodotus 2.4, 109.
3. Aristotle, *Metaphysics* 981b, trans. W. D. Ross, in *Complete Works*, ed. Barnes. On the relation of Greek science to Near Eastern civilizations see G. E. R. Lloyd, *Magic, Reason, and Experience* (Cambridge, 1979), 229–34.
4. See *The History of Science*, vol. 1, *Ancient and Medieval Science*, ed. René Taton, trans. A. J. Pomerans (New York, 1963), 109. A good brief contrast of Greek approaches to knowledge with those of the Egyptians and Mesopotamians can be found in W. K. C. Guthrie, *A History of Greek Philosophy*, vol. 1, *The Earlier Presocratics and the Pythagoreans* (Cambridge, 1962), 26–38.
5. Plato, *Phaedo* 65d–66a.
6. Both anecdotes in G. S. Kirk and J. E. Raven, *The Presocratic Philosophers* (Cambridge, 1963), 78.
7. Plutarch, *Life of Marcellus*, trans. John Dryden.
8. See G. E. R. Lloyd, *Early Greek Science* (New York, 1970), 31–32.
9. Aristotle, *Metaphysics* 983a–988b; *Physics* 204b and following; see also *Sophistical Refutations* 183b, trans. W. A. Pickard-Cambridge.
10. Lloyd, *Early Greek Science*, 12.
11. Benjamin Farrington, *Greek Science* (1944; reprint, New York, 1953), 34.
12. Herodotus 7.191, 2.20ff, trans. de Sélincourt.
13. Lloyd, *Magic, Reason, and Experience*, 232–33.
14. Xenophanes Fr. 18 Diels, trans. Freeman.
15. Alcmaeon Fr. 1a Diels, trans. Freeman.
16. Aristotle, *Metaphysics* 980a, trans. W. D. Ross.
17. In Aristotle, *Eudemian Ethics* 1216a, trans. J. Solomon, in *Complete Works*, ed. Barnes.
18. Aristotle, *Parts of Animals* 645a, trans. W. Ogle, in *Complete Works*.
19. Democritus Fr. 118 Diels, trans. Freeman.
20. Alexis Fr. 30 Kock, trans. R. W. Livingstone, in *Greek Ideals and Modern Life* (Cambridge, Mass., 1935).
21. Hesiod, *Theogony* 123–24, trans. Athanassakis.
22. Plutarch, *Life of Pericles* 32 and *Life of Nicias* 23, trans. Ian Scott-Kilvert, *The Rise and Fall of Athens: Nine Greek Lives* (Harmondsworth, Eng., 1960).

23. Diogenes Laertius 2.7, in Kirk and Raven, *The Presocratic Philosophers*, 362.
24. For other examples of Athenian restrictions of free inquiry see Robert W. Wallace, "Private Lives and Public Enemies," in *Athenian Identity and Civic Ideology*, ed. Alan L. Boegehold and Adele C. Scafuro (Baltimore and London, 1994), 128–29. Wallace goes on to argue that some of the examples of intellectual persecution are historically unsubstantiated.
25. Empedocles Frs. 1, 2 Diels, trans. Freeman; Plato, *Apology* 23a, trans. Jowett. See too Xenophanes Fr. 34 Diels; Alcmaeon Fr. 1 Diels; Heracleitus Fr. 78 Diels.
26. Heracleitus Fr. 5 Diels, trans. Freeman. Cf. too Fr. 14 Diels, condemning the excesses of the mystery religions.
27. Xenophanes Frs. 11, 15, 16 Diels, trans. Freeman.
28. In Kirk and Raven, *The Presocratic Philosophers*, 138.
29. Plutarch, *Life of Pericles* 6, trans. Scott-Kilvert.
30. Euripides Fr. 286, in W. K. C. Guthrie, *The History of Greek Philosophy*, vol. 3, *The Fifth-Century Enlightenment* (Cambridge, 1969), 229. For more examples of criticism of religion see 226–49.
31. This is how Plato summarizes the atheist position in the *Laws* 885b, trans. Jowett.
32. Protagoras Fr. 4 Diels; Critias Fr.25 Diels, trans. Freeman.
33. Heracleitus Fr. 35 Diels, trans. Freeman.
34. For this issue among the Greeks see Lloyd, *Magic, Reason, and Experience*, 126–225.
35. Parmenides Fr. 7 Diels, trans. Freeman. Cf. Anaxagoras Fr. 21 Diels.
36. Democritus Fr. 11 Diels, trans. Freeman.
37. Plato, *Republic* 529b, trans. Jowett. Plato's *Theaetetus* focuses on the issue of knowledge through sense-perception.
38. Lloyd, *Magic, Reason, and Experience*, 133.
39. Anaxagoras Frs. 21, 21a Diels, trans. Freeman.
40. Democritus Fr. 125 Diels, trans. Freeman.
41. Heracleitus Fr. 107 Diels, trans. Kirk and Raven.
42. Empedocles Fr. 3 Diels, trans. Kirk and Raven.
43. Aristotle, *Generation of Animals* 760b, trans. A. Platt, in *Complete Works*.
44. Plato, *Republic* 531a.
45. Aristotle, *Physics* 213a, trans. R. P. Hardie and R. K. Gaye, in *Complete Works*.

46. These examples in Lloyd, *Magic, Reason, and Experience,* 143.
47. Lloyd, *Early Greek Science,* 118; also Taton, ed., *Ancient and Medieval Science,* 236–37.
48. Hecataeus Fr. 1 Jacoby, trans. in Max Pohlenz, *Freedom in Greek Life and Thought: The History of an Ideal,* trans. Carl Lofmark (New York, 1966), 40–41.
49. Herodotus 2.5, trans. de Sélincourt.
50. Thucydides 1.20–22, trans. Crawley.
51. Thucydides 2.47–55, quoted at 2.48, trans. Crawley.
52. Lloyd, *Magic, Reason, and Experience,* 179.
53. Lloyd, *Early Greek Science,* 97; Taton, ed., *Ancient and Medieval Science,* 314.
54. For Hipparchus see Taton, ed., *Ancient and Medieval Science,* 311–15; Lloyd, *Magic, Reason, and Experience,* 181.
55. Lloyd, *Magic, Reason, and Experience,* 225.
56. Roy Porter, *The Greatest Benefit to Mankind: A Medical History of Humanity* (New York, 1997), 46–47.
57. Taton, ed., *Ancient and Medieval Science,* 45.
58. Porter, *The Greatest Benefit,* 56.
59. *The Sacred Disease* 1, trans. W. H. S. Jones, in *Hippocrates* (Harvard, Mass. and London, 1923).
60. *The Sacred Disease* 21, trans. Jones.
61. For this topic see Lloyd, *Magic, Reason, and Experience,* 146–69.
62. Lloyd, *Magic, Reason, and Experience,* 153.
63. *Airs, Waters, Places* 2, trans. Jones.
64. *Ancient Medicine* 1, trans. Jones.
65. *Ancient Medicine* 2, trans. Jones; see also *Epidemics III,* 15.
66. Taton, ed., *Ancient and Medieval Science,* 257.
67. Aristotle, *Nicomachean Ethics* 1176b, trans. Ross and Urmson, in *Complete Works.*
68. *Odyssey* 9.375–94, trans. Lattimore.
69. *Odyssey* 9.116–41, trans. Lattimore.
70. See Plato, *Protagoras* 320b–321a.
71. Aeschylus, *Prometheus Bound* 442–43, trans. David Grene, in *Aeschylus II.*
72. Sophocles, *Antigone* 369, 381, 392–94, trans. David Grene, in *Sophocles I.*
73. Plato, *Phaedrus* 246a ff.

74. Euripides, *Medea* 1079–80.
75. Euripides, *Hippolytus* 380–81.
76. Euripides Fr. 840 Nauck.
77. In Isaiah Berlin, "The Apotheosis of the Romantic Will: The Revolt Against the Myth of an Ideal World," in *The Crooked Timber of Humanity,* ed. Henry Hardy (New York, 1991), 219.
78. A point made by Carl Sagan, *The Demon-Haunted World: Science as a Candle in the Dark* (New York, 1996), 11.

Chapter Seven: The Birth of Freedom

1. Herodotus 7.135, trans. de Sélincourt.
2. Orlando Patterson, *Freedom in the Making of Western Culture* (New York, 1991), 42; emphasis in original.
3. "Personal" freedom and "civic" freedom are Patterson's terms in *Freedom,* 3–5.
4. Patterson, 38.
5. In Max Pohlenz, *Freedom in Greek Life and Thought: The History of an Ideal,* trans. Carl Lofmark (New York, 1966), 106.
6. Euripides, *Iphigenia in Aulis* 1400–1, trans. Walker, in *Euripides IV.*
7. A gate inscription from Persepolis, from Erich F. Schmidt, *Persepolis,* vol. 1 (Chicago, 1953), 65.
8. Herodotus 7.39, trans. de Sélincourt.
9. Herodotus 7.136, trans. de Sélincourt.
10. Aristotle, *Rhetoric* 1361a.
11. Herodotus 7.223, trans. de Sélincourt.
12. Isocrates, *Panegyricus* 151, 150, trans. George Norlin (Cambridge, Mass. and London, 1928).
13. Herodotus 5.78, trans. de Sélincourt. Later a writer in the Hippocratic corpus would also link good fighters to freedom from autocratic rule (as well as from the East's enervating and emasculating climate); see *Airs, Waters, Places* 16.
14. Herodotus 7.139, trans. de Sélincourt.
15. Pindar Frs. 76, 77 in Sir John Sandys, *The Odes of Pindar* (Cambridge, Mass. and London, 1937).
16. Isocrates, *Archidamus* 43, trans. Norlin. See too Plato, *Menexenus* 245a.
17. Aeschylus, *Persians* 192–97, trans. Benardete.
18. *Persians* 371–72, 401–4, trans. Benardete.

19. Xenophon, *Anabasis* 1.7.3, trans. Rex Warner (Harmondsworth, 1949).
20. Herodotus 7.104, trans. de Sélincourt.
21. Aeschylus, *The Suppliant Maidens* 940–45, trans. Benardete.
22. Euripides, *The Suppliant Women* 405–6, trans. Jones, *Euripides IV.*
23. Plato, *Laws* 701d, trans. Jowett.
24. Aristotle, *Politics* 1279a, trans. Jowett.
25. Aristotle, *Rhetoric* 1366a, trans. Roberts.
26. *Politics* 1291b, trans. Jowett.
27. *Politics* 1301a, trans. Jowett.
28. Mogens H. Hansen, "Liberty: Athenian vs. Modern Views," in *Dêmokratia: A Conversation on Democracies, Ancient and Modern,* ed. Josiah Ober and Charles Hedrick (Princeton, 1996), 92–93.
29. Aristotle, *Politics* 1317b, trans. Jowett.
30. Thucydides 2.37, 39, trans. Crawley.
31. Thucydides 7.69, trans. Crawley.
32. Demosthenes, *Against Androtion* 51 and *Fourth Phillipic* 70, trans. Vince.
33. Sophocles Fr. 927a, trans. Lloyd-Jones.
34. *The Suppliant Women* 436–38, trans. Jones.
35. Eupolis Fr. 291 Kock.
36. Demosthenes, *Against Meidias* 124, trans. Vince.
37. Aeschylus, *Persians* 591–94, trans. Benardete.
38. Euripides, *Hippolytus* 422–23, trans. Grene.
39. Euripides, *Ion* 671, trans. Willetts, in *Euripides III.*
40. Aristophanes, *Women at the Thesmophoria* 540–41.
41. K. J. Dover, *Aristophanic Comedy* (Berkeley and Los Angeles, 1972), 34.
42. Aelian, *Varia Historia* 2.13, 5.8.
43. Thucydides 3.36, trans. Crawley.
44. Aristotle, *Constitution of Athens* 28, trans. Kenyon.
45. Aristophanes, *Knights* 44–49, trans. Jeffrey Henderson (Cambridge, Mass. and London, 1998).
46. See Douglas M. MacDowell, *Aristophanes and Athens* (Oxford, 1995), 107–112.
47. Aristophanes, *Acharnians* 379–81, trans. Henderson.
48. *Acharnians* 659–64, trans. Henderson.

49. Aristophanes, *Clouds* 549–50, 591–94, trans. Henderson; cf. too *Wasps* 1284–91.
50. *Acharnians* 655–58, trans. Henderson.
51. Diogenes Laertius 6.69.
52. Xenophon, *Memorabilia* 4.5., trans. E. C. Marchant, in *Scripta Minora.*
53. Epicurus, Vatican Saying 77, in *Hellenistic Philosophy: Introductory Readings,* trans. Brad Inwood and L. P. Gerson (Indianapolis and Cambridge, 1988).
54. Epicurus, Vatican Saying 58, in *The Hellenistic Philosophers,* vol. 1, *Translations of the Principle Sources with Philosophical Commentary,* ed. A. A. Long and D. N. Sedley (Cambridge, 1987).
55. Epicurus Fr. 199, in Inwood and Gerson.
56. Diogenes Laertius 7.86, trans. R. D. Hicks, *Lives of Eminent Philosophers* (Cambridge, Mass. and London, 1925).
57. Diogenes Laertius 7.88, trans. Hicks.
58. Diogenes Laertius 7.121, trans. Hicks.
59. Diogenes Laertius 6.71, trans. Hicks.
60. Diogenes Laertius 6.37, trans. Hicks.
61. Diogenes Laertius 6.46, 69, trans. Hicks.
62. Plato, *Republic* 557b–558c, trans. Jowett.
63. Plato, *Republic* 560e–561c, trans. Jowett.
64. Plato, *Republic* 562c–563c, trans. Jowett. See too Plato's similar analysis in *Laws* 698b–700a.
65. Aristotle, *Politics* 1318b–1319a, trans. Jowett.
66. *The Constitution of the Athenians* 1.4–10, trans. Marchant, in *Xenophon: Scripta Minora.*
67. Isocrates, *Areopagiticus* 20, trans. Norlin.
68. Plato, *Gorgias* 483c–d, trans. Jowett.
69. Plato, *Gorgias* 484a, trans. Jowett.
70. Thucydides 5.89, 105, 115, trans. Crawley.
71. *The Constitution of the Athenians* 1.3, trans. Marchant.
72. Isocrates, *On the Peace* 14, trans. Norlin.
73. Isocrates, *Panatheniacus* 12, trans. Norlin.
74. Democritus Fr. 226 Diels, trans. Freeman.
75. Plato, *Gorgias* 452e, trans. Jowett.
76. E.g. Pericles at Thucydides 2.63; Cleon says the same thing at 3.37.
77. Thucydides 5.112, trans. Crawley.

78. See e.g. Xenophon, *Hellenica* 2.2.23.
79. *Iliad* 6.146, trans. Lattimore.
80. Pindar, *Pythian* 95, in *The Odes of Pindar,* trans. Richmond Lattimore (Chicago, 1947).
81. Simonides Fr. 520 Campbell.
82. Aristotle, *Politics* 1337a, trans. Jowett.
83. Plato, *Laws* 780a, trans. Jowett.
84. Thucydides 2.30, trans. Crawley.
85. Cynthia Patterson, *The Family in Greek History* (Cambridge, Mass., 1998), 91.
86. Demosthenes, *Fourth Phillipic* 70, trans. Vince.
87. Isocrates, *Antidosis* 24, trans. Norlin.
88. Aristotle, *Constitution of Athens* 45, trans. Kenyon.
89. Robert W. Wallace, "Private Lives and Public Enemies: Freedom of Thought in Classical Athens," in *Athenian Identity and Civic Ideology,* ed. Alan L. Boegehold and Adele. C. Scafuro (Baltimore and London, 1994), 128.
90. See Aeschines, *Against Timarchos* 28–32.
91. *Against Timarchos* 35.
92. Xenophon, *Memorabilia* 3.6.1, trans. Marchant.
93. Plato, *Protagoras* 319c, trans. Jowett.
94. Jacob Burckhardt, *The Greeks and Greek Civilization,* trans. Sheila Stern, ed. Oswyn Murray (New York, 1998), 57, 73.
95. Isocrates, *On the Peace* 14. For the unreliability of the evidence suggesting legislation that restricted the comic poets see MacDowell, *Aristophanes and Athens,* 25–26.
96. See Wallace, "Private Lives, Public Enemies," where he surveys the evidence and scrutinizes its reliability, and concludes that only two intellectuals can with certainty be said to have been prosecuted.
97. Diogenes Laertius 2.42.
98. Richard Mulgan, "Liberty in Ancient Greece," in *Conceptions of Liberty in Political Philosophy,* ed. Zbigniew Pelczynski and John Gray (New York, 1984), 8.
99. Herodotus 8.143, trans. de Sélincourt.

Conclusion: The Critical Spirit

1. Jacob Burckhardt, *The Greeks and Greek Civilization,* trans. Sheila Stern, ed. Oswyn Murray (New York, 1998), 11–12; emphasis in original.

2. Jean Pierre Vernant, *The Origins of Greek Thought* (1962; reprint, Ithaca, N.Y., 1982), 49.
3. In Xenophon, *Symposium* 4.43, trans. O. J. Todd, in *Scripta Minora.*
4. In Plato, *Phaedrus* 220e, trans. Jowett.
5. In Xenophon, *Memorabilia* 4.5.12, trans. Marchant; emphases in original translation.
6. In Plato, *Protagoras* 310e, 315b, trans. Jowett.
7. In Plato, *Republic* 531e, trans. Paul Shorey (Cambridge, Mass. and London, 1935). Socrates at this point in the *Republic* is Plato's mouthpiece, but the expression about giving an "account" (*dounai ... logon*) agrees with language used by the Socrates of earlier dialogues and Xenophon. See Shorey's note *ad loc.*
8. Plato, *Apology* 29d–30a, trans. Jowett.
9. *Apology* 38a.
10. Euripides, *Bacchae* 200–3, trans. William Arrowsmith, in *Euripides V* (Chicago, 1959).
11. *Bacchae* 268–70, trans. Arrowsmith.
12. *Bacchae* 394–96, trans. Arrowsmith.
13. *Bacchae* 505–7, trans. Arrowsmith.
14. *Bacchae* 543–44, trans. Arrowsmith.
15. Matthew Arnold, in *Culture and Anarchy,* quoted in *Selected Prose,* ed. P. J. Keating (Harmondsworth, 1970), 275, 276, 279.
16. R. W. Livingstone, *Greek Ideals and Modern Life* (1935; reprint, New York, 1969), 174.
17. Livingstone, 148.
18. The media keep alive the bogey of the "fundamentalist right," yet despite occasional short-lived victories, the religious right repeatedly fails at influencing public policy on and perception of the social issues most important to it: prayer in schools, creation science, abortion, pornography, depictions of sex and violence in popular culture.
19. Arnold, "On the Modern Element in Literature," in *Selected Prose,* 62.
20. Livingstone, 149.
21. Livingstone, 160.

Bibliography

Classical Works

Aelian. *Varia Historia*. Edited and translated by N. G. Wilson. Cambridge, Mass., 1997.

Aeschines. *Against Timarchos*. Translated by Charles Darwin Adams. London and Cambridge, Mass., 1958.

Aeschylus I: Oresteia. Translated by Richmond Lattimore. *The Complete Greek Tragedies*. Edited by David Grene and Richmond Lattimore. Chicago, 1953.

Aeschylus II. The Complete Greek Tragedies. Edited by David Grene and Richmond Lattimore. Chicago, 1956.

Apollonius of Rhodes. *Argonautica*. Translated by Richard Hunter, *Jason and the Golden Fleece*. Oxford, 1993.

Aristophanes. 2 vols. Translated by Jeffrey Henderson. Loeb Classical Library. Cambridge, Mass. and London, 1998.

Aristophanes. *Frogs*. Edited by K. J. Dover. Oxford, 1993.

Aristophanes. *The Frogs*. Translated by Richmond Lattimore. Ann Arbor, 1962.

Aristophanes. *Lysistrata*. Translated by Matt Neuberg. Arlington Heights, Va., 1992.

Aristophanes. *Peace*. Translated by B. B. Rogers. Cambridge, Mass. and London, 1924.

Aristophanes. *The Women at Assembly*. In *The Complete Greek Drama*, edited by Whitney J. Oates and Eugene O'Neill Jr. New York, 1938.

Aristotle. *The Complete Works of Aristotle*. Edited by Jonathan Barnes. Princeton, 1984.

Aristotle. *Nicomachean Ethics*. Translated by Martin Ostwald. New York, 1962.

Athenaeus. *The Deipnosophists*. 7 vols. Translated by Charles Burton Gulick. The Loeb Classical Library. Cambridge, Mass. and London, 1927-1941.

Demosthenes. Vol. 3. Translated by J. H. Vince. The Loeb Classical Library. Cambridge, Mass. and London, 1935.

Diodorus Siculus. *Diodorus of Sicily*. Translated by C. H. Oldfather. Loeb Classical Library. Cambridge, Mass. and London, 1935.

Diogenes Laertius. *Lives of Eminent Philosophers*. Translated by R. D. Hicks. Cambridge, Mass. and London, 1925.

Euripides. 5 vols. The Complete Greek Tragedies. Edited by David Grene and Richmond Lattimore. Chicago, 1955–1959.

Herodas. *Mimes*. Translated by I. C. Cunningham, in *Theophrastus: Characters; Herodas: Mimes; Cercidas and the Choliambic Poets*. Cambridge, Mass. and London, 1993.

Herodotus. *Histories*. Translated by A. D. Godley. Cambridge, Mass. and London, 1921.

Herodotus. *Histories*. Translated by Aubrey de Sélincourt. Harmondsworth, England, 1954.

Hesiod. *Theogony, Works and Days, Shield*. Translated by Apostolos N. Athanassakis. Baltimore, 1983.

Hippocrates. 4 vols. Translated by W. H. S. Jones. Loeb Classical Library. Harvard, Mass., and London, 1923–1931.

Homer. *The Iliad of Homer*. Translated by Richmond Lattimore. Chicago, 1951.

Homer. *The Odyssey of Homer*. Translated by Richmond Lattimore. New York, 1967.

Isocrates. 3 vols. Translated by George Norlin. Loeb Classical Library. Cambridge, Mass. and London, 1928–1945.

Lysias. Translated by W. R. M. Lamb. Loeb Classical Library. Cambridge, Mass. and London, 1930.

Pindar. *The Odes of Pindar*. Translated by Richmond Lattimore. Chicago, 1947.

Pindar. *The Odes of Pindar, including the Principal Fragments*. Edited and translated by Sir John Sandys. 2nd rev. ed. Cambridge, Mass. and London, 1919.

Pindar. *The Odes of Pindar, including the Principal Fragments*. Edited and translated by Sir John Sandys. Rev. ed. Cambridge, Mass. and London, 1937.

Plato. *The Dialogues of Plato*. 4 vols. Translated by Benjamin Jowett. Oxford, 1953.

Plato. *Four Texts on Socrates: Plato's Euthyphro, Apology, and Crito, and Aristophanes' Clouds.* Translated by Thomas G. West and Grace Starry West. Ithaca and London, 1984.

Plato. *The Laws.* Translated by T. J. Saunders. Harmondsworth, 1970.

Plato. *The Republic.* Translated by Paul Shorey. Cambridge, Mass. and London, 1935.

Plato. *The Republic of Plato.* Edited and translated by Francis Macdonald Cornford. Oxford, 1941.

Plutarch. *The Rise and Fall of Athens: Nine Greek Lives.* Translated by Ian Scott-Kilvert. Harmondsworth, 1960.

Seneca, Lucius Annaeus. *The Stoic Philosophy of Seneca.* Translated by Moses Hadas. New York, 1958.

Sophocles. 2 vols. The Complete Greek Tragedies. Edited by David Grene and Richmond Lattimore. Chicago, 1954–1957.

Sophocles. Vol. 3, *Fragments.* Edited and translated by Hugh Lloyd-Jones. Cambridge, Mass. and London, 1996.

Sophocles. *Antigone.* Translated by Hugh Lloyd-Jones. Cambridge, Mass. and London, 1994.

Thucydides. *The Peloponnesian War.* Translated by Richard Crawley, in *The Landmark Thucydides: A Comprehensive Guide to the Peloponnesian War.* Edited by Robert B. Strassler. New York, 1996.

Xenophon. *Anabasis.* Translated by Rex Warner. Harmondsworth, England, 1949.

Xenophon. *Conversations with Socrates.* Translated by Hugh Tredennick and Robin Waterfield. Harmondsworth, England, 1990.

Xenophon: Scripta Minora. Edited by G. W. Bowerstock and E. C. Marchant. Cambridge, Mass. and London, 1968.

Source Collections

The Ancient Egyptians: A Sourcebook of Their Writings. Edited by Adolf Erman, translated by Aylward M. Blackman. New York, 1966.

Ancient Records of Assyria and Babylonia. Vol. 1. Translated by Daniel David Luckenbill. 1926. Reprint, New York, 1968.

Campbell, D. A. *Greek Lyric.* London and Cambridge, Mass., 1982–1993.

Edmonds, J. M. *Greek Elegy and Iambus.* London and Cambridge, Mass., 1931.

Evelyn-White, Hugh G. *Hesiod, the Homeric Hymns, and Homerica.* Cambridge, Mass. and London, 1914.

Freeman, Kathleen. *Ancilla to the Pre-Socratic Philosophers.* A Complete Translation of the Fragments in Diels, *Fragmente der Vorsokratiker.* Cambridge, Mass., 1957.

Inwood, Brad and Lloyd P. Gerson. *Hellenistic Philosophy: Introductory Readings.* Indianapolis and Cambridge, 1988.

Lattimore, Richmond. *Greek Lyric.* Chicago, 1955.

Long, A. A. and D. N. Sedley, eds. *The Hellenistic Philosophers.* Vol. 1, *Translations of the Principle Sources with Philosophical Commentary.* Cambridge, 1987.

Nauck, August. *Tragicorum Graecorum Fragmenta.* Hildesheim, 1964.

Sprague, Rosamond Kent, trans. *The Older Sophists.* Columbia, S.C., 1972.

Modern Works

Ackerman, Diane. *A Natural History of Love.* New York, 1994.

Arnold, Matthew. *Selected Prose.* Edited by P. J. Keating. Harmondsworth, England, 1970.

Baldry, H. C. *The Unity of Mankind in Greek Thought.* Cambridge, 1965.

Berlin, Isaiah. "The Apotheosis of the Romantic Will: The Revolt against the Myth of an Ideal World." In *The Crooked Timber of Humanity,* edited by Henry Hardy. New York, 1991.

Black Athena Revisited. Edited by Mary R. Lefkowitz and Guy MacLean Rogers. Chapel Hill, 1996.

Burckhardt, Jacob. *The Greeks and Greek Civilization.* Translated by Sheila Stern, edited by Oswyn Murray. New York, 1998.

Burkert, Walter. *Greek Religion.* Translated by John Raffan. Cambridge, Mass., 1985.

Cantarella, Eva. *Pandora's Daughters: The Role and Status of Women in Greek and Roman Antiquity.* Translated by Maureen B. Fant. Baltimore, 1987.

Cartledge, Paul. *The Greeks: A Portrait of Self and Others.* Oxford and New York, 1993.

Chailand, Gérard. *The Art of War in World History.* Berkeley and Los Angeles, 1994.

Chelala, Cesar. "Egypt Takes Decisive Stance against Female Genital Mutilation." *The Lancet* 351.9096 (10 January 1998).

Davidson, James. *Courtesans and Fishcakes: The Consuming Passions of Classical Athens.* London, 1997.

Davis-Floyd, Robbie E. and Carolyn F. Sargent. Introduction to *Childbirth and Authoritative Knowledge: Cross-Cultural Perspectives,* edited by Robbie E. Davis-Floyed and Carolyn F. Sargent. Berkeley and Los Angeles, 1998.

Donlan, Walter. "The Tradition of Anti-Aristocratic Thought in Early Greek Poetry." *Historia* 22.2 (1973): 145–54.

Dover, K. J. *Aristophanic Comedy.* Berkeley and Los Angeles, 1972.

Ehrenberg, Victor. *The People of Aristophanes: The Sociology of Ancient Comedy.* New York, 1961.

Ellul, Jacques. *The Betrayal of the West.* Translated by Matthew J. O'Connell. New York, 1978.

Farrington, Benjamin. *Greek Science.* 1944. Reprint, New York, 1953.

Ferrill, Arther. *The Origins of War: From the Stone Age to Alexander the Great.* London, 1985.

Finley, M. I. "Ancient Slavery and Modern Ideology." In *Ancient Slavery and Modern Ideology.* New York, 1980.

Finley, M. I. "Debt-Bondage and Slavery." In *Economy and Society in Ancient Greece.* New York, 1981.

Garlan, Yvon. *Slavery in Ancient Greece.* Rev. and expanded ed., translated by Janet Lloyd. Ithaca, N.Y., 1988.

Garland, Robert. *The Greek Way of Life: From Conception to Old Age.* Ithaca, N.Y., 1990.

Garnsey, Peter. *Ideas of Slavery from Aristotle to Augustine.* Cambridge, 1996.

Gulick, Charles Burton. *Modern Traits in Old Greek Life.* New York, 1963.

Guthrie, W. K. C. *A History of Greek Philosophy.* Vol. 1, *The Earlier Presocratics and the Pythagoreans.* Cambridge, 1962.

——. *A History of Greek Philosophy.* Vol. 3, *The Fifth-Century Enlightenment.* Cambridge, 1969.

Halperin, David M. *One Hundred Years of Homosexuality and Other Essays on Greek Love.* London, 1990.

Hamilton, Edith. *The Greek Way.* New York, 1943.

Hansen, Mogens H. "Liberty: Athenian vs. Modern Views." In *Dêmokratia: A Conversation on Democracies, Ancient and Modern,* edited by Josiah Ober and Charles Hedrick. Princeton, 1996.

Hanson, Victor Davis. "No Glory That Was Greece." In *What If?* edited by Robert Cowley. New York, 1999.

——. *The Other Greeks: The Family Farm and the Agrarian Roots of Western Civilization.* New York, 1995.

——. *The Wars of the Ancient Greeks, and Their Invention of Western Military Culture.* London, 1999.

——. *The Western Way of War: Infantry Battle in Classical Greece.* New York, 1989.

Hanson, Victor and John Heath. "Who Killed Homer?" *Arion* 5.2 (1997).

——. *Who Killed Homer? The Demise of Classical Education.* New York, 1998.

Harrison, A. R. W. *The Law of Athens: The Family and Property.* Oxford, 1968.

Henderson, Jeffrey. *The Maculate Muse: Obscene Language in Attic Comedy.* 2nd ed. Oxford, 1991.

Jameson, Michael. "Private Space and the Greek City." In *The Greek City: From Homer to Alexander,* edited by Oswyn Murray and Simon Price. Oxford, 1990.

Jenkyns, Richard. *The Victorians and Ancient Greece.* Cambridge, Mass., 1980.

Jones, A. H. M. *Athenian Democracy.* 1957. Reprint, Baltimore, 1977.

Kagan, Donald. *The Great Dialogue: History of Greek Political Thought from Homer to Polybius.* New York, 1965.

Keuls, Eva. *The Reign of the Phallus: Sexual Politics in Ancient Athens.* Berkeley and Los Angeles, 1985.

Kirk, G. S. and J. E. Raven. *The Presocratic Philosophers: A Critical History with a Selection of Texts.* Cambridge, 1957.

Knox, Bernard. "The Oldest Dead White European Males." In *The Oldest Dead White European Males and Other Reflections on the Classics.* New York, 1993.

Kolchin, Peter. *American Slavery, 1619–1877.* New York, 1993.

Lefkowitz, Mary R. *Women in Greek Myth.* Baltimore, 1986.

Lefkowitz, Mary R. and Maureen B. Fant. *Women's Life in Greece and Rome.* 2nd ed. Baltimore, 1992.

Livingstone, R. W. *Greek Ideals and Modern Life.* 1935. Reprint, New York, 1969.

Lloyd, G. E. R. *Early Greek Science.* New York, 1970.

——. *Magic, Reason, and Experience.* Cambridge, 1979.

Lovejoy, Arthur O. and George Boas. *Primitivism and Related Ideas in Antiquity: A Documentary History.* Baltimore and London, 1935.

MacDowell, Douglas M. *Aristophanes and Athens: An Introduction to the Plays*. Oxford, 1995.

McLaren, Peter. "White Terror and Oppositional Agency: Towards a Critical Multiculturalism." In *Multiculturalism: A Critical Reader*, edited by David Theo Goldberg. Cambridge, Mass., 1994.

Mulgan, Richard. "Liberty in Ancient Greece." In *Conceptions of Liberty in Political Philosophy*, edited by Zbigniew Pelczynski and John Gray. New York, 1984.

Murray, Gilbert. "The Value of Greece to the Future of the World." In *The Legacy of Greece*, edited by R. W. Livingstone. Oxford, 1921.

Nussbaum, Martha. *Cultivating Humanity: A Classical Defense of Reform in Liberal Education*. Cambridge, Mass., 1997.

Ober, Josiah. *Political Dissent in Democratic Athens: Intellectual Critics of Popular Rule*. Princeton, 1998.

O'Donnell, James J. *Avatars of the Word: From Papyrus to Cyberspace*. Cambridge, Mass., 1998.

Olmstead, A. T. *History of the Persian Empire*. Chicago, 1948.

Oxford Companion to Classical Civilization. Edited by Simon Hornblower and Anthony Spawforth. Oxford, 1998.

Parke, H. W. *Festivals of the Athenians*. Ithaca, N.Y., 1977.

Patterson, Cynthia. *The Family in Greek History*. Cambridge, Mass., 1998.

Patterson, Orlando. *Freedom*. Vol. 1, *Freedom in the Making of Western Culture*. New York, 1991.

Pohlenz, Max. *Freedom in Greek Life and Thought: The History of an Ideal*. Translated by Carl Lofmark. New York, 1966.

Pomeroy, Sarah. *Goddesses, Whores, Wives, and Slaves*. New York, 1975.

Porter, Roy. *The Greatest Benefit to Mankind: A Medical History of Humanity*. New York, 1997.

Roberts, Jennifer Tolbert. *Athens on Trial: The Antidemocratic Tradition in Western Thought*. Princeton, 1994.

Roy, J. "An Alternative Sexual Morality for Classical Athens." *Greece and Rome* 64.1 (1997): 11–22.

Sagan, Carl. *The Demon-Haunted World: Science as a Candle in the Dark*. New York, 1996.

Saggs, H. W. F. *Civilization before Greece and Rome*. New Haven, 1989.

Schlaifer, Robert. "Greek Theories of Slavery from Homer to Aristotle." In *Slavery in Classical Antiquity*, edited by M. I. Finley. Cambridge, 1960.

Schmidt, Erich F. *Persepolis*. Vol. 1. Chicago, 1953.
Schofield, Malcolm. *The Stoic Idea of the City.* Cambridge, 1991.
Skinner, Marilyn B. "*Quod Multo Fit Aliter in Graecia.*" Introduction to *Roman Sexualities*, edited by Judith P. Hallett and Marilyn B. Skinner. Princeton, 1997.
Spiegel, Nathan. *War and Peace in Classical Greek Literature*. Translated by Amiel Ungar. Jerusalem, 1990.
Stockton, David. *The Classical Athenian Democracy.* Oxford, 1990.
Tallis, Raymond. *The Enemies of Hope: A Critique of Contemporary Pessimism*. New York, 1997.
Taton, René, ed. *The History of Science*. Vol. 1, *Ancient and Medieval Science*. Translated by A. J. Pomerans. New York, 1963.
Thornton, Bruce. "Cultivating Sophistry." *Arion* 6.2 (1998): 189–91.
Thornton, Bruce. "Idolon Theatri: Foucault and the Classicists." *Classical and Modern Literature* 12.1 (1991): 81-100.
Thornton, B. *Eros. The Myth of Ancient Greek Sexuality.* Boulder, Colo., 1997.
Vellacott, Philip. *Ironic Drama: A Study of Euripides*. Cambridge, 1975.
Vernant, Jean Pierre. *The Origins of Greek Thought*. Ithaca, N.Y., 1982.
Vogt, Joseph. *Ancient Slavery and the Ideal of Man*. Translated by Thomas Wiedemann. Cambridge, Mass., 1975.
Vlastos, Gregory. "Isonomia." In *Studies in Greek Philosophy,* vol. 1, *The Presocratics*. Princeton, 1995.
Wallace, Robert W. "Private Lives and Public Enemies." In *Athenian Identity and Civic Ideology,* edited by Alan L. Boegehold and Adele C. Scafuro. Baltimore and London, 1994.
Wiedemann, Thomas. *Greek and Roman Slavery.* Baltimore, 1981.
Wills, Gary. "Loving the Unlovable Greeks." *New York Times Book Review.* 15 November 1998.
——. "There's Nothing Conservative about the Classics Revival." *New York Times Magazine*. 16 February 1997.
Wright, F. A. *Feminism in Greek Literature: From Homer to Aristotle*. 1923. Reprint, Port Washington, N.Y. and London, 1969.
Zimmern, A. E. "Political Thought." In *The Legacy of Greece*, edited by R. W. Livingstone. Oxford, 1921.

Index